WORLD MIGRATION REPORT 2000

Copublished by

International Organization for Migration (IOM)
United Nations

IOM • OIM

United Nations

EDITORIAL TEAM

MANAGING EDITOR, SUSAN F. MARTIN

ASSOCIATE EDITOR, MARY ANN LARKIN

DESIGNER, MINNA NEWMAN NATHANSON

PRODUCED BY IOM

UNDER THE DIRECTION OF PETER SCHATZER

Copublished by the International Organization for Migration and the United Nations

United Nations publication
Sales No. E.00.III.S.3
ISSN 1561-5502
ISBN 92-9068-089-X

CONTENTS

TABLES

FOREWORD

Today, it is estimated that there are more migrants in the world than ever before. International migration has played a crucial role in shaping the world we know; centuries of international migration have left their mark upon nearly every part of the globe.

A growing number of people no longer remain in their countries of birth or ethnic origin but migrate the world over in search of better opportunities or safety from persecution or violence. An estimated 150 million people live outside their countries of birth or citizenship, while many others are not counted as international migrants because they live and work in another country illegally, whether on a permanent or temporary basis.

International migration has become a global phenomenon involving a wide range of sending, destination, and transit countries and a diverse group of migrants. The highly skilled worker from Australia working in Singapore, the refugee from Afghanistan in Iran, the woman from Nigeria trafficked to Italy, and the agricultural worker from Mexico working illegally in the United States are all examples of international migrants.

International migration is a complex issue because it can have an influence on relations between States. By definition, international migration involves the movement of people between two or more countries. Most of the countries of the world are now part of a global migration system where the migration policies of one State are likely to have an impact on other States. Given the global scale of international migration, its management requires increased cooperation between States.

Although many books and articles have been written on the reasons for migration in different parts of the world and on the costs and benefits of migration for sending and receiving countries, there are few studies that report in detail on global trends in migration. IOM, therefore, decided to prepare a World Report on Migration to promote a better understanding of the main migratory movements that are occurring across the globe. It is intended that this report will be published on a regular basis.

The purpose of the World Migration Report is to provide an authoritative account of contemporary trends, issues, and problems in the field of international migration. For the first time, a comprehensive review of trends in international migration in each major region of the world is presented together with a discussion of some of the main migration policy issues now facing the international community.

The book is divided into two parts. The first examines the scale of migration and characteristics of international migrants, the types of movements now underway, the factors that contribute to migration, the global contexts in which these movements occur, and the policy issues associated with these trends. The second part reviews migration trends and recent policy developments in major migration regions of the world. In nine separate regional chapters, trends in immigration and emigration are examined along with such key issues as the integration of migrants, the consequences of irregular migration, and the extent of interregional cooperation between states.

The book illustrates the nature of international migration and the enormous challenges and opportunities that current migration trends pose for governments. IOM, with a global network of over 100 offices in source, transit, and destination countries, seeks to assist governments in meeting these challenges by providing a range of services that address current migration problems and emerging migration opportunities in a practical and humane manner.

As an intergovernmental body, IOM acts with its partners in the international community to promote orderly migration and to facilitate dialogue and cooperation between States on migration matters. Through applied research, IOM seeks to further understanding of migration issues and policy developments for all those affected.

Brunson McKinley
Director General

ACKNOWLEDGEMENTS

This publication has benefited from the cooperation of many individuals from within IOM and outside. The generous support received from the Nippon Foundation through the Sasakawa Endowment Fund, has helped finance the initial work. In the early stages of the project, Reginald Appleyard and Jeffrey Crisp shared constructive ideas. In addition to the contributions by the authors of the regional chapters, the work of Susan Martin who wrote the introductory chapter and, together with Mary Ann Larkin, edited the publication was invaluable. At IOM headquarters, Jean-Paul Chardin, Brian Gushulak, Jill Helke, Yorio Tanimura and Thomas Weiss provided precious inputs. The assistance of Minna Nathanson and Angela Pedersen with the layout and of David Thompson, who did the meticulous proofreading, helped to achieve the result you have now in front of you.

Peter Schatzer

PHOTOS

COVER (TOP TO BOTTOM)
© IOM
© IOM
© IOM
© IOM
© PIERRE KING/IOM

PAGE 1 (CLOCKWISE FROM TOP LEFT)
© WENDY STONE
© VAN DE GLIND/IOM
© HOWARD DAVIES
© MARTIN FLITMAN
© IOM
© CEMIL ALYANAK/IOM
(CENTRE PICTURE)
© HARALD SIEM/IOM

PAGE 57 (CLOCKWISE FROM TOP LEFT)
© HOWARD DAVIES
© PHILIPPE GALABERT/IOM
© WENDY STONE
© RUDI MAXWALD/IOM
© IOM
© PETER SCHATZER/IOM
© IOM

GLOBAL MIGRATION TRENDS

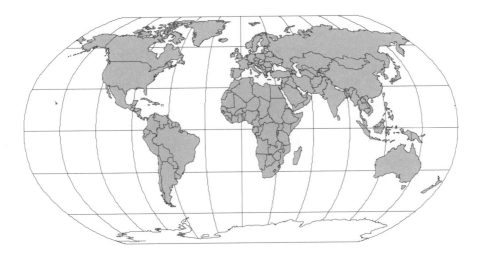

AN ERA OF INTERNATIONAL MIGRATION

INTRODUCTION

More than 150 million international migrants celebrated the turn of the millennium outside their countries of birth. They came to their new countries to work, study, join family members, or escape persecution or violence in their home countries. Most are legal residents of their new countries, but a sizeable minority are without authorization. They do not include the additional millions of tourists who visit foreign countries but return home in a few days, weeks or—at most—months.

The sheer scale of international migration gives new saliency to an age-old phenomenon. For all of human history, people have moved to find new opportunities. Whole continents are peopled by the descendants of migrants who now outnumber the descendants of the original habitants. The major world religions are founded on migration parables that include expulsion or escape, wandering, and ultimate resettlement to build the foundations of a new religion. Chinese settle-

Susan Martin, Director of the Institute for the Study of International Migration at Georgetown University,Washington, DC, USA, contributed to this chapter.

ment in South-East Asia, European colonization, the spread of Bantu-speaking populations from northern to southern Africa, all tell stories of substantial migration.

Though not a new phenomenon, many more people today have chosen or been forced to migrate than ever before, and they have gone to many more places. Significant numbers of international migrants can be found in countries as diverse as Costa Rica, Côte d'Ivoire, Germany, India, Saudi Arabia, and the United States. Equally important, the context in which international migration takes place has changed radically in the past few decades. Technological and communications changes have not only eased movements, but they have allowed migrants to retain substantial contacts with their home communities while giving would-be migrants unparalleled access to information about other countries. Economic globalization and integration means freer movement not only of goods and capital but also of services and labour. The end of the Cold War reduced many of the ideological barriers to international migration, but it also released submerged nationalistic tensions that have given rise to ethnic cleansing and other forms of forced movements.

The following sections explore the constants and the changes in global migration, beginning with an examination of the scale and characteristics of international migration, then proceeding to a discussion of the types of movements now under way, the factors that precipitate individual decisions to migrate, the global contexts in which these movements occur, and the policy issues now facing the international community.

SCALE AND CHARACTERISTICS OF INTERNATIONAL MIGRATION

International migrants are persons who take up residence in a foreign country.[1] By this definition, international migrants do not include the tourists, business travellers, religious pilgrims, or persons seeking medical treatment who make millions of visits to foreign countries each year. Rather, only those foreigners who remain for an extended stay in a new country are counted as international migrants.

OVERALL NUMBERS AND RATE OF GROWTH

The number of long-term international migrants (that is, those residing in foreign countries for more than one year) has grown steadily. According to the United Nations Population Division, only 75 million persons fitted the definition in 1965, rising to 84 million by 1975, and 105 million by 1985. There were an estimated 120 million international migrants in 1990, the last year for which detailed international statistics are available. An examination of data from selected countries of in-migration indicates that international migration continued at about the same rate of growth in the 1990s. As of the year 2000, there are an estimated 150 million international migrants.

Between 1965 and 1975, the growth in international migration (1.16 per cent per year) did not keep pace with the growth in global population (2.04 per cent per year). However, overall population growth began to decline in the 1980s while international migration continued to increase significantly. During the period from 1985 to 1990, global population growth increased by about 1.7 per cent per year, whereas the total population of international migrants increased by 2.59 per cent per year.

Even with the large and growing numbers of international migrants, fewer than 3 per cent of the world's population have been living outside their home countries for a year or longer.[2] The propensity to move internationally, particularly in the absence of such compelling reasons as wars, is limited to a small proportion of humans.

MOVEMENT ASSISTANCE

The International Organization for Migration (IOM), set up in 1951 to address the plight of refugees and displaced persons in postwar Europe, has gradually expanded both the scope and geographical coverage of its activities. IOM provides movement assistance to migrants in the broadest sense, i.e., not only persons who qualify under rules for resettlement but also persons who meet other government criteria for immigration or assistance. This extends to activities such as government-sponsored movements for purposes of labour migration and response to emergencies. Transporting persons in need of assistance remains key to IOM's overall mission. Close to 11 million migrants have been transported under the auspices of IOM. Worldwide savings resulting from transport agreements with carriers benefit migrants and donor governments in excess of US$ 85 million annually.

GEOGRAPHIC ORIGINS AND DESTINATIONS

International migrants come from all parts of the world and they go to all parts of the world. The largest numbers of international migrants are located in Asia; Europe and North America have about equal numbers; Africa, Latin America, and Oceania follow with progressively fewer numbers.

More than half of international migrants live in developing countries. Migration often occurs within the same continent. A review of labour migration from Asian countries between 1975 and 1994 reveals that, with the exception of migration from China, on average well under 10 per cent of the migrants left Asia. Refugee movements are even more localized, with the majority of refugees moving to a neighbouring country.

Even though a smaller share of international migrants go to developed countries, they tend to represent a higher proportion of the overall populations in more prosperous areas relative to developing ones. In western Europe and North America, for example, international migrants represent almost 10 per cent of the total population. Several western Asian countries and Oceania have even higher proportions of international migrants. By contrast, international migrants account for less than 1 per cent of the population in East Asia.

The United States is by far the largest recipient of international migrants, with about 25 million foreign-born residents at the end of the 1990s. Other significant receiving countries include India, Pakistan, France, Germany, Canada, Saudi Arabia, Australia, the United Kingdom, and the Islamic Republic of Iran. Together, these top 10 receiving countries accounted for 55 per cent of all international migrants in 1990 and continued to host large immigrant populations during the decade.

The industrialized countries belonging to the Organisation for Economic Co-operation and Development (OECD), in particular, experienced significant growth in their immigrant populations during the 1990s. In 1986-1987, about 36 million international migrants (some of whom subsequently naturalized) lived in the United States, France, Germany, Canada, Australia, and the United Kingdom. A decade later, more than 46 million international migrants were reported to be living in these same countries—a more than 25 per cent increase.

The States with the largest absolute numbers of international migrants do not generally have the highest proportions of international migrants within their populations. Only in Saudi Arabia and Australia do international migrants represent as much as 20 per cent of the population. The highest proportions of international migrants tend to be in small countries and territories, particularly in the Gulf region. For example, more than 70 per cent of the populations of the United Arab Emirates and Qatar are international migrants.

A number of source countries have seen significant growth in the number of emigrating nationals during the past decade. In 1987, for example, the annual outflow of workers from the four major emigration countries in South Asia (Bangladesh, Sri Lanka, Pakistan, and India) totalled just over 250,000. A decade later, almost four times that number left during the course of a single year.

The most rapid growth in the number of international migrants tends to occur as a result of refugee crises. Massive numbers of refugees may cross a border within a very short time, often into areas with little prior immigration. The more than 800,000 refugees who fled from Kosovo to Albania and the former Yugoslav Republic of Macedonia in 1999 represent one of the most recent manifestations of this phenomenon.

DEMOGRAPHICS

According to the most recent statistics on gender distribution of international migrants, about 52.5 per cent are men and 47.5 per cent are women. The largest numbers of female migrants are found in the countries with the largest overall migration. The proportion of women is higher in developed countries (almost 50%) than in developing countries (46%). There is variance by country, however. The lowest proportion of female migrants is found in the Middle East.

One of the most significant trends has been the feminization of migration streams that heretofore were primarily male. Significantly, many of the new female migrants relocate as principal wage earners rather than as accompanying family members. Castles and Miller, referencing Orlando Patterson's 1978 observation that "the greater propensity of women to move is a pattern peculiar to the New World", note that the phenomenon is now more widespread. "A key development in recent years has been the increasing feminization of migration: about 1.5 million Asian women were working abroad by the mid-1990s, and in many migratory movements they outnumber men" (6). For example, more than 60 per cent of migrants from Sri Lanka are women, employed primarily in domestic service.

TYPES OF MOVEMENTS

International migrants belong to two broad groups: voluntary migrants and forced migrants. Voluntary migrants include people who move abroad for purposes of employment, study, family reunification, or other personal factors. Forced migrants leave their countries to escape persecution, conflict, repression, natural and human-made disasters, ecological degradation, or other situations that endanger their lives, freedom, or livelihood. Among them are individuals compelled to move by government or other authorities, often in the process referred to as "ethnic cleansing."

Distinguishing between voluntary and forced migrants can be difficult. Voluntary migrants may feel compelled to seek new homes because of pressing problems at home; forced migrants may choose a particular refuge because of family and community ties or economic opportunities. Moreover, one form of migration often leads to another. Forced migrants who settle in a new country may then bring family members to join them. Voluntary migrants may find that situations change in their home countries, preventing their repatriation and turning them into forced migrants.

Despite the difficulty of categorizing different types of migrants, the process is more than an exercise in semantics. Countries have different responsibilities towards different types of migrants. For example, more than 130 countries have signed the 1951 United Nations Convention relating to the Status of Refugees and recognize that they are obliged not to return refugees to where they have a well-founded fear of persecution and to provide assistance and protection to refugees whom they admit. No similar legal obligation extends to other international migrants, although their rights while in countries of destination are protected by international human rights law, national laws, and International Labour Organization (ILO) conventions relating to conditions of recruitment and employment.

VOLUNTARY MIGRANTS

As discussed below, people move voluntarily for a host of reasons. Generally, longer-term voluntary international migrants fall into three major groupings: labour migrants; family members of prior migrants; and foreign students.

LABOUR MIGRANTS. Many of today's international migration streams began with the recruitment and employment of foreign workers. From the 1940s to the 1960s, the United States operated a guest worker programme with Mexico—the Bracero Programme. In the 1960s and 1970s, many European countries instituted their own guest worker programmes, bringing in labour from Turkey, northern Africa, and southern Europe. During the same period, the oil-rich Libyan Arab Jamahiriya and Gulf States recruited workers from other Muslim countries and from East and South-East Asia. South Africa recruited migrants from Mozambique and Lesotho to work in the mining industry.

Some migrants were recruited for seasonal work, often in agriculture. Others filled short-term labour shortages in a wider range of industries produced by burgeoning economies. Often, the international migrants were hired to perform jobs that natives would not do, particularly for the low wages or poor working conditions offered. In some situations—the oil-producing regions, for example—they provided technical skills not readily available within the native population.

Even after active labour recruitment ended, labour migration often continued. European countries withdrew their labour contracts after the 1973 oil crisis and resulting recession, but many of their guest workers remained. Employers who were pleased with the performance of their existing staff did not want to train new workers to fill posts held by guest workers; many employees who had established roots did not want to return to their home countries. When the Bracero Programme ended in 1965, migration patterns shifted towards unauthorized routes. As a recent binational study of migration from Mexico to the United States concluded, "most recently arrived legal and unauthorized Mexican migrants can find jobs in high turnover farm, manufacturing, and service jobs" (4).

Today, labour migration is highly complex. Several distinct categories of workers migrate, differentiated by their skills, the permanence of their residence in the host country, and their legal status. At the lower end of the skills spectrum, international migrants pick fruits and vegetables, manufacture garments and other items, process meat and poultry, work as nursing home and hospital aides, clean restaurants and hotels, do gardening and construction, take care of children and the elderly, and provide myriad other services. They provide these types of services in a wide range of receiving countries in almost all parts of the globe.

At the higher end of the skill spectrum, international migrants engage in equally diverse activities. They fill jobs requiring specialized skills: run multinational corporations; teach in universities; provide research and development expertise to industry and academia; practice medicine; and design, build, and programme computers—to name only a few activities. They undertake such assignments throughout the world.

National systems for admitting labour migrants vary significantly but fall broadly into two major categories: demand-driven and supply-driven. In supply-driven systems, the migrants themselves launch the admission process. For example, in Canada and Australia, point systems test the education, skills, language ability, and other characteristics that these countries see as enhancing successful integration. Although points may be given for other ties to the new country, such as family members, the point systems are aimed primarily at testing likely economic success. An applicant who meets these requirements is admitted and granted authorization for employment. In demand-driven systems, employers request permission to hire foreign workers, thereby triggering a decision to admit the migrant. Governments sometimes require that the employers demonstrate that the foreign worker will not displace native workers from jobs or adversely affect wages and working conditions. Many countries devise bilateral arrangements with other countries to regulate the movements of labour migrants. The destination country develops a list of needed occupations, and the source country recruits and screens workers for these positions.

In most countries, migrants are admitted as temporary workers and granted work authorization for specified periods. They have no right to remain in the destination country beyond the period of authorized employment. In some cases, if a permit is renewed several times, the international migrant is allowed to remain indefinitely. The traditional immigration countries—the USA, Canada, and Australia—also have mechanisms for direct admission of foreign workers for permanent settlement.

Generally, international companies moving their personnel from one country to another find few barriers to admission. Employers requesting permission to hire highly skilled international migrants also find few barriers to entry. Many countries have very restrictive policies, however, towards the formal admission of lesser-skilled international migrants for employment purposes. However, some official labour contracting systems still operate between countries. For example, the Philippines arranges employment for its nationals in dozens of countries through bilateral or less formal labour programmes.

In addition to these legal avenues of entry for labour migrants, there is unauthorized migration. Statistics on unauthorized migration are hard to find in most countries as such movements generally are clandestine, but it appears that the numbers are substantial. The United States alone estimates that it receives an additional 275,000 unauthorized international migrants each year. An unknown number enter, work, and leave within the course of a single year and are uncounted in this estimate. Unauthorized workers are found in almost as diverse a range of jobs and industries as authorized workers, with agricultural and food processing jobs, light manufacturing, construction, and service jobs being the most common types of employment. In many cases, unauthorized migrants are smuggled into countries by professional rings that specialize in human trafficking.

The rights of migrant workers are specifically enumerated in various international instruments. These instruments reflect an attempt by the international community to establish minimum standards for the treatment of migrant workers and their families, as it is acknowledged that these persons are often subject to discrimination and problems of integration. The ILO has been foremost in initiating international labour standards for the benefit of migrants. Its principal instruments are the Convention concerning Migration for Employment of 1949 (No. 97), the Migration for Employment Recommendation of 1949 (No. 86), the Convention concerning Migrations in Abusive Conditions and the Promotion of Equality of Opportunity and Treatment of Migrant Workers of 1975 (No. 143), and the Recommendation concerning Migrant Workers of 1975 (No. 151).

The most significant achievement in recent years as regards protection of migrants' rights was the adoption in 1990 by the United Nations General Assembly of the International Convention on the Protection of the Rights of All Migrant Workers and Members of Their Families. The Convention reaffirms basic human rights norms and embodies them in an instrument applicable to migrant workers and their families. It recognizes that this group of people is often in a vulnerable and unprotected position, especially given the added problems encountered from clandestine movements and trafficking in workers. The underlying goal of the Convention, therefore, is to guarantee minimum protection for migrant workers and members of their families who are in a legal or undocumented/irregular situation. Its implementation could significantly encourage basic humane treatment of all migrant workers. However, the number of ratifications is still disappointingly small.[3]

FAMILY REUNIFICATION. The second major type of voluntary migration is for family reunification. Governments often permit close family members of those already in the country to enter through legal channels, although this policy is found more frequently in the traditional immigration countries than in those authorizing contract labourers only. The anchor relative in the host country may have been married and had children at the time of arrival but left his or her family members behind. Having determined to remain in the host country, he or she petitions for family reunification. Alternatively, a citizen or international migrant already living in the host country marries a foreign national and seeks his or her admission.

The willingness of States to authorize family reunification is supported by international human rights law. Article 16(3) of the Universal Declaration of Human Rights states clearly that "The family is the natural and fundamental group unit of society and is entitled to protection by the society and the State". Splitting families apart deprives each member of the fundamental right to respect of his or her family life. As the family unit is often the principal support to its members, separating families also undermines other rights. Children and women, in particular, become vulnerable to exploitation when they are separated from their relatives.

Family reunion is often a consequence of labour migration. For example, in the years after guest worker programmes ended in Europe, most officially sanctioned international migration was for family reunion as former guest workers brought their relatives to join them. Similarly, a substantial share of the migration into the United States in the past decade was represented by the family members of unauthorized migrants who gained legal status through the Immigration Reform and Control Act of 1986.

Family reunion also causes further migration. Many would-be labour migrants learn of employment prospects through their family members in other countries and then seek authorized or, in some cases, unauthorized entry to take the jobs. Moreover, once family members obtain residence status in a new country, they are often able to bring in additional relatives through family reunification programmes—a process called chain migration. Although few countries permit legal immigration of extended family members, some migration systems do authorize admission of parents and adult siblings of already resident immigrants. For example, in one scenario, an international migrant with long-term residence sponsors his new spouse for admission; they then sponsor each of their parents, who in turn sponsor their other children, who enter with their spouses, who in turn sponsor their parents, and the chain continues.

Apart from its strong humanitarian basis and despite the potential for chain migration, family reunification is valued by host countries because it generally is an effective mechanism for helping immigrants adapt to their new society. Already-resident family members help new arrivals find jobs, housing, and other needed assistance. New immigrants may add their earnings to augment household income. Parents of immigrants often take care of young grandchildren, thereby allowing both spouses to be gainfully employed. Families pool their savings to open businesses. At the same time, however, family migration may result in fiscal costs for the host society. Aged parents may require health services or income support that immigrant families cannot afford. Immigrants often have more children than natives and, as students, the children may have special need for language or other instruction, thus increasing costs for public education—both an investment in the future and a current expenditure.

Eligibility for family reunification is not universal, however. Many contract labour arrangements preclude admission of family members. In Japan, for example, many migrants admitted on fixed-term contracts may not bring spouses and children with them. Kuwait's rules on family admissions vary by skill level and salary: only those professionals earning more than US$ 1,500 per month in the public sector and US$ 2,200 per month in the private sector receive authorization to bring their families. Admission rules often restrict family reunification for asylum seekers and those granted temporary protection, even in such traditional immigration countries as the United States.

FOREIGN STUDENTS. One of the smallest but nevertheless important groups of international migrants is students. The years after the Second World War witnessed a steady increase in the number of foreign students enrolled in colleges and universities, particularly in highly developed countries. The United States remains the principal destination for foreign students, with about 480,000 enrolled in the 1997-1998 academic year. The US share of foreign students has been decreasing, however—a measure of the growing interest of other countries in offering educational opportunities for international students.

Foreign students study a wide range of subjects at both the undergraduate and graduate levels, but certain disciplines appear to attract the greatest interest. These interests differ, to some degree, by nationality and length of study. Science, engineering (including information technology), and business management are among the most frequent areas of study for foreign students.

There are many reasons for receiving countries to encourage foreign study. Native-born students are able to interact with students from other societies and cultures. Universities gain access to a broader range of students, who are sometimes the brightest from the source countries, and also reap financial benefits, particularly where incoming foreign students pay tuition at a higher rate than students already resident in the country.

The results for the countries of origin may be more mixed. Foreign students gain access to scholarship that may not be available in their home countries. If students return home after receiving their education abroad, they may bring valuable skills and knowledge that can be applied to the economic advancement of their own countries. Of course, they may also bring home information whose loss may be detrimental to the country in which they studied, including knowledge that can be applied to weapons development. On the other hand, if they do not return, the country of origin may suffer brain loss while the host country experiences brain gain. The effect is not inevitably loss on one side and gain on the other, however. Foreign students can be the bridge that permits businesses in both countries to develop mutually beneficial economic opportunities.

FORCED MIGRANTS

A large number of international migrants have been forced to leave their home countries and seek refuge in other nations. Many left because of persecution, human rights violations, repression, or conflict. They departed on their own initiative to escape these life-threatening situations, although in a growing number of cases they were driven from their homes by governments and insurgent groups intent on depopulating an area or shifting its ethnic, religious, or other composition. In other cases, migrants were forced to move by environmental degradation and natural and human-made disasters that made their homes inhabitable for at least some period. The legal frameworks for responding to these forms of forced migration differ.

REFUGEES, ASYLUM SEEKERS, AND DISPLACED PERSONS. Refugees have a special status in international law. A refugee is defined by the 1951 United Nations Convention relating to the Status of Refugees as "a person who, owing to well-founded fear of being persecuted for reasons of race, religion, nationality, membership of a particular social group or political opinion, is outside the country of his nationality and is unable or, owing to such fear, is unwilling to avail himself of the protection of that country". Refugee status has been applied more broadly, however, to include other persons who are outside their country of origin because of armed conflict, generalized violence, foreign aggression, or other circumstances that have seriously disturbed public order and who, therefore, require international protection.

The US Committee for Refugees' 2000 World Refugee Survey (23) estimated that there were 14 million refugees at the beginning of the year, down from almost 17 million at the beginning of the decade. During 1999, significant new movements occurred, particularly from Kosovo, which also saw massive return. According to the World Refugee Survey, the largest number of refugees were in the Middle East (almost 6 million), followed by Africa (3 million), Europe (1.9 million), South Asia (almost 1.8 million), the Americas (740,000), and East Asia and the Pacific (650,000). Each of the following countries was the origin of more than 300,000 persons who were still displaced in 2000: Afghanistan, Angola, Burundi, Eritrea, Iraq, Sierra Leone, Somalia, Sudan, and the former Yugoslavia. In addition, almost 4 million Palestinians remained displaced and eligible for aid from the United Nations Relief and Works Agency for Palestine Refugees in the Near East (UNRWA). In some of these cases, the refugees had been uprooted for decades; in others they had become refugees more recently.

The number of refugees—that is, persons outside their home country—is at its lowest level in years. That does not mean, however, that the number of persons in need of humanitarian aid and protection is lower. There are a growing number of conflicts in which civilians are targets of military activity as well as war crimes and crimes against humanity. Increasingly, people in these life-threatening situations find avenues of escape closed to them. Even when they are able to leave, an increasing number find no country willing to accept them as refugees. In such recent cases, refugees who found asylum—Rwandans in eastern Democratic Republic of the Congo, Ethiopians and Sudanese in Somalia, and Liberians in Sierra Leone—were forced to flee back to their home countries because of conflict in the host country.

There has been a large increase in the number of internally displaced persons, who in the late 1990s outnumber refugees by as much as two to one. The 2000 World Refugee Survey lists more than 21 million internally displaced persons, but warns that the total number may be much higher: Sudan leads with an estimated 4 million internally displaced persons; Angola and Colombia are estimated to have as many as 1.5 million; and Iraq, Myanmar, and Turkey have as many as 1 million.

The decrease in the number of refugees reflects a second phenomenon as well—the repatriation of millions of refugees to their home countries. During the 1990s, large-scale return occurred in a wide range of countries. In Africa alone, repatriation occurred in Angola, Burundi, Eritrea, Ethiopia, Liberia, Mali, Mozambique, Namibia, Rwanda, and Somalia. Other prominent repatriation destinations were Cambodia, Afghanistan, El Salvador, Nicaragua, Guatemala, Bosnia and Herzegovina, and Kosovo. Massive relocations occurred in the Commonwealth of Independent States; millions of ethnic Russians moved to the Russian Federation and smaller numbers of other ethnic groups returned (or, in some cases, moved for the first time) to the country of their nationality.

In some cases, such movements are voluntary because hostilities have truly ended and peace brings repatriation and reintegration. Too often during the decade, however, refugees—along with internally displaced persons—returned to communities still wracked by warfare and conflict. A range of factors induces such return. Countries of asylum may be weary of hosting the refugees and place pressure on them to repatriate prematurely. Donors may also reduce their assistance in the expectation that return will soon take place. The refugees themselves may wish to restake their claim to residences and businesses before others take them, or they may wish to return in time to participate in elections. Families split by hostilities may be anxious for reunification.

Deteriorating conditions in the asylum country—rather than changes in the home country—provoke the most troubling type of repatriation. Early in the decade, increased fighting in Somalia prompted the return of Ethiopian refugees to still insecure areas; later in the decade, fighting in Zaire (Democratic Republic of the Congo) forced the repatriation of thousands of Hutus to Rwanda. This form of repatriation is disturbing for two reasons: premature return can endanger the refugees, who may move from one insecure situation into another; and such forced return undermines the entire concept of asylum, that is, a place where refugees can find protection from danger and persecution.

ENVIRONMENTAL MIGRANTS. Environmental degradation and natural disasters uproot another type of forced migrant. Unlike the refugees described above, environmental migrants do not need protection from persecution or violence, but like refugees, they are unable to return to now-uninhabitable communities. Most environmental migrants move internally, some relocating temporarily until they are able to rebuild their homes and some seeking permanent new homes. Other environmental migrants, however, cross national boundaries.

The specific environmental factors that precipitate movements vary. Mass migration may result from such natural phenomena as earthquakes, volcanic eruptions, flooding, hurricanes, and other events that destroy housing, disrupt agriculture, and otherwise make it difficult for inhabitants to stay within their communities, particularly until reconstruction is completed. For example, periodic floods in Bangladesh have uprooted hundreds of thousands of persons. Hurricanes George and Mitch provoked massive displacement in the Caribbean and Central America. While most of these flood victims are internally displaced, the recurrent environmental problems provide an impetus for external movements as well.

Man-made disasters also precipitate mass movements. Large-scale industrial and nuclear accidents—such as those in Bhopal and Chernobyl—can displace thousands of people within a very short period. Other man-made environmental problems lead to more gradual movements. Global warming, acid rain, pollution of rivers, depletion of resources, soil erosion, and desertification all hold the potential to uproot millions of people who no longer can reside or earn a living in their home communities. While some of this environmental degradation may be reversible, the most severe problems will require sustained attention and significant resources for reclamation. In the meantime, both internal and international migration can be expected.

CAUSES OF INTERNATIONAL MOVEMENTS

In looking at the causes of international migration, the key question is why certain people move when human nature appears so strongly to mitigate against uprooting. As discussed above, only about 2.5 per cent of the world's population are international migrants. Scholars examining the factors that encourage voluntary migration have derived a number of explanations. Four economic theories set out the principal causes of voluntary migration (13):

- *Neoclassical economics* "focuses on differentials in wages and employment conditions between countries, and on migration costs; it generally conceives of movement as an individual decision for income maximization." At its most basic, neoclassical economics conceives of migration in terms of supply/push and demand/pull factors. Un- and underemployment, low wages, poor working conditions, and an absence of economic opportunities motivate migration, which tends to be directed towards places in which employment, wage, and other economic opportunities are more plentiful.

- The *new economics of migration* "considers conditions in a variety of markets, not just labour markets. It views migration as a household decision taken to minimize risks to family income or to overcome capital constraints on family production activities". This theory helps explain why those who may be most affected by the supply/push factors, the poorest within the community, often are the least likely to migrate, whereas those with some opportunities at home may well consider relocating. Those with some income to lose are more likely to want to minimize their risks and they also have greater capital to use in financing the relocation.

- *Dual labour market theory* "generally ignores such micro-level decision processes, and focuses instead on forces operating at much higher levels of aggregation. The theory links immigration to the structural requirements of modern industrial economies". Under this theory, modern economies have a permanent demand for immigrant labour. Four factors are believed to perpetuate this demand. First, employers are generally unwilling to raise wages for jobs at the bottom of the skill hierarchy because those at higher levels would expect increases as well. Second, there are problems in motivating native workers to take jobs at the bottom of the hierarchy because upward mobility is absent. Third, an inherent duality in the labour market creates stable, permanent, well-paid jobs in the primary economy and unstable, temporary, poorly-paid jobs in the secondary sector. Natives tend to be attracted to the stable jobs, whereas immigrants are willing to take the less secure ones. And finally, demographic shifts have affected the participation of two segments of the native workforce, particularly women and teenagers, who traditionally had taken the secondary sector jobs. Women have shifted from being intermittent to permanent participants in the labour force, and declining birth rates have reduced the number of teenagers available for these jobs.

- *World systems theory* "sees immigration as a natural consequence of economic globalization and market penetration". In this theory, modern capitalism has penetrated economies throughout the world and created a mobile workforce able to migrate for better job opportunities. The process of economic development is inherently destabilizing for large segments of the population in newly emerging market economies, particularly as land reforms displace people from their traditional agrarian roots. Economic development also gives people new skills. Populations may move first to urban and manufacturing sectors in their own countries, but increased earnings potential may attract them to more developed economies. Further, trade and political contacts between developed and developing countries create new linkages that permit migration to take place. The movements from former colonies are one manifestation of this phenomenon; migration between countries engaged in extensive trade relationships is another.

Sociologists add to the analysis by suggesting that economic factors may initiate movements, but social factors generally sustain and even augment them. They emphasize that migration does not take place unless there are networks that link the supply of international migrants with the demand for their labour. Some networks are highly informal, involving family and community members who arrange and sometimes pay for travel, find jobs for new arrivals, and help them obtain housing and otherwise provide support.

Other networks are more formal structures. They include labour recruiters hired by businesses seeking workers. At the most extreme end of the spectrum are professional traffickers engaged in human smuggling who may arrange both clandestine entry into a new country and employment. Depending on the difficulty and duration of the travel required, traffickers provide their services at fees that can range up to US$ 50,000. Often, the smuggled migrant is expected to pay the smuggling fees with income earned in the new country.

Political scientists add still other factors to the equation. In their view, the policies of source and receiving countries matter. Although unauthorized migration is considerable, overall international movements are constrained by rules and regulations set by States. Border controls, rules regarding work authorization, penalties on illegal entry, and criteria for legal admissions all affect whether the average would-be migrant risks departure from his or her home country. Some countries set barriers on departure, including requirements for exit permission and departure fees, that determine the ease with which international migration can take place. Other countries support international migration, particularly by establishing bilateral guest worker agreements to facilitate the entry of their nationals into foreign labour markets.

These theories are not mutually exclusive: some deal with individual and household behaviour; others deal with broader societal and political influences. An individual may weigh the advantages of international migration against the needs of the entire household, but then find that migration is possible only with the help of informal or formal networks. The degree to which such help is needed may be determined by the policies of the countries of origin and desired destination. Traffickers, for example, may make the final decision about where the migrant will relocate, basing the judgement on the ease of entry as well as the macro-economic factors that determine the likelihood that the migrant will obtain employment or other assistance.

Some of the complex factors that cause and sustain international migration lead to global movements across vast distances—for example, migration from China and India to the United States or from South, East, and South-East Asia to the Gulf region. However, as mentioned above, much migration occurs within geographic regions of the world, for example: movements within North America, Central America, and the Caribbean; from eastern to western Europe; across the Mediter-ranean; within the southern cone of South America; from all parts of sub-Saharan Africa towards South Africa; from Pakistan, Bangladesh, Nepal, Sri Lanka, and Afghanistan to India; and within South-East Asia from such migrant source coun-tries as the Philippines and Indonesia towards such migrant destinations as Singapore, Malaysia, and Hong Kong.

These global and regional migration patterns are by no means static. As the causes of the movements reflect changing macro-economic conditions—as well as individual and household needs and interests—it is not surprising that coun-tries with little history of emigration become major source countries, while other nations with long traditions of emigration become immigration destinations.

MIGRATION INFORMATION

Migrants, as well as governments, need accurate, reliable, and timely information on which to base migration decisions. Too many people cross borders in an irregular fashion and make unjustified claims for asylum or residence because they are unaware of the prerequisites for the move. The public in receiving countries needs accurate information on the implications of migration to counteract xenophobia. IOM develops efficient public information campaigns targeted and adapted to specific audiences and cultural or social particularities and conducts/promotes research for better understanding of migration phenomena. Currently, IOM is conducting information campaigns in Albania, Bulgaria, the Czech Republic, Hungary, Thailand, and Viet Nam and is considering such campaigns in Russia, Cambodia, Central America, Morocco, and the Baltic States.

IMPACTS OF
INTERNATIONAL
MIGRATION

Just as the causes of international migration are complex, so too are the effects of these movements on both source and destination countries. Their impacts cannot be characterized as solely positive or negative. Often, the same factors that create benefits can also produce costs. To give a seemingly simple example, brain drain of highly skilled migrants is often described as a loss to the source country and benefit—brain gain—to the destination country. However, if the migrants help link companies in the home country with business opportunities in the new location, both countries may benefit. On the other hand, if the destination country does not utilize the skills brought by the migrants in its workforce, then the migration may well create negative impacts for both societies.

The following section dealing with the complexity of migration's impacts—economic, demographic, social, and political—focuses first on destination countries and then turns to source countries.

DESTINATION COUNTRIES

The considerable variation in the effects of international migration on destination countries is determined in part by the characteristics of the migrants, their purpose in migrating, their reception in the new country, the duration of their stay, and a complex set of other factors. Moreover, the effects at one level of analysis—for example, a locality with large numbers of immigrants—may differ substantially from those at a national level or in localities with small numbers of migrants. Similarly, short-term impacts may differ significantly from the long-term effects of migration. With the caveat that attempting to summarize briefly the nuance and range of impacts is fraught with potential problems, this section considers effects common to a range of receiving countries.

ECONOMIC EFFECTS. The economic impact of international migration is determined largely by the involvement of migrants in the economy of the destination country. When international migrants are employed, generally they contribute to the national economy of the new country. The size and importance of this contribution is determined by the extent to which the international migrants are complements or substitutes for local workers. They are complements—and produce greater benefits—if their skills and education fill gaps in the composition of the overall native labour force. They are substitutes—and hold the potential for competition with native workers—if they have similar skills and education as natives and increase, but do not diversify, the workforce.

Hence, in countries in which the characteristics of foreign workers differ substantially from the native-born—in that some are better educated while many others have lower levels of education—international migration is a net benefit to the country. A panel of the US National Academy of Sciences explains (17):

> Using a basic economic model, with plausible assumptions, we show that immigration produces net economic gains for domestic residents, for several reasons. At the most basic level, immigrants increase the supply of labour and help produce new goods and services. But since they are paid less than the total value of these new goods and services, domestic workers as a group must gain.
>
> The gains to the domestic economy come from a number of sources. On the production side, immigration allows domestic workers to be used more productively, specializing in producing goods at which they are relatively more efficient. Specialization in consumption also yields a gain.

Migration into the Gulf States follows a similar pattern, with migrants carrying out both highly skilled technical jobs as well as low-skilled service ones.

The benefits are not necessarily distributed equally to all residents of the destination country, however. The new international migrants themselves clearly benefit economically if they are able to reap higher earnings than they would have in their home country. Others who gain are natives whose skills differ from immigrants— for example, higher-skilled professionals and managers in such businesses as hotels, restaurants, garment manufacturing, and health services that keep the prices of goods and services low by hiring unskilled foreign workers. Consumers who spend less on consumer items produced by foreign workers' inexpensive labour also gain.

Those who lose economically by the entry of international migrants are the people with whom the new migrants compete for employment. In a growing economy with low unemployment, there may be few such competitors because a rising economy may be strong enough to raise all incomes. Often, however, international migration means that employers may choose among a larger number of prospective employees and offer lower wages than they might offer to attract workers in a tighter labour market. The result may be lower wages, longer working hours, and fewer benefits.

Because a significant portion of international migration involves movements of individuals with very low levels of education, unskilled workers who themselves have low levels of education have the greatest risk of economic harm. Empirically, the group that loses the most economically from continued immigration is immigrants who have already migrated. They face the greatest competition from new migrants who, coming from countries with few resources, are often willing to work at even lower wages or with even fewer benefits than their already adjusted compatriots.

The actual and perceived effects of international migration can vary significantly depending on broader economic trends in the destination country. As noted above, when an economy is growing, the capacity to absorb and benefit from new workers can be considerable. However, in times of economic recession, the tolerance for international migrants may be substantially reduced. The Asian fiscal crisis is a case in point. A number of the Asian countries hit hard by the recent economic crisis sought to reduce the number of international migrants in the workforce by implementing aggressive repatriation programmes.

Large-scale migration also can produce or reflect distortions in economies. In many of the Gulf States, for example, an extremely high proportion of natives are employed in the public sector while the vast majority of private sector jobs are held by international migrants. A similar situation exists in the Commonwealth of the Northern Mariana Islands, a US territory that controls its own immigration policy.

The workforce-related economic impacts relate primarily to countries in which the largest portion of international migrants is employed. A different set of impacts derives in countries in which many international migrants are unemployed and in need of assistance. Refugees, in particular, may experience delayed entry into the labour market, particularly when they have experienced significant traumas in escaping from their home countries or being confined in refugee camps. Receiving governments may also restrict the entry of international migrants into their job markets. At times, these policies pertain not only to unauthorized migrants but also to individuals with temporary or permanent residency, in part to avoid competition with native workers. In many countries, particularly in Europe, long-resident immigrants, including the children of foreigners born in the host country, experience high levels of unemployment even when permitted to work. Educational deficiencies, language and cultural barriers, and discrimination appear to be the principal reasons for these low levels of employment.

When a sizeable portion of the migrant population receives public support, the fiscal impacts of international migration can be significant. In many countries with generous social welfare systems, for example in Europe, international migrants are eligible for aid on much the same basis as natives. Governments often choose to house refugees and/or asylum seekers in designated camps or centres, incurring costs of shelter, food, health care, and other services. In developing countries, these costs are often shared with the international community, but developed countries tend to pay their own costs. At times, the fiscal costs are incurred by subnational government entities—provinces, states or municipalities—and tensions develop between these levels of government and national authorities.

Even when international migrants are fully employed, fiscal impacts may result from their presence. If they are employed in low-paying jobs—as is common when migrants have low levels of education—they may pay less in taxes than they and their families receive in public benefits. Moreover, governments may incur costs for services not generally needed by the native-born population. For example, schools with large numbers of immigrant children may find it necessary to introduce intensive language training classes to help the new students become ready to participate in regular courses. While these added services may be seen as a beneficial investment in the future, they nevertheless are an immediate cost of international migration. Also, health care services may see diseases that are common to the source countries from which migrants come but foreign to their own systems.

The size and duration of these fiscal impacts vary significantly according to the education, skills, and age of the migrants. The tax revenues obtained from highly skilled international migrants generally exceed their use of public-funded services. International migrants who immigrate when they are young tend to produce fiscal benefits while those immigrating when much older tend to produce fiscal costs. In countries with a high proportion of natives who are at or near retirement age, immigration of younger migrants can help offset some of the fiscal costs of providing pensions. The migrants provide additional revenue to national tax coffers that can be used to support the older natives. However, most studies show that a very large number of international migrants—far larger than is the current case—would need to enter each year to offer a significant benefit, given the rapid ageing and low fertility rates of many countries.

DEMOGRAPHIC IMPACTS. To understand this last point requires more detailed analysis of the demographic effects of international migration on destination countries. In countries with low native birth rates, international migration accounts for much of the population increase—or at least the slowing of the population decline—to be experienced over the next decades (21). International migration contributes in two ways; first, the international migrants themselves are added to the base population; second, international migrants coming from developing countries generally have higher fertility rates and, because of their relative youth, lower mortality rates than natives. Even though migrants' fertility rates tend to come down after residing in the new country for some period, in the interim they contribute to population growth. In addition to affecting total population size, international migration can dramatically affect its composition. The immigration of large numbers of young migrants can affect age distribution, although, as stated above, the numbers must indeed be very large to offset the ageing of western societies already under way.

International migration also changes the racial, ethnic, and religious composition of the destination country. As global migration has become the norm and people from all parts of the world seek admission, particularly to the industrialized countries, host populations begin to reflect the new origins of the population. Growing rates of intermarriage in many countries help mitigate against the growth of differentiated minorities separated from the mainstream population. Nevertheless, the new immigrant populations create new communities as well as new cultural, religious, and social institutions reflecting their diverse ethnic origins.

Demographic trends also can affect the receptivity of host countries to international migration. For example, lower fertility rates in combination with higher native educational levels were instrumental in causing the transition of the Republic of Korea, Japan, and Singapore from labour-exporting to labour-importing countries. Migrant labour is now relied upon for construction, domestic services, and other low-skilled employment, while higher-educated natives take up professional and white-collar occupations.

SOCIAL IMPACTS. The growing diversity of international migration contributes to a set of challenging social issues. Social impacts take many different forms and—as with other impacts—include both positive and negative effects. Thus, international migration contributes towards greater cultural diversity, translating, for example, into a wider range of cuisine, performing arts, and sporting events. Yet community tensions may arise when the migrants and the host country natives are unable to communicate effectively because they do not share a common language or social values. Substantial levels of residential segregation may limit social interaction between migrant and native populations, leading to further misunderstandings. Immigrants also may become scapegoats for other societal ills.

Crime is a social issue that demands careful attention in reference to international migration. International migrants are both targets and perpetrators of crimes in the destination countries. As targets, international migrants often reside in poor, overcrowded neighbourhoods in which crime is common. If they fear law enforcement authorities, they may be unwilling to report crimes, and thereby increase their vulnerability. International migrants also may be the victims of anti-immigrant attacks that stem from concerns about their presence in the host country.

In some cases of criminal behaviour, migration is incidental to the crime itself. For example, drug traffickers may be apprehended at the point of their illegal entry because they are attempting to smuggle prohibited substances. In other cases, international migrants may violate laws because they are unfamiliar with their host country's rules. For example, the host country may consider the migrant's traditional child-rearing customs to be child abuse. In still other cases, international migrants may seem to be committing a disproportionate number of crimes, but once their demographic characteristics are taken into account, a different picture emerges: international migrants are often disproportionately males in their late teens and early twenties, a group that tends to have higher criminal rates.

How social impacts are handled depends largely on both the policies of destination countries towards the immigrants and the likely duration of their stay. Some countries with significant levels of immigration permit only temporary admission, with no expectation that the immigrants will integrate into the local community. Even after many years of residence, the international migrants may still reside in segregated housing designated for temporary workers. Interaction between migrants and natives may remain very limited.

Other countries focus primarily on permanent admissions, with the intent that the immigrants—and certainly their children—will become full members of the society indistinguishable from natives. Most countries have some combination of temporary and permanent admissions and a range of expectations regarding the eventual social integration of international migrants.

Countries differ as well in the mechanisms used to address social impacts. For example, in the United States, issues related to social integration are left to local public institutions, such as public schools and police departments, and private sector religious, ethnic, and business organizations. There is little federal government involvement or funding. The national governments in Canada and Australia, by contrast, have more active policies that explicitly promote the preservation of social and cultural traditions while also helping new immigrants learn the language of the majority population. A number of European governments have established offices specifically charged with responsibility for addressing the social effects of migration. In Germany, for example, federal and state commissioners for foreigner affairs serve as intermediaries between the international migrant and native populations when community tensions arise.

HEALTH IMPACTS. One of the important aspects of migration is its relation to health. Health conditions, medical services, economics, local risk factors and human behaviours vary widely across the world. Those factors ultimately influence the individual and population-based health outcomes of those who reside there. The migration of people between areas of disparate health parameters can act as a bridge between these varying health environments and the consequences of these migratory movements can affect the health not only of the migrant but of the community into or through which the migrant moves.

The association between the arrival of disease and the movement of humans was recognized early in human history. The profound effects that epidemic diseases can produce following their introduction into susceptible populations have had a significant historical impact. Attempts to manage and control the importation of disease by travellers or migrants arriving from distant locations represent some of the earliest community-based public health activities in human history. The development of quarantine and the medical inspection of arrivals from disease-afflicted areas in the fourteenth century initiated processes that can still be recognized today in some nations' approaches to the medical assessment of immigrants.

Concerns with the importation of infectious diseases represented the major area of interest in migration health until the last quarter of the twentieth century. Nations and States with policies of active immigration recruitment, such as Australia, Canada and the United States, required the mandatory medical screening of immigrants, refugees, and some long-staying visitors for decades. Countries with more passive approaches to immigration put less legislative and regulatory effort into the mandatory evaluation of migrants and managed communicable disease control in these populations through their local public health systems. The use of medical criteria as a condition of granting permanent residence may help explain why some populations of migrants utilize health services at rates less than the native-born population, the so-called *healthy migrant effect*. The utilization of health services and the health determinants of mobile and migratory populations are, however, a complex issue and the impact of immigration medical screening on long-term health outcomes is not completely defined.

The growing importance of migration health is primarily a consequence of two factors. First, the size and diversity of migrant populations have expanded. Migrants and the children born to migrants make up an increasing cohort of national populations in both traditional migrant-receiving nations as well as States where migration was uncommon less than 50 years ago. Second, health outcomes and environments across the world remain markedly disparate. The incidence and prevalence of infectious and non-infectious diseases, patterns of health service utilization, poverty, education, nutrition, and behaviour—all of which influence individual and population health—vary considerably. Consequently, the translocation of large numbers of people between these disparate health environments has consequences for health care systems at both the origin of the migrants and the destination.

The movement of more people to and from locations and destinations with different health environments and health systems can create some significant challenges for the planning and delivery of appropriate health services—be they preventive, promotional, or therapeutic. Health care systems increasingly must cope with previously unusual or geographically limited illness and disease. Additionally, the increasing cultural and ethnic diversity of societies as a consequence of migration affects the social and cultural aspects of health care. Many metropolitan and national health agencies have already had to amend or develop specific programmes to meet these challenges.

The investigation and study of the health of migrants and mobile populations is an active and growing area of global interest. The results and analysis of these endeavours are being used by the health policy and planning sectors on both the national and international level as they prepare to anticipate and meet the health needs of their constituents.

In addition to the management and control of disease and illness in migratory populations, migration health activity encompasses the implications and consequences of the movement and mobility of health care providers. The global market for qualified health professionals is extensive and widespread migration of professionals, particularly if they leave the developing world for employment in the developed world, can have significant impacts on the health systems they are leaving. Alternatively, the remittances returned to the place of origin by expatriate health care professionals can be an important component of national finance. The migration of health professionals is expected to be an actively studied area in the context of globalization and the evolution of health care systems for the foreseeable future.

MIGRATION HEALTH AND MEDICAL SERVICES

Movements of people entail important aspects of public health. Migrants and mobile populations may carry health characteristics of their place of origin to new destinations. IOM has over time gathered considerable experience from medical screening of millions of individual migrants moving under IOM auspices. Based on this experience, the Organization provides appropriate treatment and preventive health services to migrants, promotes and assists in the harmonization and standardization of immigration, travel, and international health legislation/guidelines, and offers support to training and education of staff involved in migration health care.

SOURCE COUNTRIES

As in destination countries, the impacts of international migration on countries of origin are complex and its effects are both positive and negative. This section focuses on a number of different impacts, particularly economic, demographic, and social effects.

ECONOMIC IMPACTS. Promotion of international migration has been an implicit or explicit policy of many source countries. A study prepared for the World Bank concluded that among the pressures for increased international migration are "government decisions (whether explicit or implicit) to actively promote labour export as a matter of economic policy. Such policies are followed by governments as diverse as Turkey, the Philippines, South Korea, India, Pakistan, Bangladesh, Sri Lanka, Jamaica, Cuba, Barbados, Mexico, El Salvador, and Nicaragua" (18).

Remittances, or migrant workers' earnings sent back from the country of employment to the country of origin, are one reason why these countries have promoted international migration. The International Monetary Fund (IMF) estimated that US$ 77 billion was sent in remittances in 1997. The decision to remit and the amount remitted varies depending on the location of family members, earnings abroad, costs of migration, destination country living expenses, duration of stay, and other similar factors.

Remittances are important at both the national and household levels. According to one study of remittances to Latin American countries (9):

> [R]emittances may be as important to national economies as exports, which traditionally have been the greatest contributor to gross national product. Remittances to El Salvador have, on occasion, exceeded the total value of exports, and are over half the value of exports in the Dominican Republic. . . . Even in major countries like Mexico, with a strong export-oriented market, remittances equal 10 percent of the total value of its exports and almost as much as the income from tourism.

The situation is similar in other regions. Remittances to Lesotho represented about 50 per cent of gross national product (GNP). One study found that the average miner supported seven people on remittances, and only 22 percent of households had other income to supplement this form of support (16). From 30 to 80 percent of Senegalese household budgets were comprised of remittances, a situation found in other West African countries.

At the household level, most remittances are used for daily expenses, such as food, clothing, and health care, as well as for improving housing and purchasing major consumer items. A smaller proportion goes into savings and investments, such as purchasing land or starting businesses. Such uses are not uncommon, however; a study of remittance behaviour in Egypt determined that "Once-abroad migrant households in this study also show a higher propensity than nonmigrants to allocate expenditure to investments such as agricultural equipment, vehicles, commercial enterprises (stores), and especially land. This finding contradicts the widespread belief that migrants do not invest their remittance earnings" (2). In addition, consumption can have important multiplier effects on economic development, stimulating economic activity by creating increased demand for goods and services.

Although the economic benefits of remittances are clear, they can have negative consequences as well. Those receiving the remittances may be so dependent on these external resources that the continued migration of working age members of the community becomes a necessity. In turn, high emigration rates can dissuade investment in these communities because of an unavailable or unreliable workforce.

The economic impacts of emigration go well beyond remittances. International migration can also represent both a gain and loss in terms of human capital formation in the source country. International migrants may represent a brain drain for the home country, with its attendant loss of human resources. A recent study of migration from Mexico to the United States concluded (4):

> The loss of human capital is the most important cost to Mexico. . . . The loss of human capital could be estimated by looking at the costs of education, health, and social infrastructure incurred throughout the life of individuals to achieve an economically active person in good working conditions. The cost for Mexico in human capital is the 'opportunity cost' represented by having invested in preparing that person and having foregone the value added of the migrant's productive economic activity.

The same report, however, also found that international migration could present benefits in the form of productivity gains from work experience during the period of migration. "There is evidence that working experience in the United States produces additional benefits to migrants when they return to Mexico. Such a bonus would be realized as improved earnings, if they are able to capitalize on their experience acquired." The empirical study upon which this conclusion was based found that an additional year of US experience yielded a monthly return that was at least eight times higher than that of an additional year of Mexican experience.

A number of countries have made explicit use of experience gained abroad to stimulate economic development at home. For example, Indian computer scientists and programmers who work in the United States have helped formulate ties between the emerging Indian computer industry and US information technology companies.

RETURN OF QUALIFIED NATIONALS

Through return and reintegration of qualified nationals programmes, IOM is encouraging social and economic development of recipient countries. Programmes in Africa, Latin America, ex-Yugoslavia, and Asian countries have substantially contributed to fostering national human resources development and countering the effects of the brain drain. IOM screens and selects suitable candidates, finances their return, and ensures their reintegration into professional and personal environments back home and thus contributes to building indigenous capacity.

DEMOGRAPHIC IMPACTS. Because many of the principal countries of emigration have large and growing populations, international migration generally has little effect on overall population. The number of migrants relative to total population size is small in countries such as China, India, Mexico, and the Philippines. There are exceptions to this, however. A number of countries have experienced the emigration of a sizeable portion of their populations, particularly when conflict precipitated mass migration. At the height of the war in Bosnia and Herzegovina, for example, about one-quarter of the population was externally displaced, with another quarter internally uprooted.

SOCIAL IMPACTS. International migration poses many challenges to the social structures of communities with large numbers of emigrants. Families left behind may experience dislocations, with one or more members of the household absent for extended periods. Relations between spouses and between parents and children may suffer from these absences. It is not uncommon for migrants to cease sending remittances if they remain abroad for long periods, leaving their families in a vulnerable situation. Migration can also produce major changes in traditional gender roles and relationships. When men migrate, their wives fulfil new duties within the household and, at times, in the broader community and may be unwilling to give up this new authority when their husbands return. Migrating women also find new independence, whether they move to trade (as do female migrants from Mali and Mozambique), take up professional assignments (as do women from Nigeria and the Philippines), or, more typically, work in domestic service or manufacturing.

Return migration can pose problems but also opportunities. A frequent complaint in traditional communities is that members bring back unwelcome practices from the countries to which they migrated. Increased crime and gang membership may be one such ramification of international migration. In some cases, however, migrants return with knowledge of democratic practices, an unwillingness to submit to official corruption, and greater tolerance for other views and practices. These migrants can be an effective force for positive social change in their communities.

MIGRATION POLICIES: THE ISSUES OF TOMORROW

GLOBAL CONTEXTS

Four global trends have particular import for decision-making on migration matters:

- Growing economic integration and globalization;

- Changing geopolitical interests in the post-Cold War era;

- Increasing transnationalism as migrants are able to live effectively in two or more countries at the same time; and

- Changing demographic trends and gender roles.

Economic globalization is not new. Nor is the role of international migration in stimulating and being affected by global markets. More than 500 years ago, European exploration, conquest, and colonization of continents with rich natural resources was connected integrally with the growth of a new mercantile, capitalist economy. Supported by new technologies that made circumnavigation of the earth possible, migration played a critical role in the expansion of global trade. Europeans settled new territories where, too often, they used migrants as well as indigenous populations as slave labour to mine minerals, grow agricultural products, cut down trees, or engage in other activities that would fuel growing manufacturing sectors.

Today's economic globalization, however, gives new meaning to this old phenomenon. The growth in communications and transportation technologies, combined with the willingness of States to enter into binding trade commitments and businesses to establish multinational entities, permits an integration of economies that had heretofore operated in separate, differentiated spaces. As the recent Asian fiscal crisis demonstrated, problems in one part of the globe can have serious detrimental effects in places far removed.

The ramifications of economic globalization and integration for international migration are considerable, as is the role that migration plays in furthering globalization. As Saskia Sassen has written, "Immigration is, in my reading, one of the constitutive processes of globalization today, even though not recognized or represented as such in mainstream accounts of the global economy" (15). Movement of labour within the global economy, by definition, requires new thinking about the role of States in regulating migration as well as the rules and regulations that govern entry and exit. Russell and Teitelbaum make the point that "international migration is not only a factor in the competitive production of manufactures for trade, international migration is central to international trade in services" (18).

Economic trends influence both legal and unauthorized migration patterns. The growth in multinational corporations, for example, puts pressure on governments to facilitate the intercountry movements of executives, managers, and other personnel. Similarly, corporations use contingent labour and contract out assignments at an unprecedented rate. In manufacturing, it is not unusual for components of a single product to be made in several different countries. The corporate interest in moving the company's labour force to meet the demands of this type of scheduling often runs into conflict with immigration policies.

Bilateral, regional, and international trade regimes are beginning to have a profound effect on migration. The European Union's evolution of a harmonized migration regime to serve as a counterpart to its customs union is but one example. The Asia-Pacific Economic Co-operation (APEC) Committee on Trade and Investment, spurred by the Business Advisory Council, oversees exchange of information on business visa requirements and is identifying mechanisms for regional cooperation to facilitate mobility. Under review are proposals for multiple entry visas, visa waiver arrangements, travel passes, harmonization of entry conditions, and information-sharing and systems training for border management agencies (11). The North American Free Trade Agreement (NAFTA) includes potentially important migration-related provisions permitting freer movement of professionals, executives, and others providing international services from signatory countries. Although movements of lesser-skilled workers are not regulated by NAFTA, the issue is likely to be revisited as economic integration grows. In Africa, protocols on free movements of persons are under discussion in the context of the Common Market for Eastern and Southern Africa (COMESA), the Southern African Development Community (SADC), and the Economic Community of West African States (ECOWAS).

The General Agreement on Trade in Services (GATS) is another trade agreement affecting migration policy. Under GATS, for example, the US guarantees a minimum of 65,000 visas per year for admission of foreign professionals, who are authorized to remain in the country for up to three-year stays. The US has also negotiated many bilateral treaties that permit nationals of designated countries to enter on a more or less indefinite basis to conduct trade or make investments.

A further global economic trend is the development of new technologies that facilitate both virtual and actual migration of people, ideas, and work and—at least in the information technology field—also have a seemingly insatiable demand for infusion of foreign professionals with state-of-the-art skills. These new technologies make it more difficult to weigh claims of labour shortages, surpluses, and displacements, particularly when companies argue that they can provide their services (e.g., computer programming) anywhere in the world.

The growth in global trade and investment is significant for major source countries of migration as well as receiving countries. It has long been held that economic development, spurred by access to global markets and capital, is the best long-term solution to emigration pressures in poor countries. While negotiating NAFTA, President Salinas of Mexico described his hope that "more jobs will mean higher wages in Mexico, and this in turn will mean fewer migrants to the United States and Canada. We want to export goods, not people" (12). In more colourful language, Salinas cited his preference for Mexico to export tomatoes instead of tomato pickers.

Academicians exploring the relationship between economic development and emigration tend to agree that improving the economic opportunities for people in source countries is the best long-term solution to unauthorized migration. Almost uniformly, however, they caution that emigration pressures are likely to remain and, possibly, increase before the long-term benefits accrue: "The transformations intrinsic to the development process are at first destabilizing. They initially promote rather than impede migration. Better communications and transportation and other improvements in the quality of life of people working hard to make a living raise expectations and enhance their ability to migrate" (22).

Several researchers posit what economist Philip Martin refers to as an "immigration hump". As levels of income rise, emigration would at first increase, then peak, and decline—a relationship that is depicted graphically as an inverted "U" (1, 7). Martin argues that short-term dislocations will occur in such sectors as agriculture that are in need of modernization. In conjunction with the continued pull of jobs in more developed countries and networks to link workers with those jobs, migration may well increase during the transition to a more vibrant, market economy. In reference to Mexico he concluded, however, that the issue is one of timing, as unauthorized migration would otherwise continue indefinitely: despite the migration hump, "there will be less Mexico-to-US migration over the next two decades with NAFTA than without NAFTA" (12). The experience of such countries as Italy and the Republic of Korea in making the transition from emigration to immigration countries gives credence to this theory.

Trade, investment, and migration connections can be seen in Europe as well, particularly in the context of expansion of the European Union (EU). Whereas the free movement of labour was, by and large, off the table in the NAFTA negotiations (except professionals and executives, as mentioned above), issues related to labour migration are squarely part of the negotiations for EU expansion into central and eastern Europe. The EU approach links economic integration and migration in several senses. First, freedom of movement is a core principle of the EU, so that once a country is a full EU member, its nationals have the right to migrate and be treated as equals. Second, freedom of movement affects both candidates for admission and the process of admission. Once a country becomes an EU member, there is typically a seven- (Greece, Portugal, Spain,) or 10- (Italy) year wait before nationals have full freedom of movement rights.

The connections between trade and migration also arise in the context of European-North African discussions. "EuroMed" conferences bring together EU representatives and representatives of the 12 Mediterranean basin countries to discuss trade, migration, drugs, and other concerns. EuroMed has an announced goal of creating a free trade area by 2010. Under the EuroMed umbrella, the EU makes grants that aim to retard unwanted migration. For example, in May 1999 it approved Euro 4 million to support civil society in Morocco by strengthening development associations.

GEOPOLITICAL TRENDS

Most current refugee and asylum policy was formulated following the Second World War, in recognition of the lessons of the Nazi era and amid growing east-west tensions. To a large degree, refugee policy—both international and domestic—was viewed as an instrument of foreign policy. Admission of refugees for permanent resettlement, asylum for victims of persecution and repression, and international aid to victims of surrogate Cold War hostilities (Central America, Ethiopia, Viet Nam, etc.) were all part of the fight against communism.

The Cold War also made some of the solutions to refugee crises all but impossible, whether defined as attacking root causes or promoting return of refugees. With the end of the Cold War, new possibilities emerged. Many decades-old civil wars came to an end. Democratization and increased respect for human rights took hold in numerous countries around the globe. As a result, repatriation became a possibility for millions of refugees who had been displaced for years.

One of the most significant changes in recent years has been in the willingness of countries to intervene on behalf of internally displaced persons and others in need of assistance and protection within their home countries. Classic notions of sovereignty, which formerly precluded such intervention, are under considerable pressure. International human rights and humanitarian law have growing salience in defining sovereignty to include responsibility for the welfare of the residents of one's territory. Francis Deng, the Representative of the United Nations Secretary-General on Internally Displaced Persons, and his colleague Roberta Cohen argue for greater international attention to internally displaced persons:

> Since there is no adequate replacement in sight for the system of state sovereignty, primary responsibility for promoting the security, welfare and liberty of populations must remain with the state. At the same time, no state claiming legitimacy can justifiably quarrel with the commitment to protect all its citizens against human rights abuse. . . . Sovereignty cannot be used as justification for the mistreatment of populations (8).

Intervention may be expected when the actions of a sovereign State threaten the security of another State. What is new is the recognition that actions that prompt mass exodus into a neighbouring territory threaten international security. In a number of cases—beginning with resolution 688 regarding the massive flight of Kurds from northern Iraq, which authorized the establishment of safe havens in northern Iraq—the Security Council has determined that the way to reduce the threat to a neighbouring State is to provide assistance and protection within the territory of the offending State.

Humanitarian intervention has occurred in places as diverse as the Sudan, Iraq, Bosnia, Somalia, Haiti, and Kosovo. The forms of intervention range from air-lifted food drops to outright military action. The results have been mixed. Aid reached heretofore inaccessible people in many of these cases, and in Haiti and Bosnia a peace settlement lessened the immediate reasons for flight and permitted some repatriation to take place. The root causes of displacement have not generally been addressed, however, and internally displaced populations often remain out of reach. Moreover, safe havens established to protect civilians have too often been vulnerable to attack.

The need for humanitarian intervention is also linked to the end of the Cold War. In some countries rabid nationalism replaced communism, while others have become so destabilized that no government exists to protect the civilian population. Addressing these new situations is all the more challenging now that the ideological supports for generous refugee responses have unravelled. One outcome is that the principles of asylum and *non-refoulement* (non-return to places of persecution) appear to be under growing attack in Europe and North America. Further, as demonstrated in the failure of the international community to protect the so-called safe havens in Bosnia, humanitarian interests alone are often an insufficient substitute for political will.

The changing contexts of humanitarian action affect the roles and responsibilities of international organizations with regard to forced migrants. Formerly, most responsibility for handling refugee crises lay with the Office of the United Nations High Commissioner for Refugees (UNHCR), which mobilized resources from such sister agencies as the International Organization for Migration. UNHCR also partnered non-governmental relief agencies that provided on-the-ground services to refugees. Today new sets of actors increasingly are involved with UNHCR and IOM in migration emergencies.

Military contingents from numerous countries have engaged in the airlift of goods, on-the-ground delivery of food and supplies, construction of camps, military interventions to create a safe and secure environment, peace-keeping, and other like activities on behalf of forced migrants. Militaries were deployed both unilaterally and through multilateral regional (e.g., the Economic Community of West Africa Monitoring Group [ECOMOG] in Liberia) and international operations.

Human rights organizations are also involved to a greater extent today than in the past. At the international level, the Office of the United Nations High Commissioner for Human Rights (UNHCHR) supports the work of the Representative of the Secretary General on Internally Displaced Persons and provides field staff to facilitate protection. In a recent development, the Security Council charged UNHCHR with creating the conditions conducive to the return of 280,000 displaced persons in Abkhazia, Georgia.

The intersection of development agencies with humanitarian ones is seen mostly in respect to rehabilitation, reconstruction, and repatriation activities. Gaps in mandates, as well as difficulties in coordinating the transition from relief to development, are among the problems faced in post-conflict situations. A 1999 roundtable concluded that "a response to the needs of post-conflict societies organized along two artificially compartmentalized lines, namely the 'emergency/humanitarian' and 'long-term developmental', did not do justice to the fluidity, uncertainty and complexity that characterized war-torn societies" (5).

TRANSNATIONALISM

A third trend affecting migration policies is transnationalism. Partly because of the technological revolution discussed above, migrants can now far more easily live in two societies at the same time. Circular migration has been a notable aspect of migration for much of the past century. When travel was more difficult, migrants tended to live sequentially in one country or the other. Now they can maintain two homes—low-cost transportation makes shuttling between the two easy, and inexpensive communication technology permits contacts with home communities. This phenomenon is reflected in migration patterns: from North Africa and Turkey into Europe; from Mexico, Central America and the Caribbean into the United States; from China into Canada, Australia and the United States; and from Mozambique and Lesotho into South Africa.

Flows of money between immigrants and those who remain at home are another important aspect of transnationalism. As noted, remittances often exceed any other form of trade, investment, or foreign aid available to the source countries of migrants. Maintaining the flow of these resources is often an important consideration in immigration policy-making. Recently, the United States granted temporary protected status to Hondurans and Nicaraguans to encourage migrants from these countries to continue to send remittances to the victims of Hurricane Mitch.

Perhaps the most visible aspect of transnationalism is the growing acceptance of dual nationality. Several major emigration countries, including Mexico and the Dominican Republic, have shifted from opposition to active support for dual nationality. A change in Mexican law permits nationals who naturalize in another country to retain their Mexican nationality. Making a distinction between nationality and citizenship, Mexico does not permit these naturalized citizens to vote in Mexican elections. By contrast, the Dominican Republic, which also recognizes dual nationality, permits absentee voting by Dominicans who naturalize elsewhere.

Additional global trends affecting future migration pertain to demography and gender. Although worldwide fertility rates are falling, many countries in the developing world continue to see rapid population growth. In most developed countries, fertility levels are well below replacement rates—that is, couples are having fewer than two children. These countries can foresee a time in which total population will decrease, leading some demographers to refer to a looming population implosion. They also can expect an ageing population. The United Nations Population Division projects that the number of persons aged 60 or older will increase from 600 million in the late 1990s to 2 billion in 2050 (20). The population of older persons will exceed that of children for the first time in history. At the same time, the number of working age persons per each older person will decline—a process already under way in the advanced economies. In western Europe, the ratio of working-age to older persons is already four to one.

Along with these changes in population growth and age distribution are changes in the role of women in society. Women increasingly are pursuing educational opportunities, working outside of home, and participating in civil society. The 1994 Cairo International Conference on Population and Development recognized that women's education and ability to generate income are essential elements of any strategy to restrain rapid population growth. Not surprisingly, as women gain greater autonomy through education and work, they are also migrating not just as reunifying spouses but also as principal applicants for work visas.

Demographic trends affect international migration in two respects. First, they are an important factor in explaining emigration pressures in many countries. Societies with rapid population growth often are unable to generate sufficient employment to keep pace with new entries into the labour force. Environmental degradation may also result, particularly when land use policies do not protect fragile ecosystems. Such natural phenomena as hurricanes and earthquakes often have disproportionately negative effects on densely populated areas, particularly in poor countries, with large numbers displaced from homes destroyed by these events.

Second, demographic trends influence the receptivity towards and impact of migration on countries of destination. The direction of these effects is not necessarily straightforward, however. For example, a country with low fertility rates and an ageing population may benefit from the admission of working-age international migrants, but as the migrant population becomes a larger share of total population, there may be a backlash against the newcomers. This pattern is seen particularly where the migrants are of a different race, ethnicity, or religion than the native population.

The close connections between migration and other population issues was recognized at the Cairo Conference. The Plan of Action addressed a number of migration-related issues. The right of sovereign States to regulate immigration was strongly affirmed, with due regard for obligations under the Refugee Convention. National admission policies should not, however, be discriminatory in nature. The Plan of Action calls on governments to give special attention to protecting women and children migrants. The Conference urged governments to recognize the vital important of family unity in framing immigration policies. Encouragement was also given to efforts to foster the positive effects of international migration, including remittances and technology transfer.

The Cairo Conference called attention to some negative trends as well. It strongly asserted that all people should have the right to stay in, and return to, their country of origin. The right of minorities to stay within their countries was given special attention, reflecting concern about ethnic cleansing and genocide in Bosnia and Rwanda. The Conference further emphasized the need to combat trafficking in migrants, with special notice given to the need to protect women and children trafficked for sexual exploitation and coercive adoptions.

POLICY ISSUES AND DEVELOPMENTS

Issues related to international migration confront policy-makers throughout the world. These issues range from regulation of legal migration flows, particularly in the context of emerging economic globalization, to control of illegal movements in an age of mass human trafficking. Forced migration continues to be a compelling policy issue, with little sign that refugee and related humanitarian movements are anything but on the increase. The special issues raised by women migrants will continue to demand attention. So too will the health ramifications of a world on the move. Issues of immigrant economic, social, and civic integration, including citizenship, must be addressed in societies with large numbers of international migrants who have moved permanently but may not necessarily have severed their links with their home society. Finally, the ways in which governments interact with regard to international migration raise issues of how best to coordinate and cooperate in meeting the challenges of the twenty-first century.

MANAGEMENT OF INTERNATIONAL MIGRATION

Humane and orderly migration benefits migrants and society. Orderly movements of people help ensure availability of labour when the host country requires it. Regulated migration further permits family reunification with minimum delay and disruption to either the migrant households or the source and receiving countries. Migration stimulates cultural exchange and helps societies understand each other.

Given the new global economic issues, as well as problems experienced by many countries in previous attempts to regulate legal admissions of international migrants, existing policies and frameworks are being challenged. Several questions arise: When and to whom should visa restrictions apply? Who should be eligible for work and residence permits? What rights should accrue to those legally admitted for work or family purposes? Under what circumstances should family reunification be guaranteed? Which government agencies should develop and implement immigration policy? Should governments strive to harmonize their immigration policies? The answers to these and similar questions will determine the future direction of immigration policies.

Of particular note are policies related to temporary workers. The liberal democracies with highly developed economies have found sufficient difficulties in enforcing the return of temporary foreign workers for observers to posit that "there is nothing more permanent than a temporary work programme". Although permanent settlement does not necessarily present problems and can create opportunities when the workers perform valuable labour, many governments question the credibility of migration policies that lead, seemingly inevitably, to the creation of permanent new additions to the population. Yet the dictates of today's economy—with the growth in international trade, multinational operations, and contingent and contract labour even in high-skilled sectors—make it likely that there will be a continued demand for temporary labour migration.

Effective migration management also requires the capacity to curb unauthorized flows of migrants and set realistic policies for the return of migrants no longer authorized to remain. When would-be migrants and traffickers are able to violate immigration policies with impunity, the credibility of legal admission systems suffers. A public that perceives immigration to be out of control may react negatively to all forms of migration, not necessarily distinguishing between legal and unauthorized migrants.

Controlling unauthorized movements presents many challenges, particularly for democratic governments that seek to protect human rights. Strategies must, at the same time, reduce the incentives for and capacity to migrate through illegal channels while protecting the human rights of the migrants—for example, from physically harm and, if they qualify for refugees status, for protection from return to persecution. Two extremes mark the ends of the control spectrum: (1) the so-called island strategies in which control efforts are focused on borders and ports of entry and there is little enforcement inside the country; and (2) the continental strategies that evolved in western Europe, in which border controls are buttressed by internal residence and work permit systems. Most countries require some combination of strategies that prevent the entry of those without authorization, reduce access to the labour market for those without permission to work, and remove those who violate immigration laws through appropriate legal procedures.

TECHNICAL COOPERATION AND CAPACITY BUILDING

IOM technical cooperation activities and programmes complement national and international efforts to manage migration more effectively and address the concrete needs of governments to develop comprehensive and consistent responses to migration challenges in a changing international environment. IOM concentrates on four areas:
- Technical cooperation to enhance the management capacities of governments in the field of migration policy, migration legislation, and migration administration;
- Return and reintegration of skilled expatriates to counter the effects of brain drain and foster social and economic development in the country of origin;
- Exchange of experts to share knowledge and practical experience on a wide variety of migration issues; and
- Post-emergency migration management to provide countries emerging from a crisis situation with the technical expertise needed to address migration-related issues.

IOM develops its activities in partnership with governments and international organizations, particularly United Nations agencies and the European Union. Technical cooperation activities also play a key role in regional migration dialogues such as the Puebla Process and the Bangkok Symposium follow-up.

Suppressing alien smuggling and trafficking, a concern for some time, recently rose to the highest levels of policy concern in many forums. In 1993, the United Nations General Assembly adopted resolution 48/102 on the prevention of alien smuggling. It urges States to amend laws to criminalize or increase penalties for trafficking, improve procedures for detecting forged documents, prevent traffickers from using transit points, strengthen existing international conventions, and more aggressively monitor their airports and ports, and the ships and aircraft of their registry.

Migrant smuggling and trafficking is becoming one of the most explosive branches of organized crime. An estimated 700,000 to 2 million women and children are trafficked globally each year (24). The total number of migrants who are smuggled across borders is unknown, but is believed to be increasing. The organization of the smuggling of migrants appears to take many different forms. Research suggests an emerging pattern of increasing professionalization. Long-distance, intercontinental smuggling reportedly is organized by well-known ethnic crime syndicates that form strategic global alliances linked to local networks of employers and enforcers. These networks supply a full range of services from transportation to safe houses, documentation, and jobs.

The four principal approaches to combating migrant smuggling and trafficking are law enforcement activities, educational programmes, efforts to protect the rights of those who have been smuggled, and, where feasible, help in returning home. The law enforcement strategy is a mixture of disruption and deterrence, including increasing legal penalties for alien smuggling, improving intelligence, breaking up smuggling rings, increasing arrests and prosecutions of smugglers, disrupting traditional routes, and improving cooperation with domestic and foreign law enforcement officials. Additionally, attention focuses on the employers of smuggled aliens, increased enforcement of labour laws, and regulation of marriage, modelling, and escort services to ensure that they are not involved in trafficking for forced prostitution.

There are two education strategies to combat alien smuggling and trafficking: education of would-be users of smuggling and trafficking operations and training of the officials who may come across smuggling and trafficking operations. Education campaigns inform those who might use the services of a smuggler about the dangers entailed. Education campaigns to combat trafficking in women—recruited to work in legitimate occupations and then trapped into forced prostitution, marriages, domestic work, sweatshops, and other forms of exploitation—have received particular attention and support from governments. Dissemination of accurate, timely information about migration and trafficking gives would-be migrants the means to make an informed choice about migrating and thus is an important empowerment tool, diminishing the possibility of traffickers being able to exploit potential migrants' lack of knowledge.

These education campaigns aim at preventing the victimization of migrants, but once individuals do attempt entry, governments grapple with defining what standards govern their treatment: the rights of migrants attempting illegal entry to be protected from physical abuse at the hands of smugglers, other predators, and immigration officials; witness protection and other programmes for those who testify against smugglers (often, successful prosecution requires the cooperation of those who have been smuggled into the country); and programmes for the safe and orderly return of smuggled aliens to their home countries (stranded or apprehended smuggled aliens often do not have the resources to return home and abused migrants may need special help).

COUNTER-TRAFFICKING

The IOM Counter-Trafficking Programme supports IOM Member States in preventing and combating migrant trafficking, and assists and protects the migrants who are victimized. IOM operates from a basic working definition that trafficking occurs when a migrant is illicitly engaged (recruited, kidnapped, sold, etc.) and/or moved, either within national or across international borders and when intermediaries (traffickers) during any part of this process obtain economic or other profit by means of deception, coercion, and/or other forms of exploitation under conditions that violate the fundamental human rights of migrants.

IOM activities concentrate on prevention and assistance/protection and include organization of seminars and forums to raise general awareness on trafficking, share experience among the various stakeholders, disseminate results from research, coordinate/harmonize polices and measures, and create formal and informal networks dealing with the issue. Research by IOM (including publication of such reports as *Paths of Exploitation: Studies on the Trafficking of Women and Children between Cambodia, Thailand and Viet Nam; To Japan and Back: Thai Women Recount their Experiences; and Migrant Trafficking and Human Smuggling in Europe*) focus attention on the problem of trafficking, raise general awareness, and provide governments and others with essential information for developing various forms of intervention. IOM also provides training to increase the capacity of governmental and other institutions to counteract trafficking in migrants and organizes mass information campaigns in countries of origin to make potential migrants aware of the risks of irregular migration and trafficking.

IOM provides legal and medical counselling and assistance to trafficked migrants in transit and receiving countries. In cooperation with NGOs and/or ministries of health and other concerned parties, IOM seeks to address the health care needs of trafficked migrants, provides shelter and accommodation for victims of trafficking, and offers voluntary return and reintegration packages—tailored to the individual situation of the migrant—to trafficked migrants.

Events of the 1990s—most recently the interventions in Kosovo and East Timor—demonstrate that addressing humanitarian crises involving mass migration is integral to maintaining regional security and promoting sustainable development. The legal and institutional system created in the aftermath of the Second World War to address refugee movements is proving inadequate, however, to provide appropriate assistance and protection to the full range of forced migrants needing attention today.

In addition to persons covered by the 1951 United Nations Convention regarding the Status of Refugees, the humanitarian regime is faced with growing numbers of internally displaced persons who would be refugees if they crossed an international border. While some progress has been made in setting guidelines on internal displacement, as discussed above, the application of these guidelines will present challenges in the years to come. Governments will need to determine how best to prevent forcible displacement, to gain access to those who are displaced, to provide for their basic assistance and protection needs, to ensure their safety and that of those providing humanitarian assistance, and to secure such durable solutions as return to home communities or resettlement.

Also of concern are individuals fleeing generalized violence and conflict. While some regional conventions cover these victims of war under the refugee definition, many countries make distinctions between "Convention refugees"—who qualify for asylum—and others in life-threatening situations who may qualify for other forms of protection from return. In mass exoduses, in which movements occur quickly, making such distinctions is all but impossible.

Increasingly during the 1990s, governments have used various forms of temporary protection to address these complicated movements. While many developing countries in Africa, Asia, and Latin America traditionally offered temporary refuge to all persons in these refugee-like situations, the use of such processes has grown in developed countries that have heretofore generally required individual asylum adjudication. Recent experiences with temporary protection raise a number of issues including: the criteria and procedures to be used in granting temporary protection; the extent to which those granted temporary protection should have access to the asylum determination system; the benchmarks for the cessation of temporary protection; the circumstances under which return to the home country should be required; the circumstances under which other permanent solutions, such as local settlement or resettlement in a third country, should be sought; and the rights of those temporarily protected to work, public benefits, and family reunification.

WOMEN MIGRANTS

As indicated on page 7 above, about one-half of today's migrants are women. While most accompany or join family members, an increasing number migrate on their own and are the principal wage-earners for themselves and their families. These women are especially vulnerable to deprivation, hardship, discrimination, and abuse. They face discrimination because of their status both as migrants and as women. They have limited access to employment and generally earn less than men and than native-born women. Legally, many migrant women are vulnerable if their residence is dependent upon a relationship with a citizen or "primary migrant". Migrant women face real risks of physical and sexual abuse during travel and in the country of destination. The rights of migrant women all too often are violated frequently, drastically, and with impunity.

Trafficking of women for sexual exploitation is a particular problem. Measures to address trafficking should not further marginalize, stigmatize, or isolate the women who have been the victims of traffickers, thus making them more vulnerable to violence and abuse. Broad-based support programmes are needed, including individual and peer counselling, hotlines for crisis intervention, legal advice and assistance, and shelter for victims who may be endangered by criminal groups.

The increasing focus on women's rights and the special needs of migrant women in the international community has rarely been translated into policies that effectively address these needs. To move forward, three areas need attention: improving awareness and understanding of the conditions and needs specific to migrant women; ensuring equal access to projects and services so that migrant women can fully participate in and benefit from them; and designing and implementing projects and services specific to migrant women where and when appropriate.

The development of strategies and interventions designed to deal effectively with current migration health challenges is essential, and migration health programmes should provide an accurate assessment of the associated public health risks. Recently there has been increased attention to the use of medical screening for infectious diseases as a method to provide appropriate and effective treatment and intervention for these populations, rather than for identification of those to be excluded from migrating. Through such use of appropriate medical investigation it is becoming easier to manage certain diseases effectively in the period prior to migration. At a time when preventive health practices and immunization schedules vary among nations, such a strategy effectively supports the provision of interventions to migrants, thus reducing differences in the risk of disease between migrant and local populations.

International harmonization and standardization of immigration and migration health legislation and practices would lead to less complicated border and travel procedures. Effective training and education of health care providers, travel medicine practitioners, migration officers, and border services would increase the awareness of the issues, improve the health of migrants, and ensure the health of the broader population.

ECONOMIC, SOCIAL, AND CIVIC INTEGRATION

The societal interest in international migration goes well beyond the rules and regulations governing entry and exit. Equally important is what happens to migrants once they are admitted to countries of destination or return to countries of origin. Receiving countries differ significantly in the ease with which migrants can become citizens, participate in local or national elections, obtain gainful employment, and qualify for various public benefits. Availability of and access to such services as language training and cultural orientation that help both newcomers and the communities in which they settle also vary.

To some extent, the variation reflects different views of the proper role of government versus the private sector in stimulating integration. The United States, for example, follows largely laissez-faire policies, assuming that families, schools, businesses, and other local entities will help immigrants become fully functioning members of the community. By contrast, the other two traditional immigration countries—Canada and Australia—have more developed governmental structures to aid newcomers in their adjustment process.

Also underlying the variations are different notions about the integration process itself—citizenship for example. Where temporary migration is the norm, host countries may have few expectations that migrants will integrate even if they remain for long periods. Hence, they are likely to have highly restrictive provisions for naturalization, even into the second or third generation. Where permanent migration is the norm, the expectations about integration are markedly different, with relatively easy access to citizenship. In recognition that large numbers of migrants had settled permanently in their territories, a number of countries have made significant shifts in these expectations in recent years. In Germany, for example, legislation permits certain children born in Germany to automatically obtain German citizenship, with special provisions for those who will become dual nationals.

In many of the OECD countries, the economic situation of international migrants is of particular concern. Often coming from countries with less developed educational systems, and sometimes facing serious discrimination, many migrants face difficulties competing in the advanced economies. Such problems differ among countries. In much of Europe, unemployment tends to be substantially higher among foreign populations, but the generous social welfare systems provide economic support. By contrast, in the United States, there is little difference in immigrant/ native employment, but there is large and growing income inequality mostly because of the high proportion of foreign-born persons whose incomes place them in poverty.

While much of this difference reflects general economic factors in these countries, similar strategies have been recommended to aid economic integration. Literacy, host country language acquisition, and basic skills upgrading help give unskilled immigrants greater potential to succeed in advanced economies. Immigrant entrepreneurs can help revitalize the economies of immigrant communities, but they often need help in developing business plans and understanding relevant regulations, financing requirements, and other practices required of businesses. Strategies to combat racism and workplace discrimination include: identifying more precisely and acknowledging the varieties of discrimination that exist in the economy; enacting legislation guaranteeing equal opportunity; establishing mechanisms for enforcement of these guarantees; and developing measures of the extent of discrimination, so that policies can be adjusted if necessary.

REINTEGRATION OF INTERNATIONAL MIGRANTS IN SOURCE COUNTRIES

Source countries of migration differ in their capacity to reintegrate migrants who return home. In some cases, return migration is expected and governments make special efforts to help migrants invest resources earned abroad. For example, several Mexican states provide matching contributions to remitted funds used to start new businesses. These types of programmes are relatively new, however, and there is little evidence to date of their effectiveness in spurring new economic activities.

In other cases, countries are ill-equipped to support reintegration. This is particularly the case in post-conflict situations in which massive reconstruction of the economy, housing, legal systems, and political structures is needed. Further, until peace is secured and reconciliation of former opponents takes place, the security of returning populations may be problematic. Programmes to help returnees reintegrate take many forms, ranging from assistance for such immediate needs as transportation and temporary accommodation and support to longer-term strategies for ensuring economic self-sufficiency. Much of the assistance required focuses on the broader communities in which reintegration takes place: demobilization and disarming of combatants; de-mining; human rights monitoring; and restoration of basic education, health, water, sanitation, infrastructure, and judicial systems. Without progress in addressing these issues, further displacement of people can be expected.

ASSISTED RETURNS

IOM Assisted Returns activities are complementary, consisting of return programmes on the one hand and of targeted migration diplomacy on the other. IOM also plays a role as a facilitator between origin, destination, and transit countries for discussions on return and related migration issues.

In the past five years IOM has assisted more than 250 thousand migrants in returning to more than 100 countries of origin. The number of States calling upon IOM Assisted Return Services is steadily increasing, as is the variety of programmes and programme components offered. IOM Assisted Return programmes can be divided into four categories:
- Return of irregular migrants in transit;
- Return programmes generally available to all irregular migrants;
- Specific return programmes available to certain irregular migrants; and
- Return of qualified nationals.

In an increasingly interconnected world, cooperation among countries is essential in addressing such global issues as international migration. While every country has a sovereign responsibility to protect its own borders, unilateral actions are generally inadequate to the task today. Few countries can erect sufficient barriers to stop unauthorized migration, particularly if the nation wishes to benefit from such wanted migration as tourism. Moreover, commitments to human rights, including international refugee law, rightly limit a country's options with regard to certain forms of migration.

At its most fundamental, international migration involves at least two countries—the source country and the destination country. Often, international migrants transit other countries, however, to reach their destination, thereby involving other nations in the process. Given the nature of international movements, governments increasingly see benefits in bilateral and multilateral cooperation and coordination.

Regional approaches to the management of international migration hold great promise for the future as demonstrated in three examples.

First, IOM, UNHCR, and the Organization for Security and Cooperation in Europe (OSCE) organized a 1996 conference to address the problems of refugees, displaced persons, other forms of involuntary displacement and returnees in the Commonwealth of Independent States (CIS) and relevant neighbouring States.

Second, the Regional Migration Conference—the "Puebla Group"—brings together all the countries of Central and North America for regular, constructive dialogue on migration issues, including an annual session at the vice-ministerial level. The Plan of Action calls for cooperation in exchanging information on migration policy, exploring the links between development and migration, combating migrant trafficking, returning extraregional migrants, ensuring full respect for the human rights of migrants, reintegrating repatriated migrants within the region, equipping and modernizing immigration control systems, and training officials in migration policy and procedures.

Third, in East and South-East Asia, two regional migration consultation processes, are ongoing. One—the "Manila Process"—is coordinated by IOM and focuses on irregular migration and trafficking in East and South-East Asia. Since 1996, it has annually brought together 17 countries for regular exchange of information. The second—the Asia-Pacific Consultations (APC)—is co-sponsored by IOM and UNHCR. It provides for consultations among governments in Asia and Oceania on a broad range of population movements in the region. Both of these ongoing dialogues were strengthened by the ministerial-level International Symposium on Migration hosted by the Royal Thai Government in Bangkok. The search for solutions to the many migration-related problems affecting the region becomes of particular relevance in the light of the economic crisis affecting parts of Asia.

Other such processes in the making in the southern cone of South America, in southern Africa, and in the Mediterranean aim to bring together the governments of all involved countries—origin, transit, and receiving.

CONCLUSION

International migration has been an important feature of life in the twentieth century. As this overview demonstrates, it continues to present challenges and opportunities for both source and destination countries. The twenty-first century is likely to continue to see large-scale movements of people—both voluntary and forced. Most of these movements will follow the patterns established in the prior century. While some migrants will travel great distances to far-away countries, most will move within defined regional boundaries. The following chapters describe the major regional trends, examining both immigration and emigration patterns.

ENDNOTES

1. This definition is consistent with the recommendations of an expert group on international migration statistics convened in 1995. See: Statistical Division of the United Nations and Statistical Office of the European Communities, *Final Report of the Expert Group Meeting on International Migration Statistics*, New York, 10-14 July 1995 (ESA/STAT/AC/50/9).

2. With an estimated global population of 6 billion, the estimated 150 million international migrants represent 2.5 per cent of the world's population.

3. Fourteen States have ratified the convention and an additional seven States have signed it preparatory to ratification (September 2000).

REFERENCES

1. Acevedo, D. and Espenshade, T. J. (1992). Implications of a North American Free Trade Agreement for Mexican migration. *Population and Development Review*, 10:729-744.

2. Adams, R.H., Jr. (1991). *The Effects of International Remittances on Poverty, Inequality, and Development in Rural Egypt*. International Food Policy Research Institute, Washington, DC.

3. Battistella, G. and A. Paganoni (1996). *Asian Women in Migration*. Scalabrini Migration Center, Quezon City, Philippines.

4. Binational Study of Mexico-U.S. Migration (1997). *Migration between Mexico and the United States*. US Commission on Immigration Reform, Washington, DC.

5. Brookings Institution (1999). Roundtable on the gap between humanitarian assistance and long-term development. Washington, DC.

6. Castles, S. and M. Miller (1998). *The Age of Migration: International Population Movements in the Modern World,* 2nd ed. Guilford Press, New York, NY.

7. Cornelius, W.A. and P.L. Martin (1993). *The Uncertain Connection: Free Trade and Mexico-U.S. Migration*. Center for U.S.-Mexican Studies, University of California at San Diego, San Diego, CA.

8. Cohen, R. and F.M. Deng (1998). *Masses in Flight: The Global Crisis of Internal Displacement*. Brookings Institution Press, Washington, DC.

9. de la Garza, R., M. Orozco and M. Baraona (1997). *Binational Impact of Latino Remittances*. Tomas Rivera Policy Institute, Claremont, CA.

10. International Organization for Migration (1998). The migrant as traveller. *Migration and Health*, 1/1998.

11. Luther, D. (1998). Progress in recognizing and regulating global professional service providers. *Industry, Trade, and Technology Review* (publication 3134). Office of   Industries, Washington, DC.

12. Martin, P.L. (1993). *Trade and Migration: NAFTA and Agriculture*. Institute for International Economics, Washington, DC.

13. Massey, D. and J. Arango, G. Hugo, A. Kouaouci, A. Pellegrino and J.E. Taylor (1993). *Theories of international migration: an integration and appraisal.* Paper prepared for the International Union for the Scientific Study of Population, Committee on South-North Migration.

14. McNeill, W.H. and R.S. Adams (Eds.) (1978). *Human Migration: Patterns and Policies.* Indiana University Press, Bloomington, IN.

15. Sassen, S. (1998). *Globalization and its Discontents.* New Press, New York, NY.

16. Sechaba Consultants (1997). *Riding the Tiger: Lesotho Miners and Permanent Residence in South Africa.* Southern African Migration Project, Migration Policy Series, No. 2. Institute for Democracy in South Africa, Queen's University, Cape Town.

17. Smith, J.P. and B. Edmonston (Eds.) (1997). *The New Americans: Economic, Demographic, and Fiscal Effects of Immigration.* National Academy Press, Washington, DC.

18. Teitelbaum, M.S. and S.S. Russell (1992). *International Migration and International Trade.* World Bank, Washington, DC.

19. Teitelbaum, M.S. and J. Winter (1998). *A Question of Numbers: High Migration, Low Fertility, and the Politics of National Identity.* Hill & Wang, New York, NY.

20. UN Population Division (1999). *Population Ageing 1999.* (ST/ESA/SER.A/179).

21. UN Population Division (2000). *Replacement Migration: Is It a Solution to Declining and Aging Populations?* United Nations (ESA/P/WP.160), New York, NY.

22. U.S. Commission for the Study of International Migration and Cooperative Economic Development (1990). *Unauthorized Migration: An Economic Development Response.* Government Printing Office, Washington, DC.

23. U.S. Committee for Refugees (2000). *World Refugee Survey.* Washington, DC.

24. U.S. Department of State Bureau of Intelligence and Research (1999). *International Trafficking in Women to the United States: A Contemporary Manifestation of Slavery and Organized Crime.* Center for the Study of Intelligence, Washington, DC.

REGIONAL MIGRATION TRENDS

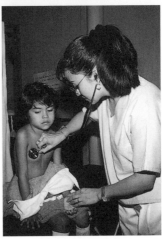

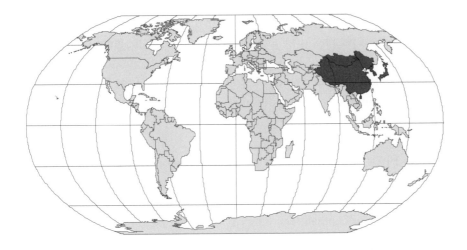

EAST ASIA

INTRODUCTION

East Asia is a region of tremendous diversity: China is the most populous country in the world and Japan is one of the largest and wealthiest economies in the world; some of the poorest people in Asia are in isolated rural parts of China (Guizhou Province, for example); some of the richest people in the world are in the global cities of Tokyo and Hong Kong. China turned away from socialist isolationism only after 1979; most of the rest of East Asia has been closely tied to North American and global capital since the end of the Second World War and particularly since the end of the Korean War in 1953. During the past decade, China persisted as one of the fastest growing economies in the world while Japan was caught in stagnation; the economies of the once dynamic Hong Kong and the Republic of Korea entered recession following the onset of the Asian crisis in July 1997. The huge economic differences within East Asia in rates of growth and in historical experience are reflected in the movements of people within, from, and to the region.

Ronald Skeldon, who will become Professorial Fellow at the School of African and Asian Studies, University of Sussex, United Kingdom, in October 2000, contributed to this chapter.

Population movements in East Asia are not simply a product of the recent past; they have always been an integral part of life in the region. The southward migration of the Chinese peoples over the centuries is one of the great themes in the region, but the movements of East Asians, particularly of Chinese peoples, out of Asia from the middle of the nineteenth century onward laid the basis for a global network of Asian migrant communities that has guided much of present migration (10, 16).

By the early 1990s, it was estimated that there were more than 30 million Chinese overseas (excluding those in Hong Kong, Macau, and Taiwan [Province of China]), some 4 million ethnic Koreans living outside the peninsula, and 1 million or so ethnic Japanese outside Japan. The majority of the overseas Chinese and Koreans were living in Asia, overseas Japanese in North and South America. Economic and demographic forces converted all but China from net exporters of population to net importers of labour.

IMMIGRATION TRENDS

The rapid economic development of parts of the East Asian region after the devastation of the Second World War and the Korean War propelled Japan, the Republic of Korea, Hong Kong, and Taiwan (Province of China) to levels of prosperity that challenged those of the developed countries of the West. This economic success gave substance to the idea of an Asian economic miracle based upon the hard work of an educated labour force under strong government direction. The transition from peasant farmers to urban, high-rise-living stockbrokers and service workers was accompanied by a transformation in fertility throughout the region. Excluding Japan, which has had a longer history of fertility decline and of lower fertility, much of the region showed a decline from an average of more than five children per woman in the late 1950s and early 1960s to fertility levels well below the replacement rate in the mid-1990s (Table 1).

This demographic transition has had a significant impact upon the patterns of migration. The single universal generalization that can be made about migration is that young adults have the highest propensity to move. When Asian economic progress first began, fertility levels were still high and newly affordable health improvements led to sharp declines in infant and child mortality. Thus, the pro-

TABLE 1.
PATTERNS OF FERTILITY DECLINE IN EAST ASIA, 1950-1990
(TOTAL FERTILITY RATES)

	1950-55	1955-60	1960-65	1965-70	1970-75	1975-80	1980-85	1985-90
China (Mainland)	6.11	5.48	5.61	5.94	4.76	3.26	2.50	2.41
Hong Kong	4.44	4.71	5.31	4.02	2.89	2.32	1.80	1.31
Japan	2.75	2.08	2.01	2.00	2.07	1.81	1.76	1.66
Republic of Korea	5.18	6.07	5.40	4.52	4.11	2.80	2.40	1.73
Taiwan[1] (Prov. of Ch.)	6.53	5.75	4.83	4.00	2.83	2.52	1.89	1.81

Note: [1]For Taiwan (Province of China) the total fertility rates refer to the final year of the period
         indicated rather than an average for the five-year period.

Sources: United Nations (1995). *World Population Prospects: The 1994 Revision* (ST/ESA/SER.A/145),
          Annex III, table, A.33. New York, NY.
          Directorate-General of Budget Accounting and Statistics, Executive Yuan (various years).
          Statistical Yearbook of the Republic of China.

portion of children in the population increased initially. Fifteen or 20 years later, those births translated into large numbers of young adults with a high propensity to migrate. But, as fertility levels fell over time so, too, did the proportion of young people in the population, and out-migration from the more developed countries of the region slowed. Rarely do demographic factors alone account for observed changes in migration patterns, but this supply factor does help explain the rise and later fall of emigration.

The impact of the shift in age structure of the population can also be seen at a macro level: rapidly expanding economies experience a shift from labour-surplus to labour-deficit conditions. Thus, demographic transition is accompanied by a migration transition. As the numbers of young people available to migrate decline and economies shift from labour-surplus to labour-deficit conditions, a shift from emigration towards immigration occurs, with that immigration coming from areas of relatively higher fertility (1, 3).

All of the most developed parts of the East Asian region experienced a transition from patterns of net emigration to net immigration, but the transition is most clearly seen in the case of the Republic of Korea (Table 2). During the late 1970s and the first half of the 1980s, the movement of workers on short-term contracts for Korean firms in the Middle East was the dominant migration from that country. Some 196,855 Koreans migrated on contract during the 1982 peak year. Permanent migration—directed almost exclusively to the United States—also grew. More than 30,000 Koreans were admitted as immigrants to the United States each year in the late 1980s. US-bound emigration was associated with the presence in the Korean peninsula of American troops who married local women, which then created the link for further family migration once the soldier and his wife were established back in the United States. Perhaps one in every nine American soldiers returned home with a Korean bride (7).

TABLE 2.
REPUBLIC OF KOREA: PATTERNS OF CONTRACT LABOUR AND PERMANENT OUTMIGRATION, 1977-1992

Date	Contract labour	Permanent emigrants	Immigrants to USA
1977	69,603	43,996	
1978	101,998	43,925	
1979	120,990	32,132	
1980	146,436	32,243	
1981	175,114	32,711	
1982	196,855	33,431	30,697
1983	184,277	32,875	31,499
1984	152,673	35,054	32,537
1985	120,245	38,686	34,791
1986	95,275	39,257	35,164
1987	86,340	42,670	35,397
1988	82,982	39,093	34,151
1989	63,647	33,066	31,604
1990	55,774	27,163	28,720
1991	45,713	19,623	20,808
1992	34,632	19,053	18,374

Sources: National Statistical Office, Republic of Korea (various years). *Korea Statistical Yearbook*.
US Department of Justice, Immigration and Naturalization Service (various years). *Statistical Yearbooks*. Washington, DC.

By 1991, the Republic of Korea's contract labour phase ended owing to the demographic changes described above. In 1997, the number of Koreans entering the United States as immigrants was less than one-third the annual rate during the previous decade. By the 1990s, the Republic of Korea emerged as an important destination of migrants, primarily from other Asian countries. The number of foreign workers increased markedly over the decade—from a few thousand in 1990, to 82,000 in December 1994 and some 267,000 in December 1997 (4, 11). With the onset of the financial crisis, estimates were that these numbers declined to about 160,000 from July 1997 to June 1998. These figures include both those in the country legally and overstayers who entered the country legally but who subsequently overstayed the period granted through their visa and became unauthorized immigrants.

Japan, Hong Kong, and Taiwan (Province of China) also became major destinations for migrants from other parts of Asia during the 1990s. The legal foreign resident population of Japan increased from about 783,000 in 1980 to 1.5 million in 1997 (22). Even at this level, the foreign population represented only 1 per cent of the total Japanese population. The majority of foreigners in Japan were long-term residents of Korean or Chinese descent. Recent immigration, however, shows admissions from a wider range of countries. The number of foreign workers in Japan is estimated to have increased from 260,000 in 1990 to 630,000 in 1996, of whom 45 per cent in the latter year were deemed overstayers.

In Taiwan (Province of China), the total number of foreign workers is estimated to have risen from 67,000 to 270,000 between 1993 and 1997, less than 5 per cent of whom are estimated to be unauthorized workers (8, 21). In 1997, foreign workers represented just over 1 per cent of the total population of Taiwan (Province of China).

In Hong Kong, the number of foreign residents at the end of 1998 was estimated to be 509,000, up from 460,000 a year earlier, and compared with 250,000 at the end of 1991 and 139,500 at the end of 1981. The actual number of immigrants to Hong Kong was higher as these figures exclude migrants from mainland China and workers who entered under one of the labour importation schemes. With Hong Kong again under Chinese sovereignty, concerns about future large-scale immigration from mainland China were renewed briefly in 1999 following a Hong Kong Appeals Court ruling that might have opened the doors to as many as 1.67 million Chinese children and grandchildren of Hong Kong residents. Beijing overturned the ruling—stemming any potential inflow—at the request of the Hong Kong government.

Although it is impossible to make a direct comparison of these migration data because of different definitions and recording methods, there are a number of common migration features throughout East Asia. First, although the absolute numbers of migrants appear significant, the migrants represent a very small proportion of the total population and labour force of host countries in this region. For example, foreign workers account generally for 1 to 2 per cent of the labour force in East Asian destinations, in stark contrast to the main destination countries in South-East Asia where migrants can account for 20 per cent or more of the total labour force.

Second, foreign workers tend to concentrate in relatively few areas and become very visible minorities in societies that have always seen themselves—rightly or wrongly—to be ethnically homogeneous. For example, in Oizumi-machi, north-west of Tokyo, almost 10 per cent of the labour force is foreign.

Third, concern over the ethnic composition of the foreign workers poses two contradictory issues for these countries. On the one hand, governments want to import labour that will fit into the local context. This desire led Japan, for example, to recruit some 140,000 *Nikkeijin* (ethnic Japanese born overseas), mainly from Brazil and Peru (14). Although these migrants looked Japanese, culturally they were Latin American, usually speaking little Japanese at first, and exhibiting very different behaviour patterns. On the other hand, the host countries' desire for greater control over foreign workers leads them to favour workers who are highly visible and who stand out from the native-born population. Excluding Hong Kong, relatively few labourers are recruited from neighbouring and labour-abundant China.

Recent East Asia migration introduced peoples with backgrounds and cultures very different from both native and earlier migrant populations. Earlier migrations primarily originated elsewhere in East Asia—Chinese to Hong Kong and Taiwan (Province of China); Koreans to Japan—while recent movements originated in these countries as well as countries in South-East and South Asia. For example, of the 270,000 foreign workers in Taiwan (Province of China) in 1997, 53 per cent came from Thailand and 40 per cent came from the Philippines (8). The principal source of foreign workers—around 150,000 in early 1998—to Hong Kong (excluding China itself) was the Philippines. While East Asian migrants still dominate movements into Japan and the Republic of Korea, workers from the Philippines, Thailand, and Bangladesh figure prominently in the flows, particularly among overstayers in the Republic of Korea.

Gender is another common thread in East Asia immigration. With the increasing participation of local women in the expanding service sector, there is a demand for domestic help in the dual-career households of the emerging middle classes that is met by importing foreign workers. This situation is most clearly seen in Hong Kong, where there are more than 150,000 women from the Philippines and significant numbers from Thailand and Sri Lanka. Many of the women from the Philippines, although highly educated, take jobs that require few skills, a situation brought on by the low remuneration for professional jobs in the economies of origin relative to the wages and conditions—free food and housing and the opportunity for additional, usually clandestine, employment—for domestic employment in the economies of destination.

One of the few types of permanent immigration allowed in the region is the movement of foreign brides into Japan and, to some extent, Taiwan (Province of China). This movement is a very small part of the total immigrant flow to those economies. It is a direct consequence of prior intense internal rural-to-urban migration that brought about rural depopulation (*kaso* in Japan) with the exodus of locally available marriage-age women from isolated rural communities to urban offices and factories. Mail order brides, mainly from the Philippines, but also from Viet Nam and Thailand, have been brought in to fill the vacuum. The social isolation of these women, the majority of whom do not speak the local languages, can only be imagined.

Throughout East Asia, migration is a tightly controlled phenomenon. All the economies implement exclusionary immigration policies that allow very few migrants to become permanent residents or to qualify for nationality. Thus, immigration is composed primarily of workers on fixed-term contracts who must return to their homeland upon termination of their contract—reminiscent of the guest worker programmes of European countries prior to 1973. A worker deemed to have overstayed the terms of the contract is deported. Throughout the region, the rights of migrants are subordinate to the will of the State and they have few of the institutions for protection available to migrants in western countries.

East Asians, aware of the saying about the European guest worker programmes that "there is nothing as permanent as a temporary worker" wonder whether contract labour will become a permanent feature of their own economies. While *Nikkeijin* are allowed to bring their families to Japan—the precursor to permanent settlement—migrants in general are not permitted family accompaniment. In

Japan, not even fourth-generation Korean and Chinese residents are considered eligible for naturalization. A major shift in public attitude and in official economic policies throughout the region would be necessary to permit long-term settlement of migrants.

Despite tight immigration controls, local labour market conditions are often influential in retaining foreign workers who otherwise would have returned home. Thus, there is a relatively sizeable number of overstayers in some countries. In Japan, for example, the need for workers in certain sectors is so great that migrants are able to stay on in their employment beyond their contract time. Though overstayers generally are visible minorities whose local integration is severely limited, authorities generally overlook their stay, to the extent that the migrant is otherwise law-abiding.

The settlement patterns of migrants in the host country often are designed to limit the possibility of future settlement: workers are brought in to do a specific job with a specific company that must house, feed, and entertain the workers on-site, essentially restricting their interaction with the surrounding population. In the case of Chinese construction workers at the Hong Kong airport, workers were restricted to their worksite until the project was over and they were sent home. Contact with the local community was discouraged. Thus, workers become dispersed in small groups throughout a host country depending on the location of a project, whether in manufacturing or construction. The spatial pattern of settlement is quite unlike other regions where migrants of the same ethnic origin find their own accommodations in concentrated ethnic communities.

East Asia is unlike North America and Australia—where native workers have moved out of the centre of major cities and have been replaced to some extent by immigrant workers. Clearly there are concentrations of immigrant labour in the largest cities, particularly around port areas and other sites where casual employment is available for overstayers. However, the numbers of immigrants are much smaller than in the countries of the West and there is little evidence of immigrants either filling a vacuum left by departing natives or pushing natives out of low-wage areas. Because so much immigration involves contract labour or is tied to specific firms in East Asia, migrants are likely to be more dispersed than in the West. With the exception of the long-established Korean or Chinese migrants, communities of new immigrants have yet to make their mark on either the urban landscapes or the patterns of movement of local populations in East Asia.

Other changes in the structure of the migration system may influence integration possibilities in the future. Rising levels of education and of expectations among the local populations of East Asia have meant that local labour is unwilling to undertake more menial jobs, leaving an important labour market niche that can only be filled by immigrant labour. Again, the possible parallels with the situation in Europe two decades ago cause discomfort among analysts and policy-makers throughout the region. Despite the recession currently affecting the region, circular patterns of labour migration can be expected to continue—if perhaps on a reduced scale—for the indefinite future.

EMIGRATION TRENDS

The largest source of unskilled labour in the East Asia region is China. International migration from China is estimated to reach 300,000-400,000 persons annually, including contract workers, emigrant settlers, students, and unauthorized workers (18). Roughly 100,000 settlers legally emigrate each year to the United States, Canada, and Australia. Estimates of the number of Chinese migrants who are smuggled illegally into these and other countries range as high as 200,000 persons per year. Excluding Hong Kong and Macau, for political and other reasons relatively small numbers of Chinese workers are recruited to work in the other economies of East Asia.

China was a relative latecomer to the international market for contract labour, participating outside the then-socialist bloc only after the reforms of 1979. Between the mid-1950s and the early 1980s, little out-migration took place. Although China essentially missed out on the boom construction years in the countries of the Middle East in the 1970s and 1980s, it was certainly aware of the experience of neighbouring economies with contract labour and the foreign exchange generated through remittances. When it opened to the wider world, China began to capitalize on its vast labour reserves and, by the early 1990s, Chinese migrants abroad generated more than US$ 6.8 billion in foreign exchange.

Recruitment agencies dominate labour migration in Asia. This is one of the most effective ways through which governments in the region avoid permanent settlement. Contract terms require the recruitment agencies to send workers home at the end of contracts. Both public and private contractors engage in recruitment, although the number of private agencies appears to be increasing. In Taiwan, contractors are responsible for both the behaviour of workers and work conditions. As the system now operates, a company desiring workers contracts an agency in a potential destination country to provide a certain number and type of worker and the agency, in turn, contacts its counterparts in the potential countries of origin. The counterparts in countries of origin then find the workers and arrange all paperwork for entry (9).

Contract workers from China generally are male, unskilled, and engaged in construction activities. For example, Chinese workers helped build the airport in Hong Kong and took part in the construction boom in Macau (both jobs have now run their course). An exception is the case of women contract workers in garment factories in Saipan, a US territory in the Marianas. In no case do families accompany contract workers. Contract labourers sent overseas originate primarily in the southern coastal provinces, although workers from the northern coastal provinces and other areas also participate in international programmes.

Perhaps 100,000-200,000 unauthorized migrants leave China every year with the help of organized smuggling rings. For obvious reasons, there are no exact sources of data on illegal migrants from China (20). The majority of unauthorized migrants appear to come from a relatively small number of source areas in southern China, principally in Fujian province. Estimates of the number of Chinese migrants smuggled into the United States each year in the early 1990s were placed at more than 100,000 people. Changle county in Fujian province is the source of most immigration to the United States, and in one village, Houyu, 80 per cent of the population reportedly is now found in and around New York. Migrants remit back an estimated US$ 100 million annually to Changle county alone (4). Senior Chinese sources in 1994 reported more than 700,000 unauthorized emigrants in recent years to Asia, Europe, Russia, and the United States. These figures remain speculative as there are other estimates of as many as 1 million persons of Chinese origin living illegally in the Siberian regions of Russia's Far East alone.

Perhaps the most striking feature of Chinese populations overseas is just how small the numbers are in comparison with the base population of China itself: 30 million Chinese migrants overseas is large in terms of absolute numbers, but small when compared with China's vast population of more than 1 billion. There was no "Great Migration" out of China to compare with the proportions leaving Europe 100 years ago, for example. However, such broad comparisons are largely meaningless, as the majority of migrants from China come from a very few areas within the country—essentially the coastal parts of Guangdong, Fujian, and Zhejiang provinces—and there the relative impact of movements overseas has been and remains great. Large parts of China, however, have not yet participated in international population movements.

While perceived poverty in the context of the rising expectations in the more open regions of the "new" China encourages many young men and women to leave, unauthorized movements are facilitated by the global network of overseas Chinese established through the migrations of the nineteenth century. This network permits the operation of a complex and constantly changing system of alternative smuggling routes from China to the countries of the West.

Perhaps the illegal movements out of China that capture the greatest attention are those of unskilled labour. Of interest are not simply the numbers—although these can be substantial—but the role of criminal organizations that appear to have turned human smuggling into a multi-billion dollar business that challenges the integrity of the borders of developed nations, particularly the United States.

The Chinese Government, like all governments in the region, condemns unauthorized migration. Numerous anti-trafficking laws were enacted in an attempt to crack down on this well-organized crime and the victimization it causes. Nevertheless, there is evidence that women (and children) are being trafficked, although they are not the only ones. At the 1995 World Conference on Women in Beijing, trafficking in women in East Asia was marked as a priority for international action. It is difficult to separate out the coercive, deceptive, and violent from other more compliant forms of trafficking. Several beginning attempts at international cooperation in the management of migration in the region, including the suppression of trafficking, were taken in early 1999 with the signing of the Bangkok Declaration. These agreements, however, are not legally binding.

The cost of arranging migration is substantial, often in excess of US$ 30,000 per head. Thus, migration is likely to be restricted to those families with access to resources. Such a sum is rarely likely to be paid up-front or in full, but the cash advance required almost certainly precludes the members of the poorest and least educated families. The organizations that have the ability to advance the sums of money required and to enforce their later collection are criminal syndicates. There is an accepted, but little documented, link between these syndicates and the trafficking of drugs. It appears unlikely that there is any single super-syndicate, but rather many small groups that operate—at times alone and at times in association. Upon arrival at the destination, migrants often are kept as virtual bonded labour in the sweatshops of the Chinatowns of some U.S. and European cities until the balance due is paid.

INTERNAL MIGRATION

After more than a decade of official control on individual mobility within China, the domestic reforms of 1979 had the unintended effect of unleashing waves of internal migration in China (2, 12). Precise figures for the number of unauthorized internal migrants in China are not available, but estimators commonly cite 100 million people on the move outside their places of registration—the floating population. The destinations for the movement are primarily the major cities of Beijing-Tianjin and Shanghai and the southern boom region around the Pearl River delta in Guangdong province. These destinations are also the same regions from which international migration occurs among a different group of people. Although more men than women move within China, much of the migration towards the Pearl River delta, in particular, is dominated by women who fill factory jobs in labour-intensive industries set up by capital from Hong Kong and Taiwan.

The intense rural-to-urban migration in China, bringing rapid urbanization, occurs against the background of rising urban unemployment as State-owned enterprises are being restructured. There is concern that the vast numbers of the floating population might contribute to social unrest if adequate employment cannot be found for them. China appears to be one of the few economies in East Asia that has been able to maintain—thus far—a relatively rapid rate of economic growth. Should this growth falter, with rural areas already burdened by surplus populations, then the "army on the move" might indeed be a factor promoting unrest. It is unlikely that internal movements will evolve directly or quickly into international flows.

A REGION IN TRANSITION

The idea of a simple shift from emigration to immigration for the countries in the East Asian region, while generally the case, shrouds important changes in the nature of the migration systems in and from the region. All the countries remain significant sources of migration of highly skilled and business migrants or of students going overseas for further study. Most of this movement is not permanent, although students or business migrants may remain overseas for long periods. In 1995, for example, almost 3 million Japanese left their country for purposes other

TABLE 3.

TYPES OF RECENT OUTMOVEMENT: JAPAN AND THE REPUBLIC OF KOREA

	Japan		Republic of Korea	
	1985	1995	1985	1995
Diplomacy	6,838	10,424	641	NA
Government and official business	20,990	41,178	4,465	22,035[1]
Short business trips	696,962	2,065,990	134,031	900,069
Employment, including assignment to overseas branches	57,236	46,239	146,823	234,188
Study and research	41,123	269,687	42,803	276,515
Emigration	34,492	89,699	38,686	16,057
Tourism	4,024,062	12,685,156	45,939	2,206,354
Others	66,663	89,752	70,76	163,534
Total	**4,948,366**	**15,298,125**	**484,155**	**3,818,752**

Note: [1]The categories of "Diplomacy" and "Government" were combined into one category in Korean official records in 1995.

Sources: Government of Japan Statistics Bureau, Management and Coordination Agency. *Japan Statistical Yearbook.*
Republic of Korea National Statistical Office. *Korea Statistical Yearbook.*

than sightseeing, up from almost 1 million in 1985. Similarly, some 1.6 million Koreans left the Republic of Korea in 1996 for reasons not related to tourism, whereas only 430,000 did so in 1990 (Table 3). The majority went overseas for business, reflecting the increasing integration of the global economic system and the influence of Asian multinational corporations in other parts of the world. Migrants from Taiwan (Province of China) and Hong Kong have dominated the business immigration programmes of Canada, Australia, and New Zealand.

Students from Japan, the Republic of Korea, and Taiwan (Province of China) have long been among the top 10 source areas for foreign students in the United States. Students from Mainland China ranked second only to Japanese students in the latter half of the 1990s. In the United States, Asian students comprise the majority of foreign students (57.7 per cent in 1997-1998). Likewise in Canada, the percentage of Asian students is also significant: 48.4 per cent in 1995 (down from 55.2 per cent in 1991 possibly as a consequence of students changing their status to permanent resident under new 1990 rules) (Tables 4A and 4B).

TABLE 4A.

ASIAN STUDENTS IN THE UNITED STATES, SELECTED EAST ASIAN COUNTRIES, 1996-1998

Country/Region	Students 1996/97	% of Total	Students 1997/98	% of Total
Japan	46,292	10.1	47,073	9.8
Mainland China	42,503	9.2	46,958	9.7
Rep. of Korea	37,130	8.1	42,890	8.9
Taiwan (Province of China)	30,487	6.6	30,855	6.4
Asia Total	260,743	56.9	277,508	57.7
World Total	**457,984**	**100.0**	**481,280**	**100.0**

Source: Institute for International Education (1998). Open Door. Washington, DC.
www.iie.org/516img/od98/ffact_02.gif Accessed on 8 September 1999.

TABLE 4B.

ASIAN STUDENTS IN CANADA, SELECTED EAST ASIAN COUNTRIES, 1991-1995

Country/Region	Students 1991	% of Total	Students 1995	% of Total
Hong Kong	13,750	17.0	5,880	8.2
Mainland China	4,460	5.5	2,850[1]	4.0
Japan	4,630	5.7	5,700	7.9
Taiwan (Prov. of Ch.)	3,490	4.3	3,550	4.9
Rep. of Korea	1,390	1.7	3,600	5.0
Asia Total	44,800	55.2	34,830	48.4
World Total	**82,240**	**100.0**	**72,700**	**100.0**

Note: [1] The decline in the number of Chinese students between 1991 and 1995 may be due
to the numbers of students who changed their status to permanent resident after 1990.

Source: Canada Statistics. International Student Participation in Canadian Education, 1993-95.
http://www.statcan.ca/daily/english/980513/d980513.htm#art1 Accessed on
8 September 1999.

These students, as well as other settler migrants to those countries, have established a pattern of long-distance commuting—the "astronaut" phenomenon—in which they establish wives and/or families at the destination while the husband returns to his place of origin to continue his job or oversee the family business (17). These migrations are giving rise to transnational communities of new identities distinct from both origin and destination communities. Where both husband and wife return to the economy of origin to continue their employment, the children established in the destination countries are known as "parachute kids". In extending families across space, despite regular commuting across the Pacific, both astronauts and parachute kids can experience intense social disruption through prolonged separation and lack of parental supervision.

The trend through time in the East Asian region, rather than a simple shift from emigration to immigration, has been towards a greater complexity in the patterns of migration and in the types of people moving. Transnational systems of circulation characterize the movements into—as well as out of—the economies concerned. This shift is the result of simultaneous increased levels of education of the local populations and decline in growth rates of the labour force. The skilled and educated participate in the out-movements as the economies expand overseas because they are reluctant to undertake the menial tasks at home that then are filled by imported unskilled workers. The construction industry in many parts of East Asia, for example, relies heavily on foreign labour.

The economic recession that gripped Asia in the 1990s has not materially affected this trend (19). It might appear that foreign workers would be among the first to lose their jobs. However, as of the first half of 1998—apart from the Republic of Korea, which had begun to repatriate illegal migrants—the direct impact of the crisis on migration in the region was relatively small. It is difficult to separate the effect of structural change in the economies—for example, the shift away from construction towards production—from any direct effect of the crisis on migration. Even in the Republic of Korea, where the repatriation of foreigners was supposed to open up jobs for newly unemployed Koreans, the result has hardly been that intended. Few Koreans have been willing to undertake the kinds of jobs filled by migrants and, even in a time of rising unemployment, the positions remain unfilled. Local workers, with their higher aspirations, are just unwilling to do the jobs at the bottom end of the spectrum—the so-called 3-D jobs: dangerous, demanding and dirty. In reality, they are unlikely to be jobs of any such kind; they are simply poorly paid, insecure, and boring. Even in a time of economic crisis, there remains a key role for international labour.

In other parts of Asia, the main impact of the crisis is likely to be upon domestic migration. When factories are closed, the newly unemployed can either stay where they are or move to look for work elsewhere. However, in the more developed economies of East Asia, the alternative of a return to the village is not a realistic option among populations schooled in urban ways. Only in China, where there is intense circulation between urban and rural sectors, would such a scenario exist and rural unemployment there is already high. In China, too, the impact of the crisis appears thus far to be small. Thus, in East Asia, the economic crisis has had little direct observable impact upon either the volume or the patterns of migration. As the crisis continues, increasing pressures in those areas hardest hit may cause migration towards East Asian economies. Overstaying and clandestine migration may increase, although with tight policies of control in place in all the East Asian economies, that impact is unlikely to be great.

China may defy such easy generalizations. A prolonged downturn is likely to have a major impact upon domestic migration, perhaps leading to the re-establishment of controls on domestic mobility and forced returns to the rural sector. It appears unlikely, nevertheless, that any but a minority of the floating population would have either the resources or the connections to move overseas. International movements, as outlined earlier, are likely to continue to be dominated by particular groups within the Chinese community that have close linkages to the Overseas Chinese, and these groups are unlikely to be domestic migrants. Overseas migration tends to originate from precisely those areas that are the targets for much of the domestic movements in southern China. Thus, increasingly, domestic migration in China is unlikely to spill over into international movements, even if some domestic migration may be to fill vacancies created through movement overseas.

CONCLUSION

In the East Asian region, there is great variation in the volumes, types, and patterns of migration, primarily as a result of the level of development of individual economies and levels of urbanization. The complexity in patterns and types of migration clearly has increased over time. Governments in the region are generally strong, with little tolerance for domestic dissent. All operate exclusionary immigration policies and permit the importation of labour only to fill specific labour needs. They are not countries of permanent immigration and migrants tend to be in vulnerable positions throughout the region—on short-term contracts, if legal, and subject to deportation, if unauthorized. Even in China, where internal movements have escalated, the majority of internal movers are technically unauthorized as they are outside their place of official registration. Internal migration can be expected to increase if China maintains its open economy, although a swing back to centralized control could certainly have an impact on population movements there. Mobility in East Asia is still much more subject to State intervention and control than in western countries of destination, even if that control appears to be eroding in places. International migration will continue to be a major issue in the region, as the developed economies maintain their demand for labour even while their societies persist in seeing themselves as homogeneous. In China—as elsewhere in the region—the tension is ever present between the desire for social order and the needs of the modern economy.

REFERENCES

1. Abella, M. (Ed.) (1994). Turning points in labor migration. *Asian and Pacific Migration Journal,* 3(1):special issue.

2. Chan, K.W. (1994). Urbanization and rural-urban migration in China since 1982: a new baseline. *Modern China,* 20(3):243-281.

3. Fields, G.S. (1994). The migration transition in Asia. *Asian and Pacific Migration Journal,* 3(1):7-30.

4. Hood, M. (1998). Fuzhou. In L. Pan (Ed.), *The Encyclopedia of the Chinese Overseas.* The Chinese Heritage Centre, The Archipelago Press, Singapore, pp. 33-35.

5. Kang, S-D. (1995). Data on international migration in Korea. *Asian and Pacific Migration Journal,* 4(4):579-584.

6. Komai, H. (1995). *Migrant Workers in Japan.* Kegan Paul International, London and New York.

7. Kuznets, P.W. (1987). Koreans in America: recent migration from South Korea to the United States, In S. Klein (Ed.), *The Economics of Mass Migration in the Twentieth Century.* Paragon, New York, NY.

8 Lee, J.S. (1998). The impact of the Asian financial crisis on foreign workers in Taiwan. *Asian and Pacific Migration Journal,* 7(2/3):145-169.

9. Martin, P.M., A. Mason and T. Nagayama (1996). The dynamics of labor migration in Asia. *Asian and Pacific Migration Journal,* 5(2/3):special issue.

10. Pan, L. (Ed.) (1998). *The Encyclopedia of the Chinese Overseas,* The Chinese Heritage Centre. Archipelago Press, Singapore.

11. Park, Y. (1998). The financial crisis and foreign workers in Korea. *Asian and Pacific Migration Journal,* 7(2/3):219-233.

12. Pieke, F.N. and H. Mallee (Eds.) (1999). *Internal and International Migration: Chinese Perspectives.* Curzon, London.

13. Sasaki, S. (1995). Data on international migration in Japan. *Asian and Pacific Migration Journal,* 4(4):565-577.

14. Sellek, Y. (1997). The phenomenon of return migration. In M. Weiner (Ed.), *Japan's Minorities: The Illusion of Homogeneity.* Routledge, London, pp. 178-210.

15. Shimada, H. (1994). *Japan's Guestworkers.* Columbia University Press, New York, NY.

16. Sinn, E. (Ed.) (1998). *The Last Half Century of the Chinese Overseas.* Hong Kong University Press, Hong Kong.

17. Skeldon, R. (Ed.) (1994). *Reluctant Exiles? Migration from Hong Kong and the New Overseas Chinese.* M.E. Sharpe, New York, NY.

18. Skeldon, R. (1996). Migration from China. *Journal of International Affairs,* 49(2):434-455.

19. Skeldon, R. (1999). Migration in Asia and the economic crisis: patterns and issues. *Asia-Pacific Population Journal,* 14(3).

20. Smith, P.J. (Ed.) (1997). *Human Smuggling: Chinese Migrant Trafficking and the Challenge to America's Immigration Tradition.* Center for Strategic and International Studies, Washington, DC.

21. Tsay, C. (1995). Data on international migration from Taiwan. *Asian and Pacific Migration Journal,* 4(4):613-619.

22. Watanabe, S. (1998). The economic crisis and migrant workers in Japan. *Asian and Pacific Migration Journal,* 7(2/3):235-254.

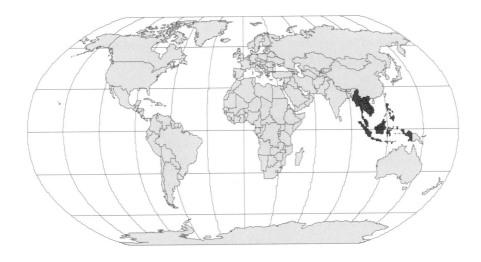

SOUTH-EAST ASIA

INTRODUCTION

Migration in South-East Asia presents a variety of forms that reflect the complexity of the region. In addition to out-migration to countries of permanent settlement, the region has temporary labour migration toward the Middle East and Asia as well as labour movements within the region. Throughout the Indo-Chinese refugee crisis the region served as a place of first asylum, and unsettled conflicts still result in temporary outflows of refugees. There are three major migration subsystems in which ad hoc migration policies produced a large number of unauthorized migrants. The recent financial and economic crisis strengthened the resolve of governments to bring unauthorized migration under control; however, bleak economic prospects only increased migration pressure. Long avoided, initial steps toward cooperation on a regional dialogue on migration are now under way.

South-East Asia is a region characterized by complex political, social, and economic dimensions. Politically, it encompasses democracies, authoritarian regimes, and a socialist government. Economically, it includes highly developed countries, emerging economies, and vast poverty. From the social perspective, it embraces a

Graziano Battistella, Director of the Scalabrini Migration Center and Editor of the *Asian and Pacific Migration Journal* based in Quezon City, Philippines, contributed to this chapter.

mixture of ethnic, linguistic, and religious traditions, highly stratified societies, and a vibrant civil community. Notwithstanding this diversity, the countries in the region rally around the organization for regional cooperation, the Association of South-East Asian Nations (ASEAN).

Considering the region's diversity, it is no surprise that migration is also a complex issue. The phenomenal growth experienced in some countries in Asia during the last two decades—accomplished with the increased mobility of capital, goods, and labour—stands in stark contrast to the poverty of neighbouring countries. Major countries of origin of migration flows, receiving countries, and countries in the midst of a migration transition are all found in South-East Asia. The region was the centre of dramatic movements of refugees for many years and currently is home to large numbers of unauthorized migrants.

The recent financial and economic crisis that began in July 1997 with the devaluation of the Thai baht was initially confined to a few countries in Asia. It became evident later that this was more than just an "Asian" crisis. Various meetings were convened to reassess the role of the Bretton Woods institutions and the wisdom and timing of the opening to global trading. More than anything else, experts stressed the need for some controls on speculative foreign investment.

The crisis affected mostly the South-East Asian region, albeit not all countries in the same way. The economies set for fast growth and reliant on foreign investments (such as Thailand, Indonesia, and Malaysia) were the countries most affected (Table 5). The drought caused by El Niño reduced agricultural productivity and compounded such other negative effects as closure of businesses, retrenchment of workers, spreading unemployment, and increased consumer prices. Signs of economic recovery became clearer in the second half of 1999, despite warnings about the danger of falling into complacency. Recovery from the social impact of the crisis will take longer, although effects on overall societal well-being (Table 6) are not immediately evident.

As well as reversals of some economic trends and reduced prospects for economic development, there are political and social consequences. The change of government in several countries created new possibilities for democratic development. However, the uncertainty of political stability complicates the adoption of economic growth policies. The lack of preparation at the sudden onset of the crisis

TABLE 5.

SOUTH-EAST ASIA: SELECTED ECONOMIC INDICATORS

	Growth rate of GDP[1]		Change in CPI[2]		Current account balance[3]		Debt-service ratio[4]		Exchange rate to the US dollar[5]	
	1997	1998	1997	1998	1997	1998	1997	1998	1997	1998
South-East Asia	4.0	-6.9	5.6	21.0	-3.3	5.2	...	...		
Cambodia	2.0	0.0	9.1	12.0	-8.4	-9.1	2.3	2.6	2,946.3	3,750.0
Indonesia	4.9	-13.7	6.6	58.2	-1.4	1.1	39.5	36.0	4,666.9	10,147.5
Lao PDR	6.9	4.0	19.3	90.1	-16.1	-10.4	9.5	11.9	1,256.7	3,045.0
Malaysia	7.7	-6.2	4.0	5.2	-5.3	8.1	6.2	0.9	2.8	3.9
Myanmar	4.6	4.0	29.7	50.0	-0.2	...	...	...	6.2	6.4
Philippines	5.2	-0.5	6.0	9.7	-5.3	2.0	11.7	11.9	29.5	40.9
Singapore	7.8	1.5	2.0	-1.5	15.2	18.2	...	...	1.5	1.7
Thailand	-0.4	-8.0	5.6	8.1	-2.0	11.5	15.6	21.3	31.3	40.3
Viet Nam	8.2	4.0	3.6	9.2	-6.8	-4.1	11.4	13.4	11,683.0	3,297.0

Notes: [1]Per cent per annum; [2]Per cent per annum; [3]Percentage of GDP; [4]Percentage of exports of goods and services; [5]Annual average.

Source: *Asian Development Outlook* (1999).

TABLE 6.

SOUTH-EAST ASIA: SELECTED SOCIAL INDICATORS

	HDI rank[1]	Population[2] (millions)	Population growth[2]	Life expectancy[2]	Literacy rate[2]	Per capita GDP (PPP)[2]
Singapore	28	3.1	2.0	77	92.2	28,780
Brunei	35	0.3	3.2	75	89.2	19,500
Thailand	59	61.4	1.5	69	93.8	6,940
Malaysia	60	22.2	2.4	72	89.3	11,700
Indonesia	96	204.6	1.6	65	84.4	3,790
Philippines	98	73.4	2.3	67	94.0	3,565
Viet Nam	122	78.7	2.3	68	91.9	1,705
Myanmar	131	48.8	2.1	60	82.0	753
Lao PDR	136	5.0	2.9	53	56.6	1,775
Cambodia	140	10.3	2.5	53	37.8	1,340

Notes: Literacy rate based on population 15 years and over; Per capita GDP in US$; HDI = Human Development Index; PPP = Purchasing Power Parity.

Sources: [1]UNDP (1998). *Human Development Report*; [2]*Asiaweek*, 30 October 1998.

complicated its impact. A false sense of security provided by years of continuous growth led governments to dismiss the need for effective social safety nets should good times change. In the face of the consequent reduced opportunities and increasing unemployment, both migration pressures and unauthorized migration are expected to grow in the short term.

Since the crisis began, the number of unauthorized migrants has grown as workers attempt to maintain their livelihood. Restrictive migration policies continue to dictate both the terms of who and how many migrants may enter a country as well as the conditions under which they may work and stay. However, short-term interests—largely business sector utilization of flexible and cheap labour—ensure that policies only determine a portion of the inflow; another portion enters without authorization or remains in the country in an unauthorized status. Reeling under the impact of the crisis, some governments made harsh decisions on migration—including lowering benefits and implementing repatriation—that caused friction on the bilateral and international fronts. As a result, there is some impetus for regional governments and international organizations to address international migration in a comprehensive and cooperative fashion.

Economic factors determine three persistent, long-term migration subsystems formed by the attraction of labour across international borders to Singapore and Peninsular Malaysia, East Malaysia and Brunei Darussalam, and Thailand. Indonesia and the Philippines constitute the main—although not exclusive—source of labour flows in the first two instances; various nations in Indochina represent the main sources of migration into Thailand.

Peninsular Malaysia and Singapore constitute the most vibrant economic sub-region in South-East Asia and thus a major attraction for migrants. Traditional commercial contacts and colonial legacies brought different streams of migrants to the peninsula, establishing large diaspora communities in Malay society. Population movements continued as a response to the demand for labour or labour shortage created by rapid development. As a migration subsystem, the peninsula receives migrants from both neighbouring countries and such more distant nations as Bangladesh. Considerable labour mobility also occurs between Malaysia and Singapore, particularly in the form of daily commuters. However, as discussed below, Singapore and Malaysia developed distinct migration policy responses to these movements.

Because of their location, history, and economic configuration, Brunei and East Malaysia—in particular the province of Sabah—constitute a different migration subsystem that coincides with the limits of the Brunei-Indonesia-Malaysia-Philippines East ASEAN Growth Area (BIMP-EAGA) established in 1994. This regional agreement recently sanctioned such labour mobility to facilitate trade, investment, and economic integration within the region. Integration is expected to result from the complementary roles played by Mindanao's agricultural development and skilled human resources, East Indonesia's and East Malaysia's untapped land, and labour demand in the East Malaysia and Brunei capitals. The region's total population is approximately 40 million people.

Cambodia, the Lao People's Democratic Republic, Myanmar, and Viet Nam are the sources for migration into Thailand and together constitute the third migration subsystem in South-East Asia. Official estimates place the number of migrant workers in Thailand (mostly from Myanmar) at 600,000; unofficial estimates exceed 1 million migrants. Other countries of the region have contributed refugees over the years. At the height of the Indo-Chinese refugee crisis, Thailand provided first asylum to Vietnamese, Cambodians, and Laotians. Vietnamese also found temporary assistance in camps in other South-East Asian countries. From 1975 to 1997, close to 1.2 million refugees received aid; more than 700,000 were resettled elsewhere; and another 400,000 voluntarily returned to their countries. The end of the Indo-Chinese exodus did not end Thailand's role as a country of first asylum. Approximately 114,000 refugees from Myanmar currently are in its territory, and Cambodian refugees cross the border to escape periodic fighting in their country.

IMMIGRATION TRENDS

As the overview demonstrated, four countries in South-East Asia constitute countries of major immigration: Singapore, Malaysia, Brunei Darussalam and Thailand.

SINGAPORE

In 1970, approximately 50,000 foreigners were working in Singapore, out of a local population of 2 million people. The number of foreigners doubled in 1980 and more than doubled again in 1990 (Table 7). By 1997, foreign workers surpassed the 500,000 mark to constitute 27 per cent of the labour force (7). It is not possible to indicate with sufficient accuracy the origin of foreign workers in Singapore, as data are not available. Nevertheless, labour migration to Singapore comes mainly from Malaysia, from nontraditional source countries such as Thai-

TABLE 7.

SINGAPORE: POPULATION AND ESTIMATED FOREIGN WORKFORCE
(thousands)

	Total population	Foreign population	Foreign workforce
1970	2,074.5	60.9	48.7
1980	2,413.9	131.8	105.4
1990	3,016.4	311.3	249.0
1991	3,089.9	327.2	261.8
1992	3,178.0	359.8	287.7
1993	3,259.4	385.6	308.5
1994	3,363.5	433.3	346.6
1995	3,467.5	481.0	384.8
1996	3,612.0	567.7	454.2
1997	3,736.7	633.2	506.6

Source: Hui, Weng-Tat (1998). The regional economic crisis and Singapore: implications for labor migration. *Asian and Pacific Migration Journal,* 7(2/3):187-218.

land, Indonesia, Sri Lanka, India, and the Philippines and from new Asian sources (Hong Kong and Taiwan [Province of China]) and Mainland China.

Both Singapore and Malaysia, although predominantly receiving countries, also experience some out-migration. Malays constitute an important minority (14 per cent in 1990) in Singapore; however, 90 per cent of them were born in Singapore. There are no exact figures on migration from Malaysia to Singapore, but an estimated revolving pool of 100,000 Malaysians, mostly from the state of Johore, are believed to work in Singapore (13).

Few Singaporeans leave to work and resettle abroad. In the early 1980s, there were approximately 2,000 emigrants each year. The figure increased to more than 4,000 at the end of the 1980s, prompting concern about brain drain. Current estimates that place the number of emigrants from Singapore at approximately 5,000 annually have led the Singapore Government to attract foreign talent (7).

Migration to Singapore is mostly temporary. Nevertheless, the Government facilitates immigration of professionals or highly skilled workers and grants them a permanent visa with the possibility of being joined by family members. The key distinction between temporary and permanent workers lies in their monthly salaries; temporary migrant workers (working permit holders) earn less than S$ 2,000 a month; professionals (employment pass holders) earn more than S$ 2,000 a month. There were about 55,000 professionals in 1997, constituting 12 per cent of the foreign workforce (7). There is little information about the return of these highly skilled migrants and about what role family may play in such decisions. Although some foreign workers remain for many years, acquiring citizenship is not discussed and rarely pursued.

Singapore has consistently encouraged the admission of highly skilled foreigners, providing incentives for them to acquire permanent residence. By contrast, the immigration of unskilled workers was discouraged, to the point of establishing a levy for employers who hired such migrant workers. The Government intended with this distinction to focus the economy on technological upgrading, rather than on low-wage, low-skilled operations. The policy did not work as expected; both dependence on foreign labour and the proportion of foreign workers increased. Instead of discouraging employers from hiring migrant workers, the rising levies placed downward pressure on wage levels of migrant workers.

Whatever reservations Singaporeans have about immigration are offset by pragmatism. They see that migrants perform jobs that local workers find undesirable and add flexibility to the labour market. For these reasons, unskilled migrants have been admitted in increasing numbers, but selective criteria specify source countries, sectors of the economy in which migrants may work, types of work permits to be granted, and administrative procedures that regulate migration (17). To avoid dependency on foreign labour, the rate of migration periodically is adjusted according to labour market needs.

Because of "its sound economic fundamentals of high savings, fiscal prudence, current account surpluses, flexible markets, strong reserves and tight regulation and supervision of domestic financial institutions" (7), Singapore coped with the economic crisis somewhat better than other countries. Nevertheless, between 25,000 and 30,000 retrenchments took place in 1998—twice what was expected at the beginning of that year. The economic slow-down also affected migrant workers. However, unlike the 1985 crisis and earlier times when migrant workers were the first to be laid off, the Government advised employers to keep their best workers, regardless of nationality (2). Because of the differential impacts of the crisis and the concentration in certain sectors of migrant workers without any possibility of replacing them, many migrants stayed on the job.

As a result, there was a reduction in unskilled migrant labour in construction, but smaller unskilled migrant job losses in manufacturing and commerce. Employers successfully argued that local labour would not take the jobs migrants were hired to do. Instead of repatriations, the Government focused on halting the entry of new workers. Migrants, however, were affected; thousands returned or were repatriated; those who remained often were forced to accept lower wages and unfavourable working conditions.

The crisis affected migrant women differently. Most women migrants are domestic workers or manufacturing—especially electronics—production workers. The domestic service sector was not as severely affected as other sectors. The presence of foreign domestic workers in Singapore allowed local women to participate in the labour market. Between 1976 and 1997, female labour participation in Singapore rose from 37.1 to 51.1 per cent. It is possible that future belt-tightening throughout the economy may reach down to the family level and result in lay-offs as well as wage reductions. Recently, however, the levy for domestic workers in Singapore was lowered to allow employers to keep domestic workers even during the crisis. Nevertheless, a slow-down in manufacturing took place and female production workers—of whom migrant women are a good proportion—were among the first to be laid off (7). Deportation of unauthorized migrants increased by one-third in 1997 and continued high in 1998, when 23,000 unauthorized migrants and overstayers were arrested (almost twice as many as those arrested in 1997) (2a).

Employment conditions for foreign workers—in regular or unauthorized status—do not differ substantially in Singapore or throughout the region. Typically, migrants work long hours, six days a week, lodge in common barracks, and have limited possibilities for social exchange. In some instances, wages of unauthorized workers exceed those of legal migrants. In most cases, however, unauthorized workers must accept what is offered them, as they have no contractual power. The single most decisive aspect in the condition of unauthorized workers is the fear of being reported to the police and being repatriated. Such fear is particularly compelling, as most unauthorized migrants have debts to be repaid and cannot afford to lose their employment. Such fear keeps them from seeking improved conditions or from seeking recourse in labour conflicts.

MALAYSIA

Current estimates of the foreign workforce in Malaysia vary because of limited availability of official data and the uncertain number of unauthorized migrants. Nonetheless, there is consensus around the estimate of 1.2 million regular migrants in the territory (Table 8). This number comprises both legal migrants who obtained regular work permits, as well as formerly unauthorized migrants who obtained legal status in several regularization programmes. As in Singapore, the majority of migrants are temporary workers. The two major countries of origin are Indonesia (64 per cent) and Bangladesh (27 per cent). Other migrants include Filipinos, Thais, and Pakistanis.

TABLE 8.
MALAYSIA: FOREIGN WORKFORCE BY OCCUPATION AND NATIONALITY, 1998

Sector	Number	Per cent	Country	Number	Per cent
Domestic help	112,373	9.3	Indonesia	716,033	63.9
Manufacturing	375,951	31.0	Bangladesh	307,696	27.5
Plantation	313,988	25.9	Philippines	24,882	2.2
Construction	245,186	20.2	Thailand	21,438	1.9
Services	134,741	11.1	Pakistan	18,052	1.6
Others	29,325	2.4	Others	32,071	2.9
Total	**1,211,564**	**100.0**		**1,120,172**[1]	**100.0**

Note: [1]The nationality of 91,392 workers was not recorded.

Source: Kassim, A. (1998). *The case of a new receiving country in the development world: Malaysia.* Paper presented at the Technical Symposium on International Migration and Development, The Hague, Netherlands, 29 June-3 July.

Migrants are employed in manufacturing, agriculture, construction, services, and domestic help. However, the occupational distribution differs according to national origin—Indonesians predominantly in agriculture and construction, Bangladeshis in manufacturing and services, and Filipinos in services.

Current immigration policy in Malaysia encourages high-skilled immigration (with no levy or bond and permission for family reunification) to contribute to the achievement of industrialization by the year 2020; restricts unskilled immigration to sectors where there is a labour shortage (sectors in which immigration is currently allowed are domestic services, export-oriented factories, agriculture and tourism); and eliminates unauthorized migration. Migration policy has been modified a number of times over the years: unauthorized migration, once tolerated, has come under increasingly greater control; after having promoted several regularization programmes to document and legalize the unauthorized population, the current policy aims at repatriating, not legalizing, all unauthorized migrants. Not only is apprehension and repatriation of unauthorized migrants (approximately 800 thousand) difficult and costly, but unauthorized migrants are essential for the economy.

Unlike Singapore, Malaysia did not formulate a coherent migration policy when labour immigration began. Instead, it responded with ad hoc provisions in response to labour market conditions. The transfer of the local workforce out of agriculture and construction led to the inflow of unauthorized migrants from Indonesia and the Philippines. Beginning with the 1984 Medan Pact with Indonesia—aimed at encouraging legal recruitment and curbing unauthorized migration—a series of policy responses was directed at excessive unauthorized migration. Examples of such policies are the revocation of the Medan Pact and the reopening of borders in 1987; OPS Nyah I [literally, operation "get rid of them"], an amnesty for domestic workers and construction workers in 1991-1992; OPS Nyah II in 1992; establishment of a one-stop agency for recruitment of foreign labour in 1995; a follow-up regularization programme in 1996; the amendment to the Immigration Act 1959/63 in 1997 (8); and the amnesty programme from 31 August to 31 October 1998 (2b). In general, unauthorized migration was tolerated during economic growth periods while stricter controls were put into effect during economic downturns.

In Malaysia, as throughout South-East Asia, unauthorized migration is not necessarily short-term. In many instances, migrants remain for years. Enforcement everywhere is spotty and depends on overall conditions, so that, for example, the chance of migration agent inspection of domestic service workers is virtually nil. By avoiding encounters with the authorities, migrants improve their chances of remaining in the country. Agents are authorized to ask for documents in public places, a deterrent for unauthorized migrants seeking a normal social life. Long-term employment in an unauthorized situation is not without penalties, however. Fees are imposed on unauthorized migrants caught or returning home. Regardless of the length of time in the country, integration into society is generally not an option for unskilled migrants anywhere in the region.

As mentioned above, migration to Sabah in East Malaysia is a distinct and separate subsystem. The Sabah region was the site of labour importation at the time of British colonial rule; it became a place of asylum for Filipinos escaping the conflict in Mindanao in the 1970s; and it has an autonomous immigration policy managed by the State Immigration Department. Throughout history, however, Sabah has been part of a geographic zone that permitted the free circulation of population for work and settlement, a custom which even colonial era border controls could not totally sever. The dependence on foreign workers, especially in the agricultural sector, is long-standing. For this reason, Sabah has somehow tolerated a significant number of unauthorized migrants.

Migration to Sabah is open primarily to Indonesians and Filipinos, but a small number of Indians, Pakistanis, and Chinese also are present. The legal migrant population in Sabah totals almost 600,000, mostly Indonesians who hold a regular work permit, Filipinos who received refugee status, and Indonesians and Filipinos who were registered during the regularization programme implemented in 1997 (Table 9). There are approximately 80,000 unauthorized migrants who did not register.

TABLE 9.
SABAH, MALAYSIA: REGISTERED FOREIGNERS BY NATIONALITY AND WORK STATUS, 1997

Nationality	Workers		Dependants		Total	
	Number	Per cent	Number	Per cent	Number	Per cent
Indonesian	170,169	75.1	124,535	66.5	294,704	71.2
Filipino	56,396	24.9	62,732	33.5	119,128	28.8
Total	**226,565**	**100.0**	**187,267**	**100.0**	**413,832**	**100.0**

Source: Kurus, Bilson (1998). Migrant labor: the Sabah experience. *Asian and Pacific Migration Journal*, 7(2/3).

Migrants work mostly in forestry and agriculture, construction, manufacturing, and domestic services (Table 10). The Department of Immigration also grants visas for those in skilled occupations, provided that local workers are not found for the same occupation. Because of the large number of dependants (close to 200,000) now in-country, it is assumed that migrants are beginning to settle and work in the informal economy.

TABLE 10.
SABAH, MALAYSIA: MIGRANT WORKERS BY OCCUPATION, 1997

	Number	Per cent
Agriculture/Plantation	17,353	52
Manufacturing	43,198	19
Services	24,494	11
Construction	17,553	8
Housemaids	7,786	3
Others	16,181	7
Total	**226,565**	**100**

Source: Kurus, B. (1998). Migrant labor: the Sabah experience. *Asian and Pacific Migration Journal*, 7(2/3).

Observers in Sabah indicate that both the number of new arrivals and the number of people who overstay their visas are rising, indicating an increase of unauthorized migration. However, it is not clear whether migrants are absorbed by the sectors least affected by the crisis, such as agriculture, or whether they simply disappear into the informal economy.

The economic crisis seriously affected Malaysia, some sectors of the economy more adversely than others: in 1998 manufacturing output was expected to shrink by 2.5 per cent, agriculture by 4.4 per cent, and construction by 3.2 per cent. Unemployment increased from 2.7 per cent in 1997 to 6.7 per cent in 1998 (14). Malaysia distinguished itself by its refusal to adopt the IMF strategy for recovery; its dissension has recently earned followers. However, not everyone in Malaysia agrees on the protectionist measures it adopted. Internal disagreement, including the incarceration of the deputy prime minister, may affect future political developments.

The impact of the crisis on migrant labour was mixed. Official figures on retrenchment of workers indicate that migrants were not disproportionately affected, as only 10.9 per cent of the 39,500 workers laid off in the first semester of 1998 were migrants (2c). However, official figures do not take into account voluntary retrenchments, unreported layoffs, and temporary employment. After the crisis erupted, the Government announced that unauthorized migrants would be repatriated and that workers in construction and services would not have their permits renewed after 15 August 1998. Subsequently, in response to employer demands, the policy was modified to allow migrants in the service sector to stay for up to six years; retrenched migrants were given the opportunity to switch to the agricultural sector.

What actually happened was that 159,000 workers left the country voluntarily from the beginning of 1998 to March 1999, while 80,000 unauthorized migrants (mostly from Indonesia) were caught and repatriated, leaving 714,000 registered foreign workers in Malaysia, down from 1 million in 1998 (2d). Very few migrants took advantage of the possibility to be hired for agricultural work, where the industry claims there are 40,000 vacancies. At the same time, there were new measures affecting migration, including an increase of the levy to MR 1,500 and mandatory contributions by migrants to the Employees Provident Fund. Domestic workers are exempt from these rulings, but other measures restrict the service sector. Employers hiring domestic workers are required to have a monthly income of at least MR 10,000 for Filipino workers (MR 3,000 for Indonesian maids) and may hire only one domestic worker.

BRUNEI DARUSSALAM

The small State of Brunei Darussalam has a population of 300,000 persons, but one of the highest per capita incomes in South-East Asia. With its oil-dominated economy, Brunei has long utilized migrant labour to respond to labour market demands. As early as 1986, temporary migrants were 32 per cent of the labour force, and by 1988, immigrant labour was 71 per cent of the private-sector workforce. As in similar economies in the Middle East, the local population in Brunei is employed in public offices and in clerical jobs. Projections for the year 2000 place immigrant employment at 35 per cent of total employment, notwithstanding the intent of the Government to reduce dependency on foreign labour (11). Although Brunei constitutes a unique entity within the BIMP-EAGA, it nevertheless belongs to this migration subsystem as most of its migrants originate in ASEAN countries, notably the neighbouring Sabah and Sarawak provinces of Malaysia and the Philippines.

THAILAND

In recent decades, Thailand assumed economic leadership within the northern part of South-East Asia. Fast development temporarily decreased Thai out-migration and quickly transformed Thailand into a labour receiving country in the international labour market. But Thailand maintains a role in labour export as well as a role as a country of first asylum for refugees in the troubled peninsula.

Thailand began its own labour migration programme in earnest in the 1980s when migrant numbers jumped from 20,000 to 125,000 in a decade. At that time, almost 70 per cent of the migrants were deployed to the Middle East, particularly Saudi Arabia. Following a diplomatic incident with Saudi Arabia in 1991 (and changes that affected a number of other labour exporting nations as well), the entry of Thai workers to Saudi Arabia dropped drastically. Thai migrants switched to Asian nations, especially Taiwan (Province of China) (136 thousand in 1997), where Thais are the dominant migrant group and work in construction jobs (10) (Table 11).

TABLE 11.
DEPLOYED THAI OVERSEAS WORKERS TO SELECTED COUNTRIES

	1993	1994	1995	1996
Saudi Arabia	5,035	4,152	2,902	1,825
Qatar	751	1,534	1,761	1,226
Bahrain	750	594	345	232
UAE	1,504	1,829	1,466	951
Kuwait	1,859	1,212	978	885
Others	2,410	7,983	10,712	15,406
Middle East	**12,309**	**17,304**	**18,164**	**20,525**
Libyan AJ	4,597	160	1,639	1,900
Singapore	1,664	2,849	3,171	17,601
Brunei	14,403	16,549	17,281	20,714
Hong Kong	5,398	5,812	5,816	4,301
Japan	5,682	8,821	8,234	10,118
Taiwan (Pr. of Ch.)	66,891	91,058	120,278	96,097
USA and Saipan	706	831	723	764
Denmark	649	49	54	12
Others	1,763	1,783	2,752	13,404
Total	**114,062**	**145,216**	**178,112**	**185,436**

Source: National Statistics Office, Office of the Prime Minister (1997). *Key Statistics of Thailand,* Bangkok.

Labour migration to Thailand is a recent phenomenon, initiated in the early 1990s. In a typical congruence of pull and push factors, migrants escaped from neighbouring country poverty to find employment in the fast-growing Thai economy. Migrants from Myanmar fled from economic difficulties and from human rights abuses. The long and porous borders between Thailand and its neighbours, an active recruiting industry, and complacent border enforcement contributed to the growth in migration from a few thousand to approximately 1 million. About 80 per cent of migrants come from Myanmar and occupy jobs in construction and agriculture. It is estimated that 50 per cent of the labour force in fisheries is Burmese (15).

Labour migration to Thailand developed without a clear immigration policy and in unauthorized fashion. To try to manage this huge number of unauthorized migrants, in 1996 the Government implemented a regularization programme allowing employers to register migrants. The initiative applied to only 43 of 76 provinces and produced just over 300,000 registered migrants. A large majority did not participate in the registration programme—either because they were not eligible or because employers were unwilling to shoulder the Government-imposed registration fee (US$ 40) and bond (US$ 200). Further, not all registered migrants renewed their registration and remained with the same employer the following year, diminishing the real impact of the regularization.

Thailand faces particular problems with migrant trafficking as it has been identi-fied as a base from which unauthorized runs of migrants begin. Traffickers more than occasionally leave migrants stranded in the country. Thai emigration is marked by trafficking in women, illegal recruitment of workers, excessive placement fees that leave workers in virtual bondage, and other abuses. In 1999, the Thai Govern-ment took the lead, sponsoring a regional conference on the problems associated with unauthorized migration.

Thailand was the most seriously affected country at the beginning of the Asian economic crisis. According to ILO, unemployment at one point in 1998 reached 2 million workers (8.5 per cent of the workforce) before ending the year at 4.8 per cent. GDP fell by 8 per cent in 1998, and was expected to fall an additional 2 per cent in 1999. Thailand also was the first to accept IMF support and stringent policies for recovery. The faithful implementation of the measures brought some stability to the economy but also weakened the recovery process and ultimately was relaxed to spur growth.

The impact of the crisis also was manifested in internal migration patterns. Approximately 188,000 left metropolitan areas to return to rural regions, particularly the north-east (6). The Government announced its intention to repatriate 300,000 unauthorized workers by the end of 1998. The operation, begun in May, led to the repatriation of 298,480 migrants by the end of that year. However, complaints from employers brought a reversal of the policy for certain industries. Some 95,000 Burmese, Laotian, and Cambodian migrants were allowed to remain until the end of the year to work in rice mills (11,000), cane plantations (23,000), rubber plantations (38,000), pig farms (3,000), and sea transport (20,000) (2e).

A ban on hiring foreign workers was to take effect. However, the ban conflicted with other measures introduced to allow migrants to remain for an additional year's labour in the textile industry (2f). At the same time, the Government encouraged Thai workers to seek employment abroad. The target for 1998 was to deploy 215,000 workers overseas. According to official estimates, more than 190,000 Thais left the country to work abroad and remitted back some 65.2 billion baht, or 340,000 baht per person. The number of Thai overseas labourers rose by 4 per cent during 1997 (2g).

EMIGRATION TRENDS

Most emigration within and from South-East Asia comes from Indonesia and the Philippines, with smaller movements from Viet Nam, the Lao People's Democratic Republic, Cambodia, and Myanmar.

INDONESIA

Indonesia developed its overseas labour contract programme in the 1980s. The programme maintained a modest outflow (less than 100,000 workers) for many years, mostly domestic workers to the Middle East and Malaysia. Their number and destinations increased in the 1990s (now surpassing 500,000 workers) (Table 12). The Indonesian community in Malaysia numbers approximately

1.4 million people. The regular overseas labour programme is overshadowed by the large number of unauthorized Indonesian migrants present in Peninsular Malaysia and Sabah. Several agreements and regularizations have not succeeded in managing the illicit movement.

TABLE 12.
INDONESIAN MIGRANTS DEPLOYED TO SELECTED COUNTRIES, 1995-1997

Country	1995 Male	Female	Total	1996 Male	Female	Total	1997 Male	Female	Total
Brunei	92	740	832	400	1,730	2,130	533	1,893	2,426
Hong Kong	50	4,155	4,205	38	2,832	2,870	39	1,980	2,019
Japan	1,366	72	1,438	2,451	87	2,538	3,218	27	3,245
Rep. of Korea	5,793	939	6,732	9,262	1,456	10,718	6,826	1,564	8,390
Malaysia[1]	11,079	18,633	29,712	5,090	33,562	38,652	194,207	123,478	317,685
Singapore	6,834	14,141	20,975	5,128	23,937	29,065	4,736	27,192	31,928
Taiwan (Pr. of Ch.)	3,460	646	4,106	6,909	1,979	8,888	6,801	2,644	9,445
Others	429	7	436	208	1	209	217	28	245
Asia Pacific	**29,103**	**39,333**	**68,436**	**29,486**	**65,584**	**95,070**	**216,538**	**158,779**	**375,317**
USA	3,305	12	3,317	1,656	0	1,656	576	0	576
Others	166	0	166	105	0	105	160	0	160
America	**3,471**	**12**	**3,483**	**1,761**	**0**	**1,761**	**736**	**0**	**736**
Europe	**64**	**0**	**64**	**739**	**28**	**767**	**576**	**1**	**577**
Saudi Arabia	5,321	38,130	43,451	7,024	108,185	115,209	8,568	108,276	116,844
UAE	107	3,805	3,912	335	6,719	7,054	80	8,982	9,062
Others	77	84	161	88	213	301	127	10	137
Middle East	**5,505**	**42,019**	**47,524**	**7,447**	**115,117**	**122,564**	**8,775**	**117,572**	**126,347**
TOTAL	**39,237**	**81,366**	**120,603**	**39,433**	**180,729**	**220,162**	**226,625**	**276,352**	**502,977**

Note: [1]1997 data for Malaysia include workers who renewed their registration in Malaysia.

Source: Ananta, A., D. Kartowibowo, N.H. Wiyono and Chotib (1998). The impact of the economic crisis on international migration: the case of Indonesia. *Asian and Pacific Migration Journal,* 7(2/3):313-338.

Ethnic, linguistic, and religious similarities facilitate the outflow from Indonesia. Marked demographic and economic disparities, geographic proximity, and well-established migration networks all contribute to the large-scale movement of both regular and unauthorized workers. Although unauthorized migration can be attributed in part to the involvement of intermediaries (illegal recruiters, travel agents, and transportation operators) in other cases Indonesians become unauthorized migrants by entering with a visitor visa and remaining illegally as workers.

Social networks play an important role among Indonesians—as they do among other migrants in South-East Asia. Access to information is crucial to migrants; migrants often base their decisions upon information coming from networks, even though outside observers consider government information more reliable. Social networks are particularly relevant in facilitating the flow of unauthorized migration. Unauthorized migration between bordering countries (such as Indonesia and Malaysia) as well as between the Philippines and Sabah and Myanmar and Thailand, relies on professional expertise in the form of recruiters and traffickers, but also on social networks to facilitate entry and to find employment. The deregulation of the recruitment industry, intended to eliminate corruption, may not prove effective, as irregular practices are embedded in the system.

The increase in emigration among Indonesians has profited the country. Migrant remittances through official channels to Indonesia amounted to US$ 828 million in 1995, declined to US$ 586 million in 1996, and increased again to US$ 1.2 billion in 1997 (1). Total remittance levels may be much higher, considering the large number of migrants who may not use banks for money transfers.

The crisis had a severe impact on Indonesia, economically and politically. Because of the economic slow-down after the currency devaluation, unemployment reached 15.4 million at the end of 1998, representing some 17.1 per cent of the 90 million labour force. More indicative of the impact, however, is the number of people who fell below the poverty line. According to Central Bureau of Statistics estimates, there are now 79.4 million Indonesians below the poverty line (39.1 per cent of the population, up from 11.3 per cent in 1996) (1).

The political turmoil generated by the crisis that brought an end to the 32-year rule of Suharto also produced ethnic strife against the well-off Chinese community. Consequently, ethnic Chinese fled by the thousands to Singapore, Hong Kong, Taiwan (Province of China), and Australia, and the international community threatened sanctions. The crisis also engendered the large-scale departure of skilled foreign workers—48,000 at the end of 1997—who had provided services in critical sectors in which Indonesians lacked the necessary skills.

Following the crisis, there were fears that large-scale return of Indonesian migrants would increase unemployment and severely limit foreign exchange earnings from remittances. However, data on such impacts are poor. Like most migrant-sending countries, Indonesia does not have a programme to employ and reintegrate returning migrants. Therefore, it is expected that migration pressure will increase again and that even more migrants will try to go abroad through illegal channels.

EAST TIMOR

Some 250,000 East Timorese fled their homes and villages after the conflict that erupted in East Timor as the result of the vote for independence on 30 August 1999. As the violence subsided and the United Nations installed an interim administration, IOM began assisting the refugees to return to their homes in East Timor. Between November 1999 and May 2000, IOM helped more than 116 thousand refugees to return to East Timor.

IOM convoys, working in cooperation with UNHCR, brought more than one-half of the returnees across the border from refugee camps in the Belu district of West Timor. At the Motaain-Batugade northern border crossing, which opened on November 7, as many as 10 thousand people a month arrived in IOM-chartered trucks and buses.

The Patricia Anne Hotung and three other IOM-operated vessels brought more than 30 thousand returnees back to Dili from West Timor's provincial capital, Kupang.

Returning to East Timor, a country where 70 percent of buildings were destroyed in the violence, was not easy. Memories of the recent past, ongoing militia activity in the West Timor camps and on the border, and uncertainty about the future traumatized the population. But for most, after months as refugees in the squalid and dangerous camps of West Timor, East Timor meant coming home and restarting their lives.

As the emergency phase winds down, efforts are concentrated on post-conflict rehabilitation through a range of interrelated projects, such as the return of qualified nationals, reintegration of demobilized combatants, mobile information and referral services, community-based rehabilitation, and migration management capacity-building. These activities form an integral part of the international humanitarian community's response to the crisis.

THE PHILIPPINES

The Government of the Philippines estimates that about 7 million Filipinos work abroad, remitting more than US$ 7 billion in 1999. The Philippines deploys migrants on contract to more than 150 countries. However, particularly in the 1970s and 1980s, the bulk of migration was directed toward the Middle East. Recently, migration shifted direction, declining in the Middle East and expanding in the East and South-East Asian markets (Table13). In 1997, for the first time, the number of Filipino migrants deployed to Asian countries was higher than that sent to the Middle East. The annual emigration flow of Filipino migrants, including those who work on the high seas, remained more than 600,000 in the 1990s. The flow to South-East Asia in 1997 was less than one-fifth of the outflow to all Asian countries and 7 per cent of total deployment. However, these figures do not include those Filipinos who go to Singapore as tourists and obtain a work permit once in the country or the unreported flow between southern Mindanao and Sabah in Malaysia. Emigrating outside the region, Filipinos represent the second largest source of legal immigration to the United States, averaging around 55,000 per year, most motivated to join family already in the USA. The Philippine Government estimates that about 1.9 million Filipinos abroad are in unauthorized migration status. Given the uncertainty in conditions of Filipinos abroad, it is difficult to assess the accuracy of this estimate.

TABLE 13.
DEPLOYED FILIPINO OVERSEAS WORKERS BY REGIONS, 1984-1997

Year	Africa	Asia	Americas	Europe	Middle East	Oceania	Trust Ter.	Other[1]	Total
1984	1,843	38,817	2,515	3,683	250,210	913	2,397		300,378
1985	1,977	52,838	3,744	4,067	253,867	953	3,048		320,494
1986	1,847	72,536	4,035	3,693	236,434	1,080	3,892		323,517
1987	1,856	90,434	5,614	5,643	272,038	1,271	5,373		382,229
1988	1,958	92,648	7,902	7,614	267,035	1,397	6,563		385,117
1989	1,741	86,196	9,962	7,830	241,081	1,247	7,289		355,346
1990	1,273	90,768	9,557	6,853	218,110	942	7,380		334,883
1991	1,964	132,592	13,373	13,156	302,825	1,374	11,409	12,567	489,260
1992	2,510	134,776	12,319	14,590	340,604	1,669	11,164	32,023	549,655
1993	2,425	168,205	12,228	13,423	302,975	1,507	8,890	41,219	550,872
1994	3,255	194,120	12,603	11,513	286,387	1,295	8,489	47,564	565,226
1995	3,615	166,774	13,469	10,279	234,310	1,398	7,039	51,737	488,621
1996	2,494	174,308	7,731	11,409	221,224	1,429	4,469	61,589	484,653
1997	3,517	235,129	7,058	12,626	221,047	1,970	5,280	72,600	559,227

Note: [1]Includes workers processed at the regional offices and air crews.

Source: Compiled from unpublished data from Philippines Overseas Employment Administration.

An estimate of the Filipino population resident in South-East Asia could be as many as 350,000, considering the uncertainty of the number of migrants in Sabah. Filipino migrants in Sabah are engaged in production, services, and entertainment as well as a variety of other occupations (Table 14). In Peninsular Malaysia and in Singapore, Filipinos predominantly work in the service sector, especially as domestic help. Thus, the Filipino population in West Malaysia and Singapore is mostly female, while in Sabah, Filipinos are present with dependents. The small stock of Filipinos in Brunei (less than 20,000) is comprised mostly of labourers and teachers.

TABLE 14.
DEPLOYMENT OF OVERSEAS FILIPINO WORKERS BY SKILL CATEGORY (NEW HIRES)

	1992	%	1993	%	1994	%	1995	%	1996	%	1997	%
Professional	72,848	28	66,105	26	74,218	29	43,976	21	36,055	18	51,228	23
Entertainers	49,996	19	42,056	16	53,292	21	23,434	11	18,487	9	25,636	12
Administrative	495	0	405	0	385	0	352	0	568	0	555	0
Clerical	4,943	2	3,801	1	3,709	1	3,386	2	3,169	2	3,534	2
Sales	2,725	1	2,576	1	2,284	1	2,090	1	1,938	1	2,560	1
Service	82,440	32	89,154	35	90,967	35	81,306	38	84,745	41	76,402	34
Maids	58,700	23	71,444	28	71,386	28	62,653	29	61,986	30	47,544	21
Caretakers	11,399	4	7,885	3	10,088	4	10,410	5	14,695	7	19,225	9
Agricultural	1,920	1	1,706	1	1,204	0	972	0	822	0	538	0
Labourers	94,525	36	92,664	36	85,816	33	81,857	38	75,683	37	83,560	38
Not classified	698	0	506	0	403	0	219	0	3,345	2	3,027	1
Total	**260,594**	**100**	**256,197**	**100**	**258,986**	**100**	**214,130**	**100**	**205,791**	**100**	**221,560**	**100**

Source: Unpublished data from the Philippine Overseas Employment Administration.

Owing to its early entry into overseas labour, the Philippines developed a complete system for migrant recruitment and contracting that has ensured its place as the number one source of contract workers in the world. The governmental system is responsible for licensing recruiters, providing information to workers, extending protection, and offering services for reintegration. The system also provides for private-sector involvement in expanding market opportunities and recruiting candidates for overseas labour. The Migrant Workers and Overseas Filipinos Act of 1995, basically a protection bill, codifies the system, gives policy direction, and mandates the deregulation of recruitment by the year 2001. Although it is regarded as a model by other labour-sending countries, NGOs and migrant associations remain critical of the overseas labour programme, which they claim diverts attention from improving the country's own development policies.

Even though the number of migrants from the Philippines remained fairly constant in the 1990s, remittances quadrupled after 1991, reaching US$ 5.7 billion in 1997, the first notable increment (31 per cent) coming between 1991 and 1992 and the second between 1994 and 1997. In 1996, remittances represented 13 per cent of GDP. In addition to moneys remitted through banks, remittances are channelled through friends and agents, and brought home personally by migrants at the end of their contracts. The more recent surge in remittances is believed to be associated with the elimination of restrictions on foreign exchange transactions and a healthy Philippine economy prior to the 1997 crisis that provided an incentive for investment at home.

Although after the crisis hit the Philippines suffered a 34 per cent currency devaluation and subsequent economic slow-down, its less exposed banking system's stability makes it generally better situated than other Asian countries. The Philippines is now beginning to attract foreign investments. This infusion of capital—together with remittances—contributes to the appreciation of the peso against the US dollar. Optimism, however, should be tempered as there are still major problems —the external debt, high unemployment, and a series of high-profile kidnappings— none of which create a favourable climate for foreign investments. Nevertheless, while other nations experienced severe negative growth in 1998, the Philippine economy posted a negative GDP growth rate of only 0.5 per cent in that year (Table 5).

Because of the variety of destinations of its migrant labour force and because not many Filipinos were in the crisis-stricken countries (with the exception of Sabah), the Philippines did not experience massive returns. Estimates projected that the number of overseas Filipinos would decline by 100,000 by the end of 1999 (5). However, after a decline in the first half of 1998, the year ended with an increase of 0.5 per cent in the deployment of workers. A drop in the flows to Malaysia, Singapore, Hong Kong, and the Republic of Korea was compensated by an increase in flows to Taiwan (Province of China), Japan, and the Middle East.

Official remittances to the Philippines declined by 16 per cent in 1998. The devaluation of the currency following the crisis discouraged migrants from remitting more than was necessary. However, prospects for 1999 were encouraging. Judging from the trends of the first six months of 1999, deployment of migrant workers in 1999 were projected to maintain 1998 levels.

INDOCHINA

Although Viet Nam—along with the Lao People's Democratic Republic, Cambodia and Myanmar—had considerable refugee and labour movements toward Thailand, it also developed its own patterns of labour migration. From 1980 to 1991, Vietnamese workers migrated predominantly to Soviet bloc countries. This movement of approximately 300,000 workers was formalized through bilateral agreements. After 1991, the administration of the labour contracts was transferred to Vietnamese companies, with the Government simply regulating and monitoring the process. The annual outflow of Vietnamese workers in the early 1990s involved approximately 60,000 people (3). In May 1999, Viet Nam signed an agreement paving the way for Vietnamese workers to go to Taiwan (Province of China). Trafficking of women to Cambodia and to the Chinese border has emerged as a concern in recent years.

Internal migration intensified because of Government programmes to relocate people from north-eastern to south-eastern provinces, but mostly because of the economic attractiveness of the more developed provinces (4). The resettlement of refugees from Viet Nam (between 1975 and 1996, 839,228 left Viet Nam, of whom 755,106 were resettled and 81,136 returned to Viet Nam voluntarily) was practically terminated with the end of the Comprehensive Plan of Action (16). Resettled refugees now constitute important communities in the United States, Canada, and Australia and serve as an attraction for additional emigration of family members (30 per cent of Vietnamese immigration to the United States is determined by family reunification).

Elsewhere in Indochina, population mobility is dominated by unauthorized migration (including trafficking) and the periodic resurgence of refugee movements; most of these movements are directed at neighbouring Thailand.

REGIONAL COOPERATION

International migration received scant attention at the regional level in South-East Asia. Some limited discussions on migration-related issues took place within meetings of the ASEAN countries and of the Brunei, Indonesia, Malaysia, Philippines-East ASEAN Growth Area (BIMP-EAGA). The wider coalition, Asia-Pacific Economic Co-operation (APEC), examined human resource development issues with particular attention to the movement of professionals—but not of unskilled migrant workers—in the region. On the initiative of the IOM, countries in the region began meeting regularly on the subject. Two discussion groups emerged:

THE BANGKOK DECLARATION ON IRREGULAR MIGRATION

We, the Ministers and representatives of the Governments of Australia, Bangladesh, Brunei Darussalam, Cambodia, China, Indonesia, Japan, Republic of Korea, Lao PDR, Malaysia, Myanmar, New Zealand, Papua New Guinea, the Philippines, Singapore, Sri Lanka, Thailand, and Viet Nam, as well as the Hong Kong Special Administrative Region . . . . Declare as follows:

1. Migration, particularly irregular migration, should be addressed in a comprehensive and balanced manner, considering its causes, manifestations and effects, both positive and negative, in the countries of origin, transit and destination;

2. The orderly management of migration and addressing of irregular migration and trafficking will require the concerted efforts of countries concerned, whether bilaterally, regionally or otherwise, based on sound principles of equality, mutual understanding and respect;

3. Regular migration and irregular migration should not be considered in isolation from each other. In order to achieve the benefits of regular migration and reduce the costs of irregular migration, the capacity of countries to manage movement of people should be enhanced through information sharing and technical and financial assistance. In this context, UNITAR, UNFPA, and IOM, joint sponsors of the International Migration Policy and Law Course (IMPLC), are invited to hold, in the near future, a course for middle to senior government officials from the region;

4. A comprehensive analysis of the social, economic, political and security causes and consequences of irregular migration in the countries of origin, transit and destination should be further developed in order better to understand and manage migration;

5. As the causes of irregular migration are closely related to the issue of development, efforts should be made by the countries concerned to address all relevant factors, with a view to achieving sustained economic growth and sustainable development;

6. Countries of origin, as well as countries of transit and destination, are encouraged to reinforce their efforts to prevent and combat irregular migration by improving their domestic laws and measures, and by promoting educational and information activities for those purposes;

7. Donor countries, international organizations and NGOs are encouraged to continue assistance to developing countries, particularly the least-developed countries, in the region aimed at poverty reduction and social development as one means of reducing irregular migration;

8. The participating countries and region should be encouraged to pass legislation to criminalize smuggling of and trafficking in human beings, especially women and children, in all its forms and purposes, including as sources of cheap labor, and to cooperate as necessary in the prosecution and penalization of all offenders, especially international organized criminal groups;

the Manila Process, focusing on trafficking; and the Asia-Pacific Consultations, focusing more on general issues of migration.

As mentioned, the Government of Thailand, in cooperation with IOM, hosted a conference on irregular migration with a view to engendering cooperation among the governments on this issue. At that meeting, the Bangkok Declaration on Irregular Migration, signed by 19 Asian governments, called for greater regional cooperation on irregular migration and trafficking and promised exchange of information on its causes and consequences (see box).

9. The participating countries and region should exchange information on migration legislation and procedures for analysis and review, with a view to increasing coordination to effectively combat migrant traffickers;

10. The countries of origin, transit and destination are encouraged to strengthen their channels of dialogue at appropriate levels, with a view to exchanging information and promoting cooperation for resolving the problem of illegal migration and trafficking in human beings;

11. Greater efforts should be made to raise awareness at all levels, including through public information campaigns and advocacy, of the adverse effects of migrant trafficking and related abuse, and of available assistance to victims;

12. Concerned countries, in accordance with their national laws and procedures, should enhance cooperation in ascertaining the identity of undocumented/illegal migrants who seemingly are their citizens, with a view to accelerating their readmission;

13. Timely return of those without right to enter and remain is an important strategy to reduce the attractiveness of trafficking. This can be achieved only through goodwill and full cooperation of countries concerned. Return should be performed in a humane and safe way;

14. Irregular migrants should be granted humanitarian treatment, including appropriate health and other services, while the cases of irregular migration are being handled, according to law. Any unfair treatment towards them should be avoided;

15. The participating countries and region should each designate and strengthen a national focal point to serve as a mechanism for bilateral, regional and/or multilateral consultations and cooperation on questions of international migration;

16. A feasibility study should be conducted on the need to establish a regional migration arrangement, linked to existing international bodies, to provide technical assistance, capacity building and policy support as well as to serve as an information bank on migration issues for the countries in the Asia-Pacific region. The countries in the region are meanwhile encouraged to utilize and strengthen the already existing bilateral and multilateral arrangements;

17. The participating countries and region will follow up on the above-mentioned issues of irregular migration at the political and senior official levels in ways which may be deemed appropriate;

18. This document shall be given the widest publicity and dissemination possible to encourage governments, non-governmental organizations, the private sector and civil society to join in a collective regional effort to alleviate the adverse effects of irregular migration and to prevent and combat trafficking of human beings, especially women and children.

Trafficking, especially in women and children, attracted the attention of various NGOs, both in Thailand and the Philippines, and some initial research has been conducted by IOM, but the problem has not received systematic attention by governments or regional forums. The level of knowledge of the trafficking phenomenon extends only to identifying trafficking routes from the Philippines and Thailand to Japan and from Viet Nam, the Lao People's Democratic Republic, and Cambodia toward Thailand and other destinations.

CONCLUSION

Migration remains an important economic and social issue in South-East Asia. Receiving countries such as Singapore, Malaysia, and now Thailand rely on it for the functioning of their economy. In addition, Singapore and Malaysia also collect revenues from levies on migrants. Countries of origin, such as Indonesia, the Philippines, and recently Myanmar, count on remittances as an essential source of foreign exchange. Migration also is a significant factor in facilitating the integration of a region with diverse ethnic origins, history, traditions, and cultures, but with increasing relations and mutual interests. These conflict with current migration policies that on the one hand are restrictive, particularly in the possibility of long-term settlement, but on the other hand are flexible in practice to favour short-term interests. For this reason, migration has potentially disruptive implications for international relations.

The region is still reeling from the adverse consequences of the financial and economic crisis that uncovered inefficiencies and irregularities in the functioning of national economies. To some extent migrants have been less affected than local workers, as they operate in occupations shunned by local workers. Significant examples exist in Malaysia and Thailand, where initial programmes of massive migrant repatriations were modified to allow certain industries (such as agriculture) to continue to operate. However, this advantage is limited to the chance of gaining employment; in working and living conditions, migrants were already at the bottom.

Among the region's migration concerns, unauthorized migration is most significant. The level of unauthorized migration is abnormally high (as much as 60 per cent in Thailand, 30 per cent in Malaysia). This is not simply an indication of migration pressures, but also of employment practices and immigration policies. International experience demonstrates that control measures are not adequate to address unauthorized migration but must be integrated into a coherent policy framework that includes domestic employment, economic development, settlement, and rights protection.

Calls for a regional dialogue on migration dilemmas have been consistently sidelined as migration policy is perceived as a domestic concern. Perhaps the Bangkok Declaration on Irregular Migration will now galvanize sufficient support for cooperative action. While ASEAN would be the natural forum for such a discussion—as its relevance increased with the current inclusion of all countries in the region—it has encountered difficulties in adopting a more effective style in resolving conflicts. ASEAN's approach to the recent tragedy in East Timor led to questions about the organization's credibility and requests for a change in style and attention to remaining trouble spots. Resisting such change or ignoring these trouble spots may bring more instability. The migration issue will not go away. Times of crisis also are times of opportunity; perhaps a new regional dialogue that includes migration will prove beneficial.

REFERENCES

1. Ananta, A., D. Kartowibowo, N.H. Wiyono and Chotib (1998). The impact of the economic crisis on international migration: the case of Indonesia. *Asian and Pacific Migration Journal*, 7(2/3):313-338.

2. *Asian Migration News*, 30 June 1998, **http://www.scalabrini.org/~smc/amnews/amnews.htm**

2a. *Asian Migration News*, 14 February 1999.

2b. *Asian Migration News,* 31 October 1998.

2c. *Asian Migration News*, 31 July 1998.

2d. *Asian Migration News*, 15 April 1999.

2e. *Asian Migration News*, 31 July 1998.

2f. *Asian Migration News*, 15 August 1999.

2g. *Asian Migration News*, 30 June 1999.

3. *Asian Migrant* (1993). Trends in Asian labor migration, 1992. 6(1):4-16.

4. Dang, A., S. Goldstein and J. MacNally (1997). Internal migration and development in Vietnam. *International Migration Review*, 31(2):312-337.

5. Böhning, W.R. (1998). Conceptualizing and simulating the impact of the Asian crisis on Filipinos' employment opportunities abroad. *Asian and Pacific Migration Journal*, 7(2/3):339-368.

6. Chalamwong, Y. (1998). The impact of the crisis on migration in Thailand. *Asian and Pacific Migration Journal*, 7(2/3):297-312.

7. Hui, W-T. (1998). The regional economic crisis and Singapore: implications for labor migration. *Asian and Pacific Migration Journal*, 7(2/3):187-218.

8. Kassim, A. (1998). *The case of a new receiving country in the development world: Malaysia*. Paper presented at the Technical Symposium on International Migration and Development. The Hague, Netherlands, 29 June-3 July 1998.

9. Kurus, B. (1998). Migrant labor: the Sabah experience. *Asian and Pacific Migration Journal*, 7(2/3).

10. Lee, J. (1998). The impact of the Asian financial crisis on foreign workers in Taiwan. *Asian and Pacific Migration Journal*, 7(2/3):145-170.

11. Mani, A. (1995). Migration in Brunei Darussalam. In O.J. Hui, C.K. Bun, C.S. Beng (Eds.), *Crossing Borders: Transmigration in Asia Pacific*. Prentice Hall, Singapore, pp. 441-455.

12. National Statistics Office (1997). *Key Statistics of Thailand 1997*. Bangkok.

13. Pang, E.F. (1992). Absorbing temporary foreign workers: the experience of Singapore. *Asian and Pacific Migration Journal*, 1(3/4):495-509.

14. Pillai, P. (1998). The impact of the economic crisis on migrant labor in Malaysia: policy implications. *Asian and Pacific Migration Journal*, 7(2/3):255-280.

15. Stern, A. (1996). Quantitative international migration data for Thailand: an overview. *Asian and Pacific Migration Journal*, 6(2):229-254.

16. UNHCR (1997). *The Indo-Chinese Exodus and the CPA*. Geneva.

17. Wong, D. (1997). Transience and settlement: Singapore's foreign labor policy. *Asian and Pacific Migration Journal*, 6(2):135-167.

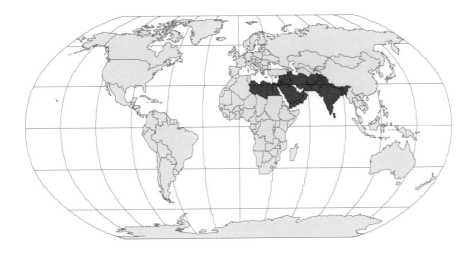

THE MIDDLE EAST
AND SOUTH ASIA

INTRODUCTION

As a migration region, the Middle East and South Asia is one of the most complex in the world today. While it is difficult to make broad generalizations about migration trends in countries as diverse as the Gulf States, Iraq, the Islamic Republic of Iran, Afghanistan, Israel, India, Pakistan, Bangladesh, and Sri Lanka, it is also true that the Middle East and South Asia are linked by history, culture, religion, and migration patterns. International migration is not new to either region, but only relatively recently have the two been brought together by the demand for labour in the oil-rich Middle East and the supply of labour from the highly populated South Asian states. Historically, however, these regions have had both immigration peaks and massive permanent and temporary outflows of population.

The most significant migration linking the two regions now involves temporary workers. The six countries of the Gulf are important host countries in the Middle

Nasra Shah, Professor, Department of Community Medicine and Behavioural Sciences, Kuwait University, Kuwait, and Mary Ann Larkin, an independent consultant to the Institute for the Study of International Migration, Georgetown University, Washington, DC, USA, contributed to this chapter.

East for temporary migrants and provide employment for millions of foreign workers. A majority of these workers comes from South Asia. Nearly 1 million workers from South Asia emigrate each year to the Middle East, mostly from Bangladesh, India, Pakistan, and Sri Lanka.

There are significant levels of labour migration among South Asian countries and from them to South-East Asia. On a far smaller scale, highly educated Indians and Pakistanis have long migrated to the United Kingdom and other regions once under its rule. Today, permanent migration from these countries is directed to the United States, Canada, Australia, and the United Kingdom.

Israel is important to any discussion of migration in the Middle East. Israel admitted nearly 1 million Soviet Jews as well as smaller numbers of Ethiopian Jews during the past decade. In addition to its permanent immigration programme, Israel also has become an important destination for temporary foreign workers.

Several major flows of refugees and asylum-seekers also originate in the Middle East and South Asia as old conflicts are rekindled and new conflicts emerge. Palestinian refugees left stateless upon the establishment of Israel and now numbering 3.3 million persons have yet to find a permanent home (37). The 1991 Gulf War led to the return of an estimated 300,000 Palestinians to Jordan; these returnees had been living mostly in Kuwait and held Jordanian passports. Palestinians remain in various other countries in the region. Discussions of their return to Palestinian-controlled territory are under way as part of the final status negotiations outlined in the Oslo Peace Accords.

More than 2.5 million Afghan refugees are in Pakistan and Iran, down from more than 5 million in the early 1990s (35). More than 500,000 Iraqi refugees are in Iran. The Tamil separatist movement in Sri Lanka led to refugee flight. Many repatriated over the course of the 1990s, but occasional outbreaks of fighting cause renewed flows; more than 100,000 Sri Lankan refugees were in India in 1999 (35). The disputed territory of Kashmir continues to be a source of conflict between India and Pakistan; they have fought three wars over the territory since 1947. Nuclear tests carried out by India and then by Pakistan made the political situation tense and increased the potential for refugee outflow.

Although the numbers of asylum seekers from South Asia are quite small, this migration attracts public attention, especially in Europe. The number of Bangladeshis, Pakistanis, and Indians seeking asylum in Europe has rarely exceeded 10,000 annually during the last two decades. The political conflict in Sri Lanka generated relatively more asylum seekers than other conflicts. About 75,000 Sri Lankans (Tamils) sought refuge in Europe during the 1980s and 1990s (9).

The region has faced repeated natural disasters in the form of floods—especially in low-lying Bangladesh—that cause massive deaths and casualties and force the temporary displacement of hundreds of thousands of individuals.

Recognizing the diversity in the flows in the Middle East and South Asia, this chapter does not attempt to tell the entire story of this migration. Rather, it focuses on several major trends in the region: labour migration into the Gulf States, particularly from the principal emigration areas in South Asia; permanent and temporary migration into Israel; and forced migration, with a particular focus on the world's three largest refugee populations—Palestinians, Afghans, and Iraqis.

LABOUR MIGRATION TRENDS

Most labour migration in this region gravitates to the Gulf States. These States focus primarily on temporary labour migration and recruit increasingly from the South Asian countries of India, Pakistan, Bangladesh and Sri Lanka.

IMMIGRATION TRENDS

Six countries comprise the Gulf Cooperation Council (GCC)—Bahrain, Kuwait, Oman, Qatar, Saudi Arabia, and the United Arab Emirates. With the exception of Saudi Arabia, each has a small national population that necessitates the inflow of foreign workers. Oil is the major source of revenue for all the Gulf States, and conditions rise and fall on its fate. The economic boom in the region brought about by the rise in oil prices in the 1970s caused an immediate need for workers in all categories of industry. Owing to British links, South Asian migrants have had a small foothold in jobs in the region since the 1930s, but their opportunities widened further with increased demand. Foreign workers in the Gulf were primarily of Middle East origin, but following the Gulf War in 1990-1991, even more opportunities for South Asian workers opened up as hundreds of thousands of workers from countries that supported Iraq in the conflict were not welcomed back.

A number of economic, demographic, and political factors underlie the attraction of migrants to the Gulf. One characteristic unique to the Gulf is the extremely high percentage of non-nationals in their populations, especially in their labour forces (Table 15). More than one-quarter of the labour force in most countries is expatriate, ranging from 28 per cent in Saudi Arabia and Oman to more than 75 per cent in Qatar. The proportion of non-nationals was even higher earlier in the 1990s. Policies are in place in all countries to maintain or increase birth rates in order to reduce dependency on foreign labour. As a result, increasing numbers of nationals enter the workforce each year. Population growth rates have been quite high starting from a low base, although there has been some recent evidence of fertility decline (7, 1).

TABLE 15.

TOTAL POPULATION BY NATIONALITY AND PERCENTAGE OF NON-NATIONALS IN THE LABOUR FORCE

Country	Population, 1996[1] Total	% national	% non-national
Saudi Arabia.	19,814,330	72.3	27.7
Kuwait (1997)[2]	2,152,775	34.6	65.4
Bahrain	566,726	62.6	37.4
Qatar	568,242	23.5	76.5
UAE	2,392,927	26.9	73.1
Oman	2,240,073	72.4	27.5
Total	**27,735,073**	**48.6**	**51.4**

Sources: [1]ESCWA (1997). *Demographic and Related Socio-Economic Data Sheets, Economic and Social Commission for Western Asia as assessed in 1996*. United Nations publication.
[2]Public Authority for Civil Information (1997). *Directory of Civil Information: Population and Labour Force*. Kuwait Government.

Among other reasons for the high foreign labour demand are the low wages for the work carried out by foreign workers, the variety of skills foreign workers offer, and their willingness to work in dirty, dangerous, and demanding (3-D) jobs that nationals shun. In addition, a whole range of intermediaries in host countries as well as countries of origin earn financial benefits from arranging labour migration. Within the host country, trading in residence permits benefits the sponsor. In Kuwait, as in other GCC members, labour is sometimes brought in not to satisfy genuine economic activity but to earn transfer fees (16).

Although the Gulf countries differ in terms of the level of infrastructure development that necessitates foreign workers, steady demand for skilled and unskilled workers continues. Kuwait reached a plateau in its construction boom, but other Gulf countries are still building. Oman, for example, requires a greater percentage of construction workers among the foreign workers it employs while Kuwait demands a greater contingent of service workers in its mix.

Another major reason for the high demand for foreign labour is the structural imbalance in the labour force participation of national workers. In some countries, such as Kuwait, the Government guarantees a job to each national. Thus, native-born workers are employed overwhelmingly in the public sector—about 94 per cent in Kuwait and 93 per cent in Saudi Arabia. Some tensions are evident in attempts to employ the growing national population as, for the first time, Gulf countries are facing rising unemployment levels (31). In Kuwait, the private sector employs about 75 per cent of the total labour force, but only 1.3 per cent are Kuwaiti (21).

South Asians now predominate in the foreign work force in the Gulf. In 1997, for example, the expatriate labour force in Kuwait was 65 per cent Asian, 33 per cent Arab, and only 2 per cent other nationalities (21). A similar breakdown is evident in other Gulf States.

Data on South Asian migrants demonstrate a pattern of growth that began in the 1970s and became particularly strong after the 1991 Gulf War (Table 16). Twice as many Indian labour migrants went to the Middle East in 1992 as migrated in 1991, for example, and labour migration to the Middle East also rose considerably from other major countries of origin in South Asia. The largest numbers of migrants from South Asia are from India. Data (Table 17) illustrate the magnitude of migration, specifically to the Gulf. At least 750,000 temporary workers from just four countries in South Asia migrated to the GCC countries in 1994, among them Indian (405,000), Bangladeshi (133,000), Pakistani (114,000), and Sri Lankan (111,000) migrants. Since then, the numbers of South Asians working in the Middle East has remained substantial, although migrants—especially from Sri Lanka and

TABLE 16.
ANNUAL OUTFLOW OF LABOUR MIGRANTS, 1976-1997

Year	Bangladesh		India		Pakistan		Sri Lanka	
	Total	% to ME	Total	% to ME	Total	% to ME	Total	% to ME
1976	6,092	91.3	4,200	na	41,690	95.7	1,200	100.0
1977	6,225	98.2	22,900	na	140,445	99.6	12,500	100.0
1978	22,809	99.7	69,000	na	129,553	99.0	17,700	100.0
1979	24,465	98.9	171,000	na	118,259	99.9	25,900	100.0
1980	33,275	97.7	236,200	na	118,397	97.9	28,600	100.0
1981	55,787	96.5	276,000	na	153,081	99.0	57,400	100.0
1982	62,805	99.0	239,545	93.6	137,535	99.8	22,500	100.0
1983	59,216	98.3	224,995	96.9	120,031	99.7	18,100	100.0
1984	56,794	98.5	205,922	96.4	93,540	99.9	15,700	na
1985	77,714	98.8	163,035	98.4	82,333	99.9	12,400	na
1986	68,704	99.0	113,649	96.1	58,002	99.6	15,800	na
1987	55,016	99.0	125,356	97.2	66,186	99.8	16,127	94.7
1988	68,570	98.3	169,844	97.7	81,545	99.8	18,973	93.8
1989	107,294	93.6	126,786	95.1	95,863	98.0	24,724	na
1990	103,814	97.4	141,816	94.2	113,781	98.0	42,624	na
1991	147,131	97.7	192,003	96.0	142,818	99.8	65,067	94.5
1992	188,103	93.2	416,784	96.7	191,506	99.7	124,494	90.3
1993.	244,590	70.4	438,338	95.5	154,529	99.2	129,076	90.0
1994	186,903	72.4	425,385	95.1	114,019	98.9	130,027	85.0
1995	187,543	74.8	415,334	93.0	122,840	94.5	170,131	83.3
1996	211,620	na	414,214	93.7	127,784	93.0	162,572	85.1
1997	230,765	na	416,424	92.8	153,929	96.0	149,843	84.6

Notes: na = not available; ME = Middle East

Sources: Stahl, W. and R.T. Appleyard (1992). International manpower flows in Asia: an overview. *Asian and Pacific Migration Journal.* 1(3/4):417-476.
Bangladesh: 1990 and 1995, official data; 1991-1994, R.A. Mahmood (1995). Data on migration from Bangladesh. *Asian and Pacific Migration Journal,* 4(4):531-541; 1996 and 1997, R. Amin (1998). *Enhancing capabilities of emigration countries to protect men and women destined for low-skilled employment: the case of Bangladesh.* Paper presented at the Technical Symposium on International Migration and Development organized by the United Nations ACC Task Force on Basic Social Services for All, The Hague, Netherlands, 29 June-3 July.
India: 1976-1981, D. Nayyar (1989). International labour migration from India: a macro-economic analysis. In R. Amjad (Ed.) *To the Gulf and Back, Studies on the Economic Impact of Asian Labour Migration.* New Delhi: ILO/ ARTEP; 1990-1992, S.K. Sasikumar (1995). International labour migration in India. *Asian and Pacific Migration Journal,* 4(4):555-563; 1993-1997 from Annual Report, Ministry of Labour.
Pakistan: 1989-1993, F.I. Azam (1995). Emigration dynamics in Pakistan: an overview. *International Migration,* 33(3/4):729-762; 1994, F.I. Azam (1995). Data on international migration from Pakistan. *Asian and Pacific Migration Journal,* 4(4):585-588; 1995-1996, O.P.F. [Overseas Pakistanis Foundation] official data.
Sri Lanka: 1990-1991, Official data; 1992-1994, K. Yapa (1995). Data on international imigration from Sri Lanka. *Asian and Pacific Migration Journal,* 4(4):601-612; 1995, G. Gunatilleke (1998). Macroeconomic implications of international migration from Sri Lanka. In R. Appleyard (Ed.), *Emigration Dynamics in Developing Countries, South Asia.* Ashgate for IOM/UNFPA, Aldershot, England; 1996-1997, *Statistical Handbook of Foreign Employment 1998.*

TABLE 17.
MAJOR DESTINATIONS OF SOUTH ASIAN MIGRANTS

Sending countries	Receiving countries				
	Saudi Arabia	Other GCC[1]	Other Arab	Others	Total
Bangladesh (1994)					
Number	91,385	41,990	2,258	51,270	**186,903**
%	48.9	22.5	1.2	27.4	**100**
India (1994)					
Number	265,875	139,034	na	20,476	**425,385**
%	62.5	32.7		4.8	**100**
Pakistan (1997)					
Number	78,327	69,508	76	6,018	**153,929**
%	50.9	45.2	0.05	3.9	**100**
Sri Lanka (1997)					
Number.	48,123	78,615	15,414	7,691	**149,843**
%.	32.1	52.5	10.3	5.1	**100**

Note: [1]Other GCC countries include Bahrain, Kuwait, Oman, Qatar, and the United Arab Emirates.

Sources: **Bangladesh:** R.A. Mahmood (1995). Data on migration from Bangladesh. *Asian and Pacific Migration Journal,* 4(4):531-541.
India: Government of India, Ministry of Labour. *Annual Report 1995-96.* p. 98.
Pakistan: O.P.F. [Overseas Pakistanis Foundation] official data.
Sri Lanka: *Statistical Handbook of Foreign Employment, 1998.*

Bangladesh—have begun to diversify their destinations to include South-East Asian countries (Table 17).

These data reflect the number of registered migrants arriving in the Middle East. The actual flow, including unauthorized workers, is much higher. No precise figures of unauthorized migrants exist, but insight into the magnitude of the problem may be found in the level of expulsions each year. For example, the United Arab Emirates expelled more than 160,000 unauthorized workers in a three-month period in 1996 (17), and Saudi Arabia reportedly expels from 350,000 to 450,000 unauthorized residents each year (17).

The major nationalities of the foreign workforce in the Gulf changed as a result of the Gulf War. Migrants from countries that supported Iraq in the conflict were expelled from Kuwait and other Gulf countries. The departure of 350,000 Palestinians from Kuwait and the expulsion of 750,000-800,000 Yemenis from Saudi Arabia began to change the nationality composition of foreign workers. Kuwait banned the return of five nationality groups—Iraqis, Palestinians, Jordanians, Yemenis, and Sudanese (26). In the labour market vacuum that occurred, Asians and Egyptians were the major beneficiaries.

Despite the employment of temporary labour migrants, Gulf countries do not encourage nor accept permanent immigrants. Increasingly concerned about the high levels of foreign workers—especially unauthorized workers—governments began to impose restrictions. Their concerns about the possible permanence of these workers stem, in part, from the experience of several countries with Palestinian workers who remained over many years. Palestinian families were formed and reunited from abroad, but even these migrants' children born in the Gulf were considered foreigners by law. Prior to the Gulf War, one-third of the foreign population of Kuwait was born in-country, mostly of Palestinian parents.

Citizenship and nationality are closely guarded in the six Gulf States, all of which are governed by kings or emirs who inherit political power from within the influential families of the region. Each of these countries evolved from clan-based forms of social organization that opened up to democracy. To varying degrees, the GCC nations share a social and economic philosophy of providing for their citizens through free or highly subsidized social programmes, including education, health care, housing, and employment. Such policies are predicated upon having a small population.

Development plans indicate the need to reduce overall dependence on outside labour. Because of the near-total concentration of nationals in the public sector, with foreigners occupying nearly all employment in the private sector, one of the major government policies is to encourage employment of nationals in the private sector. Rising unemployment among nationals adds to pressure for these changes. A related policy restricts the employment of foreign workers in the public sector by the imposition of a hiring limit of 35 per cent foreign workers in government offices and departments. Recent reports state that the GCC nations intend to "replace 75 percent of foreign workers with their own citizens by 2020" (6). Even more important is the need to stop unauthorized migration. Governments took steps to curb visa trading that encourages the inflow of unauthorized foreign workers. Governments also became increasingly selective in granting visas to foreigners and in maintaining control over the migration process. Documentation controls register the exit—as well as the entry—of foreign workers.

Host countries in the Gulf restrict migrants to fixed-term (renewable) contracts that link migrants to employers. Migrants are not permitted to transfer to another employer during a specified time without permission and may not change residence to work for another employer. If caught in Kuwait, for example, migrants are imprisoned and later deported. Migrants are discouraged from bringing family and only those professionals earning high salaries (US\$ 1,500/month, public sector; US\$ 2,200/month, private sector) receive authorization for spouse and children.

In an attempt to control the growing migrant population that is necessary to run the economy, yet discourage its permanent settlement, mass repatriations have taken place in recent years (Table 18). From mid-1996 to mid-1998, all six Gulf nations declared periods of amnesty during which they allowed unauthorized workers to leave or regularize their status without facing jail or fines. The United Arab Emirates took the lead in offering an amnesty after the issue was discussed at a ministerial meeting in the Gulf; other nations quickly followed suit.

TABLE 18.
AMNESTY RETURNEES FROM THE SIX GCC COUNTRIES, 1996-1998

Country	Total repatriated
Saudi Arabia	752,241
UAE	200,000
Bahrain	32,365[1]
Oman	24,000
Kuwait	11,502
Qatar	3,000
Total	**1,023,108**

Note: [1]Asians who applied to leave the country or regularize their status.

Sources: **Saudi Arabia and Qatar**: *Migration News,* September 1998.
UAE: *Kuwait Times*, 2 December 1994, p.4.
Bahrain: *Migration News*, November 1997.
Oman: *CISNEWS*, June 1998.
Kuwait: *Kuwait Times*, Saturday, 20 December 1997, p.1.

Labour recruitment is mainly arranged by licensed private and public agents in the country of origin and host countries. In some instances, however, a migrant is legally hired directly by an employer in the host country through connections with family and friends. Not all agents are licensed and visa trading is common, even among licensed agents.

Surveys of migrant workers and returnees indicate that for a large majority, labour migration to the Gulf is a positive experience (8). Skilled workers earning higher amounts of income generally express higher levels of satisfaction. Despite the downward trend in salaries, migrants are able to earn wages that are several times higher than possible in their home country. A majority would like to stay as long as possible and make efforts to bring in as many of their friends and relatives as they can. For workers and their families who become used to higher levels of income, there seems no better alternative than to maintain the Middle East job, by whatever means possible. Workers are willing to undergo a fair amount of hardship for the sake of their families. About 70 per cent of the time, migrants are married but unaccompanied. Absence of the migrants (usually husbands) has been found to create marital and social problems only in a minority of families.

While the experience of most migrants is favourable, there is need for protection of workers' rights. When abuse occurs, recruitment agents and employers are the two major violators. The former arrange migration for at least half of all workers, and agents are known to charge up to 10 or 15 times more than officially allowed. In some cases, workers are abandoned in the host country or a third country of transit. All the countries of origin have attempted to streamline the movement and registration of overseas migrants.

Labour laws of some host countries (e.g., Kuwait) do not cover certain categories of workers, such as housemaids. Sometimes, minimum wage standards exist as part of host country legislation but are not implemented because of a tight labour market in which many migrants compete for limited jobs. Humanitarian advocacy for a minimum wage, adequate housing, and other facilities for migrants is likely to be at odds with labour market realities. Even when they have grievances and the labour law of the host country theoretically protects them, workers rarely organize or complain unless the situation becomes really desperate, for example, being unpaid for four to six months, severely beaten, or raped.

Certain categories of workers, especially housemaids, require special protection not now available. Even though a large majority (about 80 to 85 per cent) of housemaids appear to be satisfied with their migration experience, abuse is a reality in all Gulf countries. Among the major countries that export female domestic workers, only the Philippines collects and publishes systematic data on the types of abuse suffered by housemaids reporting such violence. The usual complaints are non-payment of wages, long working hours, and general mistreatment. However, cases of beatings and verbal abuse constituted almost 20 per cent of all complaints in 1994; cases of rape about 3 per cent (29). Runaway maids present a special problem. Embassies of some countries set up shelters to accommodate them. In Kuwait, for example, India, Sri Lanka, and the Philippines have such shelters. At any one time, 200 to 400 runaway maids seek refuge at the Sri Lankan embassy, which allows them to stay at its premises but lacks resources to adequately house or feed them.

UNAUTHORIZED MIGRATION

One factor that perpetuates the demand for foreign workers is a hidden economy whereby private sponsors (*kafeels*) engaging in visa trading in the host countries are the major beneficiaries. Agents often secure more visas than required, with or without the employer's knowledge, and sell the excess visas. Because a migrant must have some type of visa to enter the country, visa trading is a common and lucrative business. The visa document designates whether an individual is authorized to work in-country; dependents and visitors are not permitted to work. In addition to the initial fee paid for a visa, a worker must pay the *kafeel* an agreed sum to renew the residence visa, usually every two years. Some benefits of this system also accrue to intermediaries in the sending countries.

The selling or buying of a visa is illegal. In Kuwait, the procurement of a work visa from a *kafeel* willing to sell it does not guarantee a job. If a migrant worker arrives without a job, the worker tries to find one through the social network or in response to advertisements. The *kafeel* must provide a release to transfer the residence status to the new employer. However, a transfer cannot be made unless a person has been in the country for at least two years. Thus, when a migrant takes up the job for an employer who is not the *kafeel*, the individual becomes an unauthorized worker.

Another situation in which migrants become unauthorized workers is by overstaying the term of their visa. While some unauthorized workers have been present historically in the Gulf, stern action to deal with them has been taken during the past few years. Each of the GCC countries announced periods of amnesty during which workers could either leave or regularize their stay. Punishments for living in the Gulf without proper authorization include fines ranging from US$ 240 in Oman to US$ 26,000 in Saudi Arabia and jail terms ranging from one to six months in different countries. More than 1 million persons were repatriated during the past two years from the GCC countries as a result of the amnesty programmes (Table 18).

EMIGRATION TRENDS

In 1947, India gained independence from the United Kingdom and Pakistan was partitioned into two wings, East and West. East Pakistan separated in 1971 and became the independent nation of Bangladesh. These events shaped the subsequent direction of migration within South Asia. Historical links to the United Kingdom and other Commonwealth nations provide an emigration avenue for the relatively affluent and professional sectors in these countries. However, most migration movements within and from South Asia today are related to labour migration across borders and outside the region to the Middle East.

While there was some labour migration from South Asia to the Gulf as far back as the 1930s under British rule, a remarkable upsurge in such movement occurred after the 1973 oil embargo. Bangladesh, India, Pakistan, and Sri Lanka lead the region in out-migration. During 1994-1995, it is estimated that 4 to 5 million workers from these countries were overseas, mainly in the Middle East (Table 17). Substantial outflows continued, with small yearly fluctuations. In 1997 alone, nearly 1 million migrants from Bangladesh (231,000), India (416,000), Pakistan (154,000), and Sri Lanka (150,000) left home to join their compatriots working abroad.

As these data reflect only documented migrants, they are likely to underestimate the real numbers by 30 to 50 per cent. The total stock of South Asian migrants abroad, including unauthorized migrants, is not known, although it is believed to be increasing. A very rough estimate of unauthorized migration can be based on deportation or the numbers of migrants in jail on visa violations. However, these data are often confidential and difficult to obtain. The Sri Lankan Government estimates that as many as 100,000 unauthorized migrants are overseas, including 10,000 in Japan and 20,000 in Italy (11).

Until the early 1990s, more than 90 per cent of all registered workers from South Asia moved to the GCC countries. This situation remains true today for Indians and Pakistanis, but Bangladeshis and Sri Lankans now move to other destinations (Table 17); about 28 per cent of Bangladeshis sought non-GCC destinations in the mid-1990s. By 1996, the Bangladesh Government had registered 1.5 million temporary labour migrants, an average of 100,000 migrants per year, to 59 countries around the world, mostly in Asia (18). Some 5 per cent of Sri

Lankans sought non-GCC destinations in the mid-1990s. Malaysia is a major new destination for Bangladeshis, while Lebanon, Jordan, the Maldives, and Singapore are new hosts to Sri Lankan migrants (36).

All four of these South Asian countries have high participation in temporary labour migration, but permanent settlement abroad is common only among Indians and Pakistanis. About 1.5 million persons of Pakistani origin are estimated to reside in North America and the United Kingdom, and some 220,000 Bangladeshis in the United Kingdom (18). Emigration of Pakistanis to the United Kingdom and the United States continues, based primarily on family reunification. Indian professionals and technical workers migrate in large numbers more or less permanently to jobs in the United States, the United Kingdom, Canada, and Australia. The annual outflow of permanent migrants currently is estimated at about 50,000 (22). In all, an estimated 15 million Indians live abroad. The impact of these numbers on India, however, is relatively insignificant given the total population of about 1 billion. In recent years, the Indian Government has encouraged expatriates to invest in their home country, particularly in India's emerging information technology sector.

Starting in the 1980s, there were new flows of South Asian migrants to southern Europe that took on permanent characteristics (38). By 1990, some 49,000 citizens, mostly from the four nations profiled here, were registered as legal residents of Italy; in Spain, some 8,000 legal residents were of Asian nationality.

Numerous factors underlie the decision to migrate. In addition to the strong demand for labour in the Middle East outlined above, conditions at home help set the stage for migration. Key among the push factors that motivate migration is the desire to improve one's standard of living. The lack of opportunity at home, combined with the lure of higher wages and the encouragement of friends and family who migrated earlier, work together to facilitate migration. The population of these four countries alone totals more than 1 billion people (Table 19). The 1997 Human Development Report recorded that in South Asia there are more people affected by poverty than any other region (32). Some 48 per cent of Bangladeshis and 47 per cent of Pakistanis are faced with various forms of deprivation as judged by the United Nations Development Programme human poverty index. Although the economies were growing at rates between 4.5 per cent in Bangladesh and 6.1 per cent in Pakistan from 1980 to 1993, and the Asian crisis did not have the

TABLE 19.
**SELECTED DEMOGRAPHIC AND SOCIOECONOMIC INDICATORS
FOR MAJOR SENDING COUNTRIES**

Indicators	Bangladesh	India	Pakistan	Sri Lanka
Total population, 1997 (in millions)	122.2	969.7	137.8	18.7
Population growth rate (%) 1994-2000.	1.6	1.6	2.7	1.0
GNP annual growth (%) 1980-1993	4.5	5.0	6.1	4.6
GNP per capita (US$) 1994	220.0	320.0	430.0	640.0
Human poverty index[1] value (%) 1990-1996	48.3	36.7	46.8	20.2
Adult literacy rate (%) 1994	37.3	51.2	37.1	90.1

Note: [1]The index is based on the percentage of people not expected to survive to age 40, adult illiteracy rate, and percentage of population without access to safe water and health services, and of underweight children under age 5.

Sources: UNDP (1997). Human Development Report. pp. 126-127, 147-148, 164-165, 194-195, 202-203; Population Reference Bureau (1997). *Wall Population Data Sheet* (for the total population).

devastating effects in South Asia that it had elsewhere (13), population growth exceeded the capacity of the economies to employ new entrants into the workforce each year. It is estimated that 40 per cent of the labour force of Bangladesh is unemployed or underemployed, while for the Pakistani labour force, the figure is 12 per cent.

Labour migrants do not come from the poorest or most destitute groups within the country, nor is unemployment normally a reason for migration. Migrants generally are more enterprising and fit individuals who can afford the ever-increasing financial costs of migration. Surveys of return migrants indicate that a majority of migrants were employed prior to migration, although unemployment appears to involve certain segments of the immigrant population. Unemployment among migrants varied from an estimated 11 per cent in Pakistan to 38 per cent in Kerala, India. Overall unemployment in Kerala deserves special mention as one-half of all emigrants from India originate in this state. More than 30 per cent of the labour force in Kerala is unemployed. Among migrants with secondary or higher education, unemployment was even higher at 50 per cent in the 1970s and nearly 66 per cent in 1996 (19). There are many disparities between the South Asian countries of origin and their Gulf country hosts. The population size difference is notable. The combined population of the four major sending countries is 45 times larger than the combined population of the six GCC countries. Differences in income also are phenomenal: the per capita income is 29 times higher in Saudi Arabia and 74 times higher in the United Arab Emirates than in Bangladesh. Labour demand exists in host countries for the plentiful supply of workers who are available and are willing to work under harsh conditions in jobs that the nationals are neither trained for nor willing to accept.

The wage differential between the home country and the Middle East is a tremendous pull—unskilled workers from Sri Lanka earn eight times more in the Middle East, while unskilled workers from Bangladesh earn about 13 times more. Further, foreign wages can be worth significantly more at home at times of currency devaluations. It is thus not surprising to find that 50 to 60 per cent of return migrants would like to re-emigrate. Many of the unemployed are return migrants waiting to return to the Middle East.

The formation of informal networks of friends and relatives facilitates movement and allows migration to become a self-perpetuating phenomenon. Case studies of housemaids from Sri Lanka clearly demonstrate the outward expanding nature of social networks. In one case, 18 primary migrants arranged for the employment of 154 others, indicating a multiplier of 8.5 (11). Not all communities have an equal propensity to migrate, as the exceptionally high concentration of emigrants from Kerala demonstrates.

In Kuwait, a 1996 survey among 800 skilled and unskilled male migrants from South Asian countries also showed the salience of social networks (28). Of all migrants interviewed, work visas had been arranged through friends and relatives for 34 per cent; Pakistanis (56 per cent) registered the highest rate of assistance from networks.

Networks provide several advantages, including social support to the migrants and their families back home, a place to stay if needed, and financial or other assistance. Migrants assisted by a network are also more successful in earning a higher salary and in overall job satisfaction (30). Further, the survey revealed that networks reduce the financial cost of migration; a smaller percentage of those who migrated through the network (63 per cent) had to pay for their visa, compared to workers who migrated using recruitment agents (94 per cent). However, network migration was risky in the sense that more of such workers migrated without a job offer in hand and more migrants were in an unauthorized status because of the type of entry visa they held. Among Sri Lankans, effectively organized social networks absorb unauthorized migrants readily and encourage repeat temporary migration (11).

The Governments of Bangladesh, India, Pakistan, and Sri Lanka are highly pro-emigration. Labour migration often is viewed as a panacea to help to resolve problems of unemployment and poverty. Remittances from overseas workers are a life-saver for the economies of some countries and a powerful force in shaping government policies. Sri Lanka and Bangladesh, in particular, pursued active migrant promotion campaigns that led to diversification of destinations, especially in Asia.

Emigration rules and procedures were revised during the 1970s or 1980s as migration volume increased. Each country also developed an administrative machinery to regulate outflows, ensure worker welfare, and promote further worker emigration. Data on annual outflows now are routinely collected by migration bureaus, although their accuracy varies.

A separate government bureau provides oversight of the labour contracting process and regulation of recruitment agents. While rules and procedures exist for punishing fraudulent agents, many loopholes remain. What is reported to and handled by the protectorate offices in sending countries is usually only a fraction of the instances of abuse. Migrant workers often are unwitting parties to exploitation when they are willing to pay the higher fee in order to get a visa. On the positive side, government-established welfare funds in each country provide assistance for migrants' families at home against the death of migrants overseas or for family use for education or housing. The Bangladesh Government also turned its attention to halting the trafficking of women and children by instituting criminal penalties; the Government is also providing some oversight of working conditions in host countries.

The governments attempt to maintain close ties with the host governments and to minimize controls on labour outflows. Pakistan, for example, waived minimum wage and return passage conditions of employment. Among the four countries, India dedicates the least effort because international migration is small compared to internal migration within India and involves a relatively smaller portion of the overall population. Nevertheless, India, too, waived the need for emigration checks of semi-skilled workers in order to preserve workers' share of the overseas labour market (26).

Return flows are not documented in any of these countries of origin. Some programmes exist to help migrants invest in land or housing on return, although governments generally do not have return or reintegration programmes. Research from India and Pakistan suggests that the savings and skills of returnees usually are not adequately utilized (4, 20).

A majority of migrant workers from all countries, except Sri Lanka, is male. In the case of Sri Lanka, most studies report the percentage of women among all labour migrants to be 60 per cent or higher. Recent data suggest an increasing feminization of the registered migrant workforce—72 per cent of the migrants in 1992 and 75 per cent in 1997. One major reason for this is the increasing demand for housemaids in additional countries. When examining the gender composition of migrants from other countries, it should be remembered that published data are based on registered migrants and do not cover undocumented workers. Research from Kuwait shows, for example, that in April 1996 there were 40,000 Indian women domestic servants employed in Kuwait, even though they are not reflected in published statistics in India, nor does the Indian Government permit the legal movement of such workers to Kuwait. As the workers are not allowed to migrate, the Indian embassy does not certify their movement, unlike that of workers who have legal permission to move (29).

In 1994, a small minority of emigrants from the four countries were professionals —doctors, engineers, judges, teachers, computer operators, and managers. Professionals range from 1 per cent in Pakistan to 6 per cent of the migrant workforce in Bangladesh. More than one-half of all workers from each country are unskilled or semiskilled workers, employed as labourers, servants, cleaners, and gas station attendants. Even with the slowing down of the construction boom in the Gulf, a large percentage of migrant workers are still absorbed in unskilled occupations, given the labour market structure in the Gulf.

Outside the Gulf in Singapore, Pakistan, Thailand, and India, low-skilled, temporary migrants from Bangladesh work in various industries, including the construction and hotel/restaurant industries and personal services (female domestic service workers). In Malaysia, Bangladeshi migrants work in assembly and small manufacturing plants. A different flow of Bangladeshis who are educated and have some religious qualifications occupy positions in religious institutions in India and Pakistan (18).

The relationship between population size and the number of migrants appears to account for much of the differential impact of international migration on these four countries of origin. Migrant numbers, especially from India, may appear quite large in comparison to the population of the host countries, but generally are not significant given the populations of the countries of origin. At the other extreme, about one-third of workers in Sri Lanka participate in labour migration.

Dependence on migrant remittances as a contribution to the national coffers as well as to family income is unmistakable (Table 20). The amounts remitted home vary, but reliance on this source of income was once strong in Pakistan and is strong today in Bangladesh. In 1994, remittances from overseas workers accounted for 34 per cent of the revenues from all goods and services exported from Bangladesh. In the three other countries, the contribution of remittances to the economy ranged from 14 to 17 per cent. The funds are channelled through both banks and non-official channels. Resources are most commonly used to purchase consumer items, homes, or land, or to celebrate weddings and other occasions.

Migration results in a skills drain on the local economy. The loss of certain skills even results in some wage increases. Nevertheless, given the levels of unemployment in society—especially among returnees—migration does not appear to have major negative impacts on the economy of the country of origin.

TABLE 20.
MIGRANT WORKER REMITTANCES AND PERCENTAGE OF EXPORTS,
1980 AND 1994

Country	Net workers' remittances (Million US$)	Remittances as percentage of revenues earned from exports of goods and services
Bangladesh		
1980	197	20.2
1994	1,090	33.9
India		
1980	2,786	22.6
1994	4,976	14.2
Pakistan		
1980	1,748	58.1
1994	1,446	17.2
Sri Lanka		
1980	152	11.3
1994	698	17.1

Source: World Bank (1996). *World Development Report.* New York, NY, Oxford University Press. Table 16, p. 218.

IMMIGRATION TRENDS IN ISRAEL

Israel is the principal country of permanent immigration in the Middle East. Jews from many countries have migrated to Israel since its creation in 1948; major countries of origin include Poland, Romania, Iraq, Iran, Morocco, and Tunisia (3). Over the past decade, a surge in migration to Israel occurred following the relaxation of emigration restrictions on Jews in the former Soviet Union. Also, Israel had encouraged temporary migration of foreign workers from countries such as the Philippines, Romania, and Thailand since 1993. The migration of foreign workers was necessitated by curtailed access from the West Bank and Gaza, which traditionally supplied Palestinian workers (37).

By law, Israel must accept immigrants of Jewish origin without numerical restriction. Formed in 1948 with fewer than 1 million inhabitants, the nation encourages and facilitates this immigration. The first wave of immigration in the 1950s from North Africa and Asia soon doubled the population. Between 1960 and 1989, immigration declined to an average of 10,000-15,000 per year, mostly from North America and western Europe.

The peak in recent immigration occurred in the early 1990s when Russia lifted emigration restrictions. Nearly 200,000 immigrants were admitted in 1990, and 176,000 in 1991. Thereafter, immigration averaged 80,000 annually. Between 1989 and 1997, a total of 848,000 immigrants arrived in Israel, 85 per cent of whom were from the former Soviet Union. During this period, the other major source of immigration was Ethiopia—some 30,000 Ethiopian Jews.

The current surge in immigration from the former Soviet Union—and Russia in particular—is due primarily to conditions in the countries of origin. The Russian economic crisis and drop in the value of the rouble left many persons with little recourse but to emigrate in search of a better life. Un- and under-employment is high in Russia, particularly among highly educated professionals. Further, one-third of the immigrants reported a surge in anti-Semitism in Russia.

Israel's approach to permanent immigration in the 1990s has been described as a policy of direct absorption. The arrivals are provided with a stipend for the first year to be spent as they wish for housing, education, clothing, and other needs. The Ministry of Immigrant Absorption offers employment programmes (including placement services, re-training, and small business training), housing and mortgage assistance, local integration assistance, education and language training for children and adults, and programmes to reinforce Jewish identity. The Government implements affirmative action policies for immigrants from Ethiopia and southern Russia who generally are less educated and less prepared for the Israeli labour market.

By the end of 1990, housing shortage was acute (14). Public housing construction was planned for the outlying areas of the country where population was sparse, while privately-backed construction proceeded in more central areas. Security concerns appear to have played a part in the Government's settlement decisions. Nevertheless, subsequent surveys of immigrant housing patterns revealed that the new Russian immigrants preferred to live in the central and urban areas of the country, which was similar to the Israeli-born settlement pattern (14). Lower salaries and fewer job opportunities in the remote areas appear to underlie immigrants' preferences, despite the lower cost of housing. Those immigrants who do choose housing in outlying areas often rent apartments, rather than purchase homes as those in the central areas do, which indicates that they may be less permanently settled.

Recent Russian immigrants to Israel overwhelmingly are highly educated professionals. The 1990 wave doubled the numbers of academics, more than doubled the numbers of medical doctors, and nearly tripled the number of engineers. Engineers continue to constitute a significant share (approximately 10 per cent) of all immigrants. From 1994 to 1997, some 67 per cent of immigrants from the former Soviet Union were of working age (18-65 years of age); 21 per cent were younger than 18 (15).

Downward mobility has been recorded among most migrants from Russia, as they find their abilities and experience rate lower in comparison with Israeli standards. Some 40 per cent of Russian immigrants who came first were obliged to change their occupation after arrival in order to find employment—although virtually no physicians were forced to do so. Those who arrived later in the 1990s had to switch occupations even more often; less than one-third of these scientists and academics currently work in their original occupation; less than 30 per cent of professionals and technical workers continue in their chosen occupation. Studies show that the rate of excess supply in the professional fields will continue into the future, leading to longer and longer times for immigrants to reach full integration.

Even as Israel was struggling to absorb the permanent immigrants from the former Soviet Union and Ethiopia, the country was beginning to import temporary workers from other parts of the world. Israel had been reliant on Palestinian labour from the occupied territories of Gaza and the West Bank; then that workforce was suddenly cut off. The Israeli labour market has been highly stratified by ethnicity, with Arab workers primarily occupied in low-wage, low-skilled jobs. Numbering 100,000 in the mid-1980s, half of the Gaza workforce and a third of the workforce of the West Bank worked in Israel. However, in 1993, the borders were closed temporarily as a response to a wave of terrorist attacks. Without access to these workers and with the pressing need to construct immigrant housing, the Israeli Government reluctantly agreed to employer demands to admit foreign workers.

By mid-1996, the Israeli Government had issued work permits to 104,000 foreign workers, mostly from Romania (construction), Thailand (agriculture), and the Philippines (domestic service) (5). Additionally, some 40,000 Palestinian workers from the occupied territories worked in Israel, including both authorized and unauthorized workers. Government sources indicated that 50,000 to 100,000 unauthorized foreign workers worked in the country in 1996.

Labour restrictions in Israel apply to Palestinians as well as to workers brought in from other countries. Palestinians must have work permits that tie them to specific employers and are subject to strict security restrictions. These workers must return to the territories each night, cannot form or participate in a labour union, and have unemployment insurance deducted from their pay—although they are not entitled to such benefits. Other foreign workers also are required to have a work permit, but enforcement of immigration and labour restrictions is considerably relaxed. In 1995, only 950 unauthorized workers were deported and only 242 employers were fined for labour violations (5).

While there is little controversy about the presence of the foreign temporary workers, concerns are raised about their potential permanence. Some urban workers settle and bring their families to join them, but they are a distinct minority. Some enclave settlement patterns are evident in cities. Polls in Israel reveal acceptance of the need for foreign workers (61 per cent) and a majority (55 per cent) indicated willingness to live in the same neighbourhood as foreign workers (5). Nevertheless, human rights groups in Israel protested against the treatment of foreign workers, citing the few legal rights given to them and the tendency to summarily deport workers involved in labour disputes.

FORCED MIGRATION TRENDS

In South Asia, the various shifts involved in nation-building over the years were accompanied by massive bloodshed, loss of life, and extensive forced population movements. The countries of both the Middle East and South Asia continue to be wracked by forced migration stemming from political events, civil conflict, and environmental disasters. Today, the number of refugees from new and renewed civil conflicts in various countries of the region fluctuates.

Nevertheless, several of the longest lasting and most tragic refugee situations in the world—involving the Palestinian, Afghani, and Iraqi populations—are in the Middle East or straddle the Middle East and South Asia. These groups represent the world's three largest refugee populations (35).

The Palestinian refugee problem is by far the oldest; some refugees have been displaced for more than 50 years. Large numbers of Palestinian refugees are found throughout the region, the largest numbers in Jordan (1.46 million), the West Bank and Gaza Strip (1.3 million), the Syrian Arab Republic (366,000), and Lebanon (365,000). Unlike other refugees who are aided and protected by UNHCR, the Palestinians are the responsibility of UNRWA, which maintains refugee camps and provides funding for education, health care, employment programmes, and other services.

As noted above, negotiations are currently under way between Israel and the Palestinian Authority in the West Bank and Gaza about the future of the Palestinian refugees. Under the Oslo Peace Accords, this issue was placed on the agenda of the final status negotiations, along with other highly controversial issues.

The Afghan refugee situation has also been prolonged, though it has ebbed and flowed since the fall of the Soviet-controlled Government in 1992. At the height of displacement, about 5 million refugees had left Afghanistan, primarily for Pakistan and Iran. As of the end of 1998, about 4 million had returned. Nearly 1.4 million repatriated in the first nine months after the change in government and another 1 million returned in 1993. Then repatriation slowed, largely because of continued insecurity in Afghanistan. New refugee movements and continued large-scale internal displacement occurred as fighting intensified. Military offences by the Taliban, in combination with their highly restrictive moral codes and restrictions on women's rights, produced still further forced migration within and out of Afghanistan. Today, there are about 2.6 million Afghan refugees and as many as 1 million internally displaced persons.

The third largest group of refugees is from Iraq; more than 580 thousand persons from Iraq are refugees, about 530 thousand of them in Iran. Another 1 million persons are internally displaced in Iraq, including about 800 thousand Kurds in a northern Iraq zone protected by the United Nations since the end of the Gulf War. Many of the Iraqis have been in Iran for decades where they received, by and large, a gracious welcome. Most were expelled from Iraq during the Iran-Iraq war because of suspected Iranian heritage. With the continued presence of both Iraqi and Afghan refugees, the welcome is growing thin. While they have been largely self-sufficient for much of their stay, recent Iranian Government restrictions on work authorizations have significantly increased unemployment.

CONCLUSION

Migration will continue to figure prominently in the Middle East and South Asia, although there are signs that movements may diminish over time. In the early 1990s, more than one-half of all workers in the Gulf were foreign. While the GCC countries had a general policy of reducing the number of expatriates, the economy traditionally sustained a relatively high demand. A slowdown and reversal in the demand may now be imminent for two major reasons. The Gulf economies experienced a slowdown as a result of the fall in oil prices and most host countries suffered from budget deficits. At the same time, there was a rapid increase in the indigenous labour force resulting from the high birth rate. New entrants to the labour market demand the promised public sector employment. Unemployment among nationals raises difficult political questions about the wisdom of importing large numbers of foreign workers, resulting in additional attention in policy planning. The repatriation of unauthorized workers is one concrete sign of the changed mindset. If the receiving countries are able to implement their restrictive policies, outflows from South Asia to the Gulf will decline markedly in the next few years. The persons most affected by these policies will be unskilled and semi-skilled workers. It appears, however, that the demand for housemaids will continue unabated.

For their part, South Asian governments continue to rely on migration to resolve employment pressures and on remittance income to fuel their economies. Bangladesh and Sri Lanka have begun to recognize the need to diversify their labour migration programmes; however, they have not focused at home on optimizing the talents and resources of returning migrants. Other South Asian nations still rely on Middle East destinations almost exclusively, particularly for lower-skilled migrants. Governments cautiously balance conflicting goals—to maximize labour exports and to seek fair and just treatment for migrants.

Although Israel has seen a surge in migration during this past decade, it is unclear whether the trend will continue. Political and economic stability in the former Soviet Union could well diminish the push factors causing many Soviet Jews to emigrate. Greater security within Israel, which awaits a successful end to the final status negotiations with the Palestinians, would increase Israel's immigration "pull," but it may also reduce the need to import temporary foreign workers to do jobs previously performed by Palestinians.

Unlike other developing regions, such as Latin America and South-East Asia, which have seen a decline in forced migration during the past decade, refugee movements and internal displacement continue to exert substantial pressure in the Middle East and South Asia. In the absence of long-term solutions to the underlying causes of these movements, it is unlikely that significant progress will be made in ending forced migration.

REFERENCES

1. Al-Rashoud and Farid, S. (1997). *Kuwait Family Health Survey 1996,* Preliminary Report. Ministry of Health, Kuwait, and Council of Health Ministers of GCC States, Riyadh.

2. Amawi, A. (1998). *Releasing the development potential of return migration: the case of Jordan.* Paper presented at the Technical Symposium on International Migration and Development, The Hague, Netherlands, 29 June-3 July.

3. Appleyard, R. (1991). *International Migration: Challenge for the Nineties.* International Organization for Migration, Geneva.

4. Azam, F-I. (1995). Emigration dynamics in Pakistan: An overview. *International Migration* (Geneva), 33(3/4):729-762.

5. Bartram, D.V. (1998). Foreign workers in Israel: history and theory. *International Migration Review,* 32(2):303-25.

6. *CIS News* (1998). 14 September.

7. Farid, S. (1996). *Transitions in demographic and health patterns in the Arab region.* Paper presented at the Arab Regional Population Conference, organized by the International Union for the Scientific Study of Population, Cairo, Egypt, 8-12 December.

8. Gunatilleke, G. (Ed.) (1991). *Migration to the Arab World: Experience of Returning Migrants.* United Nations University Press, Tokyo, Japan.

9. Gunatilleke, G. (1995). The economic, demographic, sociocultural and political setting for emigration. *International Migration,* 33(3/4):667-687.

10. Gunatilleke, G. (1998a). Macroeconomic implications of international migration from Sri Lanka. In R. Appleyard (Ed.), *Emigration Dynamics in Developing Countries: South Asia.* Ashgate for IOM/UNFPA, Aldershot, England.

11. Gunatilleke, G. (1998b). The role of networks and community structures in international migration from Sri Lanka. In R. Appleyard (Ed.), *Emigration Dynamics in Developing Countries: South Asia.* Ashgate for IOM/UNFPA, Aldershot, England.

12. Hockstader, L. (1999). From motherland to promised land: fleeing austerity, antisemitism, Russian arrivals reshape Israel. *The Washington Post*, 28 June, p. A13.

13. International Monetary Fund (1998). *World Economic Outlook*. Washington, DC. **http://www.imf.org/external/pubs/ft/weo/weo1098/pdf/1098ch2.pdf** Accessed on 12 August 1999.

14. Lipshitz, G. (1998). *Geographical dispersion and housing policies for immigrants*. Paper presented at the Third International Metropolis Conference, organized by the Metropolis International Project Team, Israel Metropolis Conference Organizing Committee, and JDC-Brookdale Institute, Zichron Yaacov, Israel, 30 November-3 December.

15. Ministry of Immigrant Absorption, Israel (n.d.) **http://www.moia.gov.il/english/statistika/statist/table/table0.html** Accessed on 13 May 1999.

16. Kuwait Ministry of Planning (1997). Human Development Report.

17. *Kuwait Times* (1996). 22 May.

18. Mahmood, R.A. (1995). Emigration dynamics in Bangladesh. *International Migration* 33(3/4):699-728.

19. Nair, G.P.R. (1998a). Dynamics of Middle East migration from Kerala. In R. Appleyard (Ed.), *Emigration Dynamics in Developing Countries: South Asia*. Ashgate for IOM/UNFPA, Aldershot, England.

20. Nair, G.P.R. (1998b). *Releasing the development potential of return migration*. Paper presented at the Technical Symposium on International Migration and Development, The Hague, Netherlands, 29 June-3 July.

21. Public Authority For Civil Information (1997). *Directory of Civil Information: Population and Labour Force*. Kuwait Government.

22. Premi, M.K. (1998). Migration dynamics in India. In R. Appleyard (Ed.), *Emigration Dynamics in Developing Countries: South Asia*. Ashgate for IOM/UNFPA, Aldershot, England.

23. Rogers, R. (1992). The future of refugee flows and policies. *International Migration Review*, 26(4):1112-1143.

24. Sasikumar, S.K. (1995). International labour migration in India. *Asian and Pacific Migration Journal*, 4(4):555-563.

25. Shah, N.M. (1994). Arab labour migration: A review of trends and issues. *International Migration*, 32(1):3-28.

26. Shah, N.M. (1995). Emigration dynamics from and within South Asia. *International Migration*, 33(3/4):559-625.

27. Shah, N.M. (1997). *Emigration dynamics in South Asia: major findings and policy recommendations*. Paper presented at the 12th IOM Seminar on Migration: Managing International Migration in Developing Countries, Geneva, 28-29 April.

28. Shah, N.M. (1998). The role of networks in migration to Kuwait among South Asian males. In R. Appleyard (Ed.), *Emigration Dynamics in Developing Countries: South Asia.* Ashgate for IOM/UNFPA, Aldershot, England.

29. Shah, N.M. and I. Menon (1997). Violence against women migrant workers: issues, data and partial solutions. *Asian and Pacific Migration Journal*, 6(1):5-30.

30. Shah, N.M. (2000). Relative success of male migrant workers in the host country, Kuwait: Does channel of migration matter? *International Migration Review*, 34(1):59-78.

31. United Nations (1998). *International Migration Policies.* New York, NY.

32. UNDP (1997). *Human Development Report.* New York, NY.

33. UNHCR (1999). *Country profiles.* Geneva. **http://www.unhcr.ch/world/asia/india.htm** Accessed on 27 August 1999.

34. UNHCR (1995). Migrant trafficking: Sri Lankan experience. In *State of the World's Refugees,* Oxford University Press Oxford. **http://www.unhcr.ch/refworld/pub/state/95/box5_2.htm** Accessed on 27 August 1999.

35. US Committee for Refugees (1999). *World Refugee Survey.* Washington, DC.

36. Yapa, K. (1995). Data on international migration from Sri Lanka. *Asian and Pacific Migration Journal*, 4(4):601-612.

37. Zlotnik, H. (1998). International migration 1956-96: An overview. *Population and Development Review*, 24(3):429-69.

38. Zlotnik, H. (1993). *South-North migration since 1960: The view from the South.* Paper presented at the International Population Conference, organized by the International Union for the Scientific Study of Population, Montreal, Canada, 4 August-1 September.

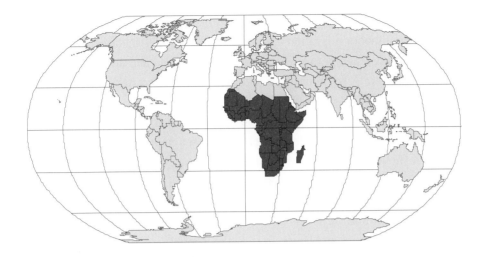

SUB-SAHARAN AFRICA

INTRODUCTION

Every type of migration is found in sub-Saharan Africa. A host of factors—historical, demographic, economic, political, ecological and ethnic—come together to generate these movements. Labour migrants who were unskilled, semi-skilled, and professional, as well as nomads, unauthorized migrants, refugees and internally displaced persons travelled mostly to traditional destinations within the region until recent years.

These traditional subregional migration patterns developed over time: labour migration—authorized and unauthorized—characterized migration in West Africa; contract labour migration predominated in southern Africa; East Africa —especially the Horn of Africa and recently the Great Lakes region—is noteworthy for its massive refugee movements, with the greatest numbers of forced movements in East Africa. These established movements are now giving way to new migration patterns.

Aderanti Adepoju, Chief Executive of the Human Resource Development Centre, Lagos, Nigeria, contributed to this chapter.

Internal and international migration in sub-Saharan Africa now takes place in the context of social and economic transformation. Recent economic and political crises triggered labour migration and refugee flows to destinations with no prior links to countries of emigration. As the crises intensified and unemployment and poverty worsened, flows intensified and increasingly were made up of women, including highly skilled professionals migrating in their own right and sometimes travelling great distances. The formation of subregional economic communities influenced these new trends. Under their auspices, a number of initiatives to permit the free movement of persons among countries are under discussion, although the acceptance and implementation of such policies is not yet universal.

The major host countries in this region are the Côte d'Ivoire in western Africa, Gabon in central Africa, and Botswana and the Republic of South Africa in southern Africa. The major countries of origin are Mali and Burkina Faso in western Africa and Lesotho in southern Africa. Because so much is under transition in Africa, the in-between countries both receive and send migrants (Ghana, Nigeria, Senegal), former migrant-receiving countries are now migrant-sending countries (Uganda, Zambia, Zimbabwe), and others generate and/or host refugees (Burundi, Ethiopia, Liberia, Malawi, Mozambique, Rwanda, Somalia, Sudan, United Republic of Tanzania, etc.).

Data are a perennial problem for researchers and policy-makers who attempt to understand the characteristics and impacts of these migration phenomena. Data on international migration remain fragmentary and incomplete. Census data tend to undercount births and, while they record length of residence, they do not capture migration. Specialized migration surveys are based on small samples and tend to be location-specific. Available data provide some insights into causes of migration, but little on aggregate stocks and flows. Data on refugees are generally more readily available than data on conventional migrants, although the reliability of data sources varies. In general, data are not comparable across countries. Problems inherent in assessing major migration movements in sub-Saharan Africa—from unauthorized movements to legal cross-border movements—mean that researchers must tap into a variety of data sources to begin to understand the phenomenon. Data noted in this chapter should be understood to provide only an approximate picture of the magnitude and characteristics of migration in the region.

IMMIGRATION TRENDS

As mentioned above, the principal countries of immigration in Africa include South Africa, Botswana, Côte d'Ivoire, and Gabon. The most extensive data relate to migration trends in South Africa, but some information is available on the other major receiving countries.

REPUBLIC OF SOUTH AFRICA

Labour migration has been a dominant feature in South Africa. The rate of in-migration increased dramatically following the demise of the apartheid regime in 1994. New inflows are more diversified than in the past, consisting of both skilled and unskilled migrants. Migrants are motivated in part by declining conditions in their home countries, but also by expectations of employment and an improved standard of living under the new Government in South Africa.

Overall data on the volume of migration in South Africa are not available and probably unknowable (13). A few experts' estimates of pieces of the migration picture provide a snapshot of the importance of the different types of flows into some sectors and regions of the country and some basic insights into the migration process.

The annual inflow into South Africa from other countries in southern Africa is estimated to have increased from just under 500,000 in 1990 to more than 3.5 million in 1995 (13). Under temporary work permits, contract labour in South African mines is the most established of these flows into the country. Approximately 200,000 foreign migrant workers—or about one-half of the total mine workforce—labour in the mines each year. Labour brokers recruit and contract another 100,000 migrants each year as casual or temporary workers in other industries. Contracts are governed by South Africa's bilateral treaties with Mozambique, Lesotho, Botswana, Swaziland, and Malawi.

South Africa admits a small percentage of permanent residents, refugees, and asylum seekers each year, although inflows consist mainly of temporary migrants. Skilled migration into South Africa experienced unprecedented growth in the past few years. After the change in government, the influx in migration included doctors and engineers from Cuba and Europe, who are in high demand. Other workers from sub-Saharan Africa also flocked to South Africa from Nigeria, Senegal, Sierra Leone, the Democratic Republic of the Congo, Kenya, and Uganda. Quite different from the traditional labour migrants, these individuals were mostly skilled professionals—teachers, university professors, doctors, lawyers, nurses, and engineers. Some of the nationals of these countries entered the then nominally independent homelands clandestinely during the period of apartheid. Traders and students from the Democratic Republic of the Congo followed in 1991-1994 as their country's economy, government, and society virtually collapsed. Traditional migrants from the satellite States of Lesotho, Swaziland, Botswana, Malawi, and Mozambique were mostly unskilled farm labourers and mine workers. Women—now highly visible in cross-border migration—move primarily for trading (buying and selling) and visiting relatives (16).

Countless foreign workers enter South Africa without authorization. An estimated 3.5 million unauthorized persons were in South Africa in 1997 (30). Deportation data are often used as a proxy for roughly gauging the increase/decrease in levels of unauthorized migrants; in 1996, more than 181,000 migrants were deported, up from 91,000 in 1994 (Table 21). Of the latter group, 75 per cent were Mozambicans, with the remainder from Nigeria, Sierra Leone, Ethiopia, and Zambia. This represented a dramatic increase in the number of unauthorized migrants deported under the post-apartheid Government. The number of residence visa overstayers also increased exponentially during the 1990s (Table 22). While no exact figures on unauthorized migration exist, the Government is aware that 750,000 persons who entered South Africa on temporary visas were not recorded as having departed (12). Because of the relatively open and vast borders, however, many individuals do enter and leave the country without inspection.

TABLE 21.
DEPORTATIONS OF UNAUTHORIZED IMMIGRANTS
FROM SOUTH AFRICA, 1992-1996

Year	Number deported
1992	83,109
1993	97,223
1994	90,900
1995	157,695
1996	181,230

TABLE 22.
RESIDENCE PERMIT OVERSTAYERS IN SOUTH AFRICA, 1992-1996

Year	Number of overstayers
1992	83,960
1993	82,243
1994	84,243
1995	128,778
1996	233,472

Mozambicans represent the largest migrant group in South Africa. An estimated 350,000 were there in the early 1990s while conflict still raged in their own country (13). An estimated 90,000 Mozambican refugees remained in South Africa at the close of the UNHCR repatriation programme in 1996 (37). Some 120,000 Mozambicans had contracts in 1995 to work in agriculture; many of them were recruited from among Mozambicans already in South Africa.

Migrants from Lesotho are dependent on work in South Africa. An estimated 100,000 Lesotho workers labour in the mines of South Africa, representing some 40 per cent of the predominant Basotho tribe's male workforce (29).

Among the factors attracting migrants to South Africa is its economy and the wide disparity between incomes in South Africa and those of its neighbours (Table 23). South Africa's per capita income in 1996 was four times larger than in the other 11 member States of the Common Market for Eastern and Southern Africa (COMESA) combined and accounted for two-fifths of the GNP of all sub-Saharan Africa. Per capita income at that time in South Africa was 35 times that of Mozambique (31). Even when South Africa erected electrified barbed-wire fences along its lengthy borders with Mozambique to control the influx of refugees and immigrants, desperate migrants risked entry.

In 1994, South Africa ended apartheid, the racially based system of government biased toward the white minority. Almost immediately, immigration policy initiatives were taken to eliminate the most severe violations of the rights of unauthorized migrants as condoned by the 1991 Aliens Control Act. The reforms were codified in the 1995 Amendments to the earlier Act. Nevertheless, immigration restrictions remain strict, and few legal means exist for the temporary entry of

TABLE 23.
GDP PER HEAD IN SELECTED SADC COUNTRIES, 1993

Countries	GDP per head, 1993
South Africa	2,800
Botswana	2,700
Namibia	1,600
Swaziland	1,000
Lesotho	750
Angola	680
Zimbabwe	640
Zambia	400
Malawi	250
Tanzania (United Rep.)	105
Mozambique	100

foreign workers. Although its policies are still under review, South Africa is currently described as having a two-gate immigration policy. The first gate regulates the admission of permanent immigrants and skilled temporary immigrants. Other temporary entrants allowed include visitors, business persons, students and individuals seeking medical care. The second gate gives to white farmers and the mining industry virtually the only authority to recruit and contract unskilled and semi-skilled labour under bilateral agreements with the countries of origin. Employers must secure work permits for foreign migrants; their numbers almost quadrupled between 1992 and 1996 (Table 24).

TABLE 24.
NEW TEMPORARY WORK PERMITS ISSUED IN SOUTH AFRICA,
1992-1996

Year	Number of new permits
1992	5,581
1993	5,741
1994	8,714
1995	11,053
1996	19,498

In a 1996 amnesty program, South Africa granted residence to about 124,000 nationals of southern African countries, among them 85,500 migrants from Mozambique, nearly 20,000 from Zimbabwe and over 8,000 from Lesotho who had been living in the country since 1986 (25). Another 51,000 foreign miners also were granted residency rights. Many migrants eligible for amnesty on the basis of years worked did not always apply for it. Participation rates were considered especially low among Mozambicans, who were said to have had plans to return permanently to Mozambique and felt secure enough in their jobs to decide not to apply (14). Under law, persons who enter on temporary visas may not change their status in-country and may not naturalize, regardless of the number of years of residence.

During the past few years, two different task forces created by the Ministry of Home Affairs recommended changes to migration law and policy. Their reports reflect criticisms that the Amendments to the Aliens Control Act did not go far enough to remove the racially biased immigration policies of the past. The 1999 White Paper on International Migration, as did the 1997 Green Paper before it, analysed the role of labour migration in South Africa. The analysis noted both the loss of skilled manpower in critical areas owing to out-migration and the recent entry of unauthorized migrants. The core of the 1999 White Paper recommendation is that the Government should shift the balance of immigration enforcement from border controls against unauthorized immigration to workplace inspection. The newest recommendations would streamline visa categories but continue the long-standing concessions to the mining and agricultural industries' needs for foreign labour.

Immigration is a very sensitive policy issue in South Africa; xenophobic reactions against immigrants are rampant. The domestic unemployment situation helps fuel these reactions. The predominant perception is that immigrants compete with nationals for scarce job opportunities. Perhaps no more than 7 per cent of young people who complete their education find work in South Africa, and an estimated 40 per cent of the country's workforce—6 million persons, mostly black—were unemployed in 1995, up from 30 per cent in 1980. South Africa's share of total world gold output shrank from 50 per cent in 1980 to just 23 per cent in 1995. Moreover, underground gold is becoming increasingly costly and complicated to extract and additional mechanization has reduced labour input by miners from the traditional sources: Lesotho, Botswana, Swaziland, Malawi, and Mozambique (31). It is estimated that economic growth of 7 per cent (in contrast to the current less than 4 per cent) would be required merely to create jobs for new school graduates, leaving untouched the backlog of unemployed.

Reactions against immigrants are also based partly on the clustering of foreign workers in particular skilled occupations, such as professors, scientists, and managers, and in particular sectors, such as informal trading, where they come in contact with South African workers. Migrants have been accused of criminal activities, causing unemployment, depressing wages, and marrying local girls solely to obtain residence certificates. The reality is that immigrants carry an increasing proportion of the work load in agriculture, construction, and services. The data do not prove, however, that this concentration has had an overall negative impact on wages for the local workforce (13).

Unauthorized migrants remain unprotected under the law. Expulsion is immediate. Employers take advantage of this situation by offering lower wages and poor working conditions to migrants. Women and children especially are exploited in agriculture, where they receive the lowest wages and are frequently exposed to hazardous substances (13). Employers reportedly rarely face sanctions. On the positive side, since 1994, government oversight has led to significant improvements in the physical working conditions in the mines.

Comparatively less policy emphasis is placed on outflows from South Africa since the change in government. Frightened by the alarming rate of criminal violence and frustrated by the loss of privileges, several thousand white professionals have emigrated since the transition to majority rule (Table 25). The first outbound wave included the emigration of managers, technicians, doctors, and other professionals and their families to Canada, Europe (especially the United Kingdom), the United States, and Australia. The second wave of emigrants from South Africa consisted of white farmers. Some 39,000 South Africans emigrated between 1994 and 1997. About 11 per cent of the top managers and 6 per cent of the middle managers resigned in 1997 in order to emigrate (31). The outflow of key professionals prompted the Government to insist that departing physicians refund the cost of their medical training as a measure to stem the outflow of scarce medical personnel. The exodus left vacancies that are a prime attraction for professionals and technical personnel from other African and more distant countries.

TABLE 25.
INTERNATIONAL MIGRATION OF PROFESSIONALS
IN SOUTH AFRICA, 1994-1997

Year	Immigrants	Emigrants
1994	1,075	1,900
1995	775	1,680
1996	777	1,950
1997	450	1,600

BOTSWANA

In recent years, Botswana emerged as a major country of immigration in southern Africa. A small country of about 1.5 million inhabitants, its economy recorded rapid and steady growth in the past decade. Hence, it attracted numerous migrants, especially highly skilled professionals. The world's largest diamond producer, Botswana is a democratic, stable, prosperous country. It had the world's fastest growing economy between 1975 and 1990, and its 1997 per capita GDP was among the highest in sub-Saharan Africa. Yet the country lacks skilled manpower and relies on skilled immigrants in many areas, including about 500 professors on the staff of its only university. The country does not have a migration policy per se, but it relaxed its laws concerning entry visas and residence in the early 1990s. Along with many other countries, Botswana instituted localization policies after independence in an effort to conserve available employment for nationals.[1] The country has now embarked on a massive training of its nationals to replace foreign labour with nationals (10).

CÔTE D'IVOIRE

Côte d'Ivoire has always been a major country of immigration as a result of its vast and varied natural resources, diversified and modernized export, agriculture, and plantation economy, efficient infrastructure, and modern industries. In 1995, there were 4 million immigrants out of a population of 14 million in the Côte d'Ivoire. The country's domestic labour force is small and about one-quarter of its waged labour force are foreigners.

This immigration was deliberately planned. The country's first president—ignoring the arbitrary borders drawn by colonial powers—encouraged immigration from the country's poor neighbours. Immigrants from Burkina Faso, Nigeria, Liberia, Senegal, and Ghana flooded the plantations and took up menial jobs that the local population scorned. Immigrant workers were accompanied by their families and were allowed to marry cross-culturally, settle, and vote. By 1993, the majority of immigrants were from Burkina Faso (49 per cent) and Mali (20 per cent) (Table 26). Some 75 per cent of immigrants are illiterate. Despite their lower standard of education, 73 per cent are employed.

The Government's liberal immigration policy of more than three decades has now been ended, as much by economic expediency as by politics. Unemployment, crime, and the AIDS epidemic were blamed on the influx of immigrants. The economic downturn and increasing unemployment among young nationals were used as excuses for the recent shift in Government policy to apprehend and deport unauthorized migrants. Additionally, political changes dictated that immigrants be disenfranchised, especially Muslims who had for decades been allowed to settle with their families and to vote. The Government policy to register and issue special identity cards to foreigners was widely viewed as a first step in a series of actions aimed at apprehending and deporting illegal immigrants. In 1998, in a further measure against immigrants, Parliament approved a three-fold increase in annual residence fees for foreigners, while reducing the fee for nationals by 90 per cent.

TABLE 26.
IMMIGRANTS IN CÔTE D'IVOIRE BY COUNTRY OF ORIGIN, 1993

Country of origin	Number
Burkina Faso	822,787
Guinea	131,030
Mali	336,737
Niger	49,060
Senegal	23,150
Benin	43,491
Ghana	111,803
Liberia	94,213
Togo	27,709
Others	46,065
Total	**1,686,045**

GABON

Gabon, a small country of 1.2 million people, is rich in natural resources—oil, forests, and manganese—but has a shortage of manpower. The country relies on contract labour and immigrants to supplement the domestic labour force. The population growth rate is low, 63 per cent of the adult population is literate, 73 per cent of the total population lives in urban areas and more than 40 per cent in the capital city. Gabon is the third producer of manganese and the sixth producer of wood in the world. The agriculture sector has been neglected, resulting in rural exodus of young people to the cities. Per capita income of US$ 4,450 is among the highest in sub-Saharan Africa.

There are more than 160,000 immigrants in Gabon. Most immigrants come from Mali, Equatorial Guinea, Nigeria, Senegal, Benin, Cameroon, and Togo. About a quarter of the wage earners are expatriates from other countries in Africa and Europe. In recent years, many immigrants and refugees entered Gabon from Burundi, Rwanda, the former Zaire, and the Congo to seek asylum and to look for work. The war and political instability in these countries forced thousands of their nationals to migrate to Gabon where they hoped to secure a better life and greater security.

Unemployment increasingly poses a challenge in Gabon: in 1996, about 20 per cent of the active labour force was unemployed. Of the estimated 20,000 persons entering the labour force annually, not more than 4,000 are able to secure jobs in the formal market (23). The petrol sector is the main engine of the economy, thus rendering it very vulnerable to external shocks.

The Government adopted a policy of localizing employment opportunities in response to the increasing unemployment. In 1991, a presidential decree was issued to safeguard jobs for nationals. Since then, the policy of "Gabonizing" the labour force has been pursued with vigour (34). In September 1994, the Government enacted laws that required foreigners to pay residence fees or leave the country by the middle of February 1995. At the end of the deadline, about 55,000 foreign nationals were expelled from the country while 15,000 legalized their residency.

EMIGRATION TRENDS

Migration in Africa falls into two major categories: forced movements of refugees and internally displaced persons; and labour migration.

REFUGEES AND INTERNALLY DISPLACED POPULATIONS

Refugees and internally displaced persons constitute the vast majority of African peoples on the move. Once centred in the Horn of Africa, refugees became even more highly visible in the Great Lakes region and in West Africa. The series of wars and conflicts in these regions also generated millions of internally displaced persons within national borders. All over sub-Saharan Africa, the explosion of ethnic violence uprooted millions of people. Estimates by UNHCR placed the number of refugees and those in refugee-like situations in Africa in 1999 at 6.5 million (35). From 1969 to 1990, 17 of the world's recorded 43 civil wars that created major refugee populations were in Africa, including four struggles for autonomy or independence. These included "high intensity" civil wars in Angola, Liberia, and Mozambique. In Sudan, Somalia, Rwanda, and Burundi, ethnic tensions played visibly important roles in such conflicts. Ethnic rebellion was recorded in 17 countries of the region. Sustained refugee flows are rooted in such ethnic conflicts (28).

The focus of refugee flows in 1997-1999 was in western Africa. Prolonged internal conflicts in Liberia sent nearly 500,000 refugees to the Côte d'Ivoire and Guinea, the majority of whom have since repatriated. More than 400,000 refugees from Sierra Leone were still being assisted in 1999 in Guinea and Liberia. Conflicts in Guinea-Bissau produced hundreds of thousands of internally displaced persons and several thousand refugees fled the country. In the Great Lakes region, Burundi and Rwanda are the major source of refugees. Conflicts in the Democratic Republic of the Congo in 1997 and the Congo (Brazzaville) in 1998 also generated thousands of refugees. UNHCR reported that the flow of Congolese to the United Republic of Tanzania was the most regular flow of refugees anywhere on the continent in mid-1999. Events before, during, and after the 1994 genocide in Rwanda triggered the outflow of nearly 2 million refugees, to add to the 1 million Rwandan Tutsis already relocated outside the country. The sudden return of nearly 700,000 Rwandan refugees from eastern Zaire (Democratic Republic of the Congo)

in late 1996 and the follow-up forced repatriation of 500,000 or more others from the United Republic of Tanzania were equally dramatic (36).

Overall, recurrent internal instability in the 1990s resulted in numerous population displacements. As the region is torn by civil strife and abuse of human rights by totalitarian regimes, the number of internally displaced persons escalates and millions of refugees seek asylum in neighbouring countries. The dire situation of refugees in sub-Saharan Africa—the large numbers, the traumatic conditions they face, and the colossal proportions of humanitarian assistance they require— captured the attention of the international community.

LABOUR MIGRATION

Other forms of migration (temporary labour migration, brain drain, and unauthorized migration) thrive and, unlike refugee flows that are virtually confined to the region, increasingly are becoming extracontinental.

Deteriorating conditions in sub-Saharan Africa changed intraregional labour migration: economies are saddled with debt and unemployment; population growth rates are soaring; most governments are too weak or tyrannical to govern effectively; a few fledgling democracies fight for stability; and natural causes or development gone awry lead to ecological damage. Together, these factors make the status quo intolerable for many people who must migrate for their own and their family's survival.

In many parts of sub-Saharan Africa, the existence of a stressful economic environment combines with declining real incomes to create a perception that the local economic future is dismal. This perception, in turn, contributes to the sustained exodus of skilled and unskilled persons—both men and women. While data on the proportions of skilled and unskilled workers in these flows are unavailable, the outflow of professionals and skilled workers to various African countries, Europe, the USA, and Canada is on a scale not experienced before.

The migration of highly qualified and experienced workers from Zimbabwe, Zambia, Senegal, Ghana, Uganda, and Nigeria to South Africa, Europe, North America, and the Middle East intensified in the 1980s and 1990s. A World Bank study noted, for example, that owing to the state of the depressed economies in Africa some 23,000 qualified academic staff emigrated each year in search of better working conditions. It is estimated that about 10,000 Nigerian academics are employed in the United States alone (38). Paradoxically, about 100,000 non-African experts now work in sub-Saharan Africa, a number far greater than at independence and about the same as the number of Africans working in western Europe and North America. According to IOM data, these foreign experts, whose work is tied to development assistance in the region, now occupy positions not available to qualified Africans and account for 35 per cent of the region's annual official development aid.

The traditional male-dominated, long-term, and long-distance migration in sub-Saharan Africa is becoming increasingly feminized in the 1990s. Anecdotal evidence shows a striking increase in migration by women who traditionally had remained at home while men moved around in search of paid work. Significant proportions of women are migrating independently to fulfil their own economic needs rather than simply joining a husband or other family members. The migration is not confined by national borders: professional women from Ghana, Kenya, Nigeria, and Zambia now engage in international migration, often leaving spouses behind to care for the children. In Nigeria, for example, most female migrants are professionals. Women nurses and doctors were recruited from Nigeria to work in Saudi Arabia; some women take advantage of handsome pay packages in the United States and Canada to accumulate savings to carry them through harsh economic conditions at home; others migrate with their children to pursue studies abroad, as the educational system in Nigeria has virtually collapsed (5).

In Côte d'Ivoire, migration of women from Burkina Faso, Ghana, and Nigeria intensified in spite of the looming economic crisis in this traditional host country. This is explained by the tradition of women to cluster in the informal commercial sector, less affected by economic crisis, unlike men who primarily work in the waged sector as agricultural labourers, white-collar service workers, etc. As jobs became tighter during the 1990s and as remittances dropped, many families increasingly relied on women's participation in the economy and on their farming activities (20). Where men lost jobs through retrenchments, women were forced to seek additional income-generating activities in an attempt to maintain a constant family income.

Migration throughout sub-Saharan Africa now is being adopted by households as a survival strategy to supplement dwindling resources. Such households select and invest in a migrant who has the greatest potential for supporting the entire household through remittances. Propelled by the economic crisis, migration today has become an increasingly important coping mechanism for the survival of the family (5).

Dual-residence strategies are now commonplace to ensure that families maintain their extended structure in the face of losses due to migration. Remittances are an integral part of migration linkages and networks. African migrants maintain strong economic and other links with their home communities. During their migration career, internal as well as international migrants visit home periodically, provide support for newly arrived migrants from home, and send money and consumer items to families at home. At the macro level, remittances are an important source of foreign exchange, as in other regions.

Several major countries of origin of migration from various parts of sub-Saharan Africa are profiled below. The list is by no means exhaustive but provides an overview of emigration trends in selected countries.

LESOTHO. Lesotho is a small country of 1.8 million people with no viable natural resources, completely surrounded by South Africa. In 1996, 45 per cent of men in the workforce were employed in South Africa's mines, down from 51 per cent in 1984. About 7 per cent of Lesotho nationals—77 per cent of whom were male— lived outside the country in 1996. Nearly all emigrants (96.8 per cent) were in South Africa (33).

Only 10 per cent of the land in Lesotho is suitable for agriculture. Landlessness has therefore been the primary emigration pressure. With a per capita GNP of US$ 590 in 1994, Lesotho is one of the poorest countries in southern Africa. About 85 per cent of the resident labour force are subsistence farmers. The dependence on emigration for employment and remittances from mine workers is a major development challenge for Lesotho: in 1996, remittances contributed 24.4 per cent to GNP. South Africa's policy of recruiting mine labour from within its borders has limited access of new migrants to employment in the mines. During the apartheid era, some foreign investors and diplomatic missions relocated to Lesotho from South Africa and generated local employment, but the trend has since reversed. Even at an optimistic growth rate of 6 per cent per year, the wage sector could at best provide jobs for no more than 20 per cent of the job seekers, excluding the anticipated returnees from South Africa.

The Government of Lesotho has articulated no policy to integrate return migrants. Employers do provide a lump sum to capitalize return migrants for self-employment. Climate constraints and stiff competition from cheaper exports from South Africa limit the prospects of revitalizing the economy through the development of arable agriculture, such as the Lesotho Highlands project. This internationally funded project is the third major employer of labour; however, its importance could decline after the completion of construction-related activities.

During the past few years, the following issues have engaged the attention of policy-makers: the health of the returning migrants and their spouses; the need for miners to transfer skills acquired to Lesotho's mining industry located in the southern part of the country; and the need to pay more attention to the education of young boys. The latter is in response to the decline in unskilled employment in South Africa for men (traditionally girls remain in school while boys are prepared for mine work).

MALI AND SENEGAL. With a population of about 11.5 million persons, Mali is one of sub-Saharan Africa's poorest countries and a major emigration country. It is estimated that the country accounted for at least one-fourth of all inter-African emigrants in 1993; between 1976 and 1987, an estimated 1.4 million Malians emigrated. The Kayes region produces the majority of international migrants from Mali.

In the early 1990s, an estimated 3.7 million Malians were resident in major destinations around the world, with the largest single concentration (27 per cent) in Côte d'Ivoire (Table 27) (9). Short-term migration is undertaken for trading in neighbouring countries in the Sahel or other parts of western Africa; longer-term migrants seek to establish residence and find employment in Cameroon, the Democratic Republic of the Congo, Gabon, and the Central African Republic.

There is some evidence to support a pattern of replacement migration, whereby migrants of rural origin move to towns to occupy positions vacated by others who have emigrated abroad. This is the case of emigrants from Mali and Burkina Faso to France, the Côte d'Ivoire, and Gabon and from Senegal to France. In some

TABLE 27.

COUNTRIES OF DESTINATION OF MALIAN EMIGRANTS, 1991

Countries	Emigrants
Côte d'Ivoire	1,000,000
Sahel	2,000,000
Central Africa	500,000
Gulf States	154,650
Europe	103,605

instances, immigrants from neighbouring countries occupied positions vacated by nationals of the host countries who themselves had emigrated abroad. Often the result is a step-by-step migration pattern from rural areas to the cities, and then to another country.

One of the primary emigration pressures in Mali relates to land. Most of the population consists of subsistence farmers, yet only 10 per cent of the land is suitable for agriculture. Researchers explain that the principal problem is lack of access to arable, productive land capable of producing enough to sustain a family, not just in good years, but through frequent, successive years of drought or other disaster. Poverty, joblessness, and illiteracy are pervasive. Because of the lack of economic alternatives, the region is dependent on seasonal migrant labourers who travel to Senegal, Côte d'Ivoire, and other major labour shortage areas of western Africa (21).

For generations, Sahelians—especially Malians—migrated to France to engage in menial work. Emigration to France was, and remains, a family enterprise, with each successive generation of migrants prepared and supported by its predecessors. Despite breaking with the culture, religion, economy, and living conditions of their homeland, most migrants still feel obliged to remit money home regularly. Given the increasing restrictiveness of the traditional host countries, however, Malian migrants have been returned in large numbers from Saudi Arabia, France, and the Libyan Arab Jamahiriya, among other countries. Emigration to France from Senegal and Mali is an option today only for those experienced migrants with ample contacts and potential support.

Labour migration to Saudi Arabia and the Libyan Arab Jamahiriya also declined in recent years, following reports of mistreatment of Malians and difficulties in remitting money home. Malians and other Sahelians are under intensive pressure to explore alternative destinations within Africa. The economic and cultural barriers are less pronounced for intra-African migrants who, even when earnings are lower, tend to take their families with them. The post-apartheid waves of migrants from Senegal, Mali, Nigeria, and Sierra Leone to South Africa consist mostly of street vendors and traders ready to tap the relatively affluent market (9). Their governments created new ministries to assist emigrants and potential emigrants with information about living conditions abroad as well as employment and residence requirements. Emigrants are encouraged to send money home regularly and consular offices in the major receiving countries were expanded to deal with the problems faced by their nationals there.

A large proportion of Sahelian—especially Senegalese—migrants are traders. Such migrants, breaking with tradition, are exploring non-conventional destinations with no linguistic, cultural, and colonial ties. For example, Senegalese traders initially migrated to Zambia; when the economy of that country collapsed, migration shifted to post-apartheid South Africa. Senegalese also move to Europe—Italy, Portugal, Germany, Belgium, and Spain. Finding the situation of immigrants in Europe increasingly intolerable because of the increasingly vocal and popular xenophobic environment, some immigrants—mainly petty traders—crossed the Atlantic to the United States in search of greater opportunities (Table 28).

TABLE 28.
SENEGALESE EMIGRANTS IN SELECTED COUNTRIES OF DESTINATION, FEBRUARY 1997

Country	Estimated population	Legally registered
Côte d'Ivoire	150,000	45,000
USA	15,000	3,200
Italy	60,000	
Mali	30,000	8,424
Gabon	33,725	
France	60,000	45,000
Gulf States	10,976	7,560
Germany	5,000	1,400
Egypt	30,000	2,000
Guinea	15,000	6,676

One notable example of migration for trade is that of the Mourides from Senegal to New York. These migrants travelled initially to France and in the 1980s to the United States where they established themselves in petty commerce. The first Francophone Africans to arrive *en masse* in New York in the early 1980s, they started as street vendors. Despite sustained harassment by the city administration, the group later established itself in a particular neighbourhood of the city. With the momentum of the social network, the tide of follow-up migration burgeoned.

The importance of remittances for the families at home is substantial. ILO household budget surveys reveal that in Senegal dependence on emigration and remittances is highly significant—from 30 to as much as 80 per cent of family income is covered by moneys remitted by emigrants. Similar findings were reported for Mali, Lesotho, and to a lesser extent, Burkina Faso. For example, in the Kayes region of Mali, the contribution of migrants to the regional economy during the last decades has helped in filling the gaps of assistance to a region subject to successive droughts in the 1970s and 1980s that accelerated the aridity of the land. The resulting migration pressures make this region the principal emigration basin towards the rest of Africa, Europe (principally France), Asia, and America. The remittances not only sustain families, but are shared for the community and village building of schools, health centres, cooperatives, and water supply systems.

KENYA, UGANDA, AND THE UNITED REPUBLIC OF TANZANIA. Few data are available on the magnitude and characteristics of migration from Kenya, Tanzania, and Uganda. Migration flows amongst these three East Africa countries are the predominant movements, consisting of temporary agricultural contract workers, temporary professional and skilled workers, and unauthorized migrants. Kenya and Tanzania are basically immigration countries, although like Uganda—which now exhibits more emigration than immigration—they are all countries of origin of significant migrant populations. Skilled labour and professionals emigrate from East Africa primarily to southern Africa, Europe, and the United States (27).

Kenya, Uganda, and Tanzania share a history of open borders that dates to the colonial period and that facilitated migration among the three countries. Linguistic similarities (English and Swahili) and close ethnic ties also facilitate their interaction. Ethnic groups often span borders created for the ease of colonial administration. Early economic integration initiatives after independence in the early 1960s maintained the open-door policies that were later enshrined in the East Africa Community (EAC) in 1967. The volume and type of migration vary with both political and climatic conditions. Current policies favour freedom of movement.

Migration policies in East Africa varied with political change. Borders opened and closed depending upon political conditions and international relations amongst the three nations from about 1977 to 1996. Current policy favours regional economic integration, export-led growth, and economic restructuring, including implementation of Free Movement of Peoples, the Right of Residence and Establishment—the term for the near Africa-wide proposal for free labour mobility.

Southern Africa offers strong attractions for temporary professionals from Uganda, Kenya, Tanzania and other countries in East Africa. Large numbers of secondary school teachers and university lecturers, as well as Kenyan doctors and nurses, migrated to Botswana as a result of economic restructuring policies that made finding employment in their own country's key education and health professions difficult (3).

NIGERIA. In transition to a democratic State, Nigeria plays a complex and important role as both a source country of immigration and a leader in resolving refugee crises in western Africa. The roots of Nigeria's emigration go back to the colonial period when Nigerian migrants moved within and outside western Africa. As early as 1931, the Nigerians in Ghana numbered more than 67,000. During the same period, Nigerians also headed to Europe to engage in educational activities, with many remaining after their studies (19).

After the 1980s, emigration to Europe and North America accelerated; Nigerians also sought economic opportunities in South Africa and the Middle East. Emigration occurred for a complex array of reasons, including "economic mismanagement, its population explosion, the unfulfilled expectations instilled by previous governments, the high rate of unemployment, and the extreme extent of environmental degradation" (24). At the same time, internal migration from rural to urban areas was "fuelled by drought, famine, the devastation of rural areas, and the strong belief that towns and cities offer better opportunities" (19).

REGIONAL MIGRATION TRENDS

In sub-Saharan Africa, several new trends in migration are apparent: both international migration destinations and the characteristics of international migrants diversified; longer-term circular and replacement migration was more common; women joined the ranks of international migrants in increasing proportions; trafficking in migrants increased owing to restrictive immigration policies in host countries; and international migration arrived on the policy agendas of national governments and—increasingly—regional cooperative organizations. These changes affected migrants in all socio-economic categories. Rural-to-urban migration was commonplace for several decades and often occurred across arbitrarily placed colonial borders. Those individuals with money or connections migrated to distant areas that shared linguistic and colonial ties. Now, highly skilled professionals who once migrated to traditional destinations in Europe, the United States, and the Gulf States of the Middle East are finding South Africa and Botswana viable migration alternatives. Low-skilled unauthorized migrants find their way to the north through intermediate countries en route to new destinations in southern Europe, the Middle East, and Asia.

The factors associated with the continuity and changes in migration movements within and from the region are complex and interrelated. One important factor was the implementation of structural adjustment plans (SAPs) by several countries of the region as they attempted for more than a decade to set their economies right. Conforming to IMF and World Bank conditions, many countries reduced the size of the public sector—the dominant employment sector—through retirement, retrenchment, and redundancies; the private sector followed suit. As a result, heads of household found themselves out of work, adding to the existing unemployment pool—mostly young males (6).

As long as political and economic conditions remain precarious and perceptions of future economic conditions are considered equally dismal, the propensity to emigrate in sub-Saharan Africa will be sustained. Internal, intraregional, and international migration responds essentially to the same underlying factors—the pull of opportunity and network contacts and the push of distinctly poor prospects at home. Poverty is as compelling a motive for migration for many Africans as is the pull of enhanced living conditions in developed countries.

Since the beginning of the 1990s, fewer migrants have been able to find stable and remunerative work in traditional destinations within the region. Many migrants no longer adhere to the classical labour migration patterns and explore a much wider set of destinations than those in which seasonal work was found. There has been increasing diversification of destinations among Sahelian international migrants, who have migrated to various African countries, Europe, and North America (20).

Temporary, long-term circular migration to a variety of alternative destinations has intensified (2). With economic success not necessarily guaranteed even with circulation between two places, more migrants find they have to move among several places in order to eke out a living. A pattern of step migration—in which new migrants to urban areas often take jobs left by those individuals who migrate out of the country—is evident among both unskilled migrants from Mali and Senegal and foreign professionals in South Africa.

As already noted, the traditional pattern of male migration, in which wives and children remain at home, has changed in recent years; a significant proportion of single and married women now emigrate alone in search of secure jobs in neighbouring and developed countries of the north. Such migration of women is likely to intensify as a result of the deteriorating conditions in the region. Conditions for women, however, are still difficult, as they still remain marginalized and vulnerable at origin and destination.

Young migrants are adopting more sophisticated, daring, and evasive methods to penetrate the tight border controls in the north. Movements are more clandestine, involving more risky passages and trafficking via more diverse transit points, for example, through Morocco to Spain. Some enter the host countries as tourists or students and later work and live there without officially changing their status. Others travel through an intermediate country such as Gambia, Cape Verde, or Guinea to obtain false documentation for a fee and then invariably travel via a third country en route to Spain, Portugal, Italy, or the Libyan Arab Jamahiriya. While some continue with the traditional two-step move from a village to a coastal city and then to Europe, many others pursue varied itineraries to reach an ultimate destination in Europe (21).

Trafficking in illegal migrants, a hitherto rare practice, is on the increase and a larger number of young persons are now involved in daredevil ventures to gain entry into Europe. Individual stowaways engage in life-threatening travels, hiding on ships to southern Europe and recently to East Asia. Unscrupulous agents also exploit desperate youths with promises of passages to Italy, Spain, and France. Many of these youths are stranded in Dakar; other migrants who make it to Europe are apprehended and deported on arrival or soon afterwards (4). In May 1966, some 200 Kenyans were stranded in Saudi Arabia after being tricked by traffickers who promised them lucrative jobs. After the 1973 advent of large-scale tourism in Gambia, trafficking was in young boys. Older women—mainly from Europe—came to Gambia to marry young Gambian boys; many of these young men have since found their way home.

Migrant trafficking is just beginning to attract attention in sub-Saharan Africa. Currently, there is little evidence that trafficking is an organized activity. Local media treat evidence of trafficking as the clandestine work of individual operators. Governments have not established the adoption of measures to combat migrant trafficking as a priority, as they did, for example, in their anti-drug trafficking efforts.

Increasingly in the 1990s, international migration policy is a topic for discussion and action in the plethora of emerging subregional organizations for economic cooperation. At the end of the 1980s, African leaders recognized that accelerated development could not be achieved without pooling together natural and human resources for their mutual benefit. Nations fragmented by artificial borders viewed economic cooperation as a viable means to enlarge market size and facilitate movement of goods, services, labour, and capital (8). Towards this end, several subregional economic organizations were created or revitalized during the 1990s.

Among these organizations is the Common Market for Eastern and Southern African (COMESA), founded in 1993 to continue economic cooperation and integration efforts begun in 1981 by the Preferential Trade Area for Eastern and Southern Africa. The 1992 Windhoek Treaty established the Southern African Development Community (SADC) on the outline of an earlier union, and for the first time welcomed the post-apartheid Government of South Africa into its fold. In August 1995, the leaders of eastern and southern Africa revitalized SADC to create, among other aspects, a free trade community, with free movement of people and a single currency by the year 2000 (29). Among a number of other cooperative economic organizations already in existence in central and western Africa are the Economic Community of West African States (ECOWAS), established in 1975. The momentum of the new work of these associations led to the 1993 Abuja Treaty that formalized the agreement to create an African Economic Community by the year 2025. It is considered a landmark treaty on the road to all-African regional integration.

Free mobility of labour, residence, and establishment—the subject of diplomatic protocols among African countries for more than two decades—was formally addressed in protocols of each of these cooperative organizations. This is not to say that there is total agreement on how to address international migration, which is just one of a number of issues under discussion by these multilateral communities. ECOWAS has to a large extent implemented the Protocol for the Free Movement of Persons, although member States remain lukewarm about the rights of residence and establishment. Within COMESA, member States have been implementing a strategy of gradual visa relaxation since 1985, but have not yet eliminated all visas. Both COMESA and SADC prepared and discussed phased-in approaches to implementing free labour mobility, but member States have achieved agreement only on the first phase, which includes limited-duration, visa-free entry. The remaining phases of the strategies considered by many countries as too controversial for implementation at this time include respect for the right of residence, right of establishment, and creation of a European-like arrangement of open internal borders among the members of the respective economic areas. When SADC member States agreed in 1993 to abolish visa requirements for travel within SADC countries, for example, Zimbabwe and South Africa declined to implement the plan at that time out of fear that they would be overwhelmed by unauthorized immigration (8). South Africa, in particular, is aware that if people were allowed by the protocol to move freely, the dominant immigration tide would flow to South Africa.

A variety of contradictions characterize the subregional organizations. Over the course of various economic crises, many countries enacted a series of localization laws that restrict foreigners, including nationals of community States, from employment in certain economic activities. Countries often belong to more than one cooperative community and are caught between their conflicting policies. In many cases, these multi-country organizations are dominated by the economy of a single country: South Africa in SADC, Gabon in the Central African Customs and Economic Union (UDEAC), Côte d'Ivoire in the West African Economic Community (CEAO), Nigeria in ECOWAS and the Democratic Republic of the Congo in the Economic Community of the Great Lakes (CEPGL). These imbalances often spark xenophobic reactions among nationals of the dominant countries, as well as mistrust and suspicion of dominance by nationals of the smaller countries. Expulsions and deportations are common policy measures directed at unauthorized migrants throughout sub-Saharan Africa. Remarkably, these deportations occurred both before and after the formation of subregional organizations. It is usually impossible to distinguish between foreign migrants in a particular country. Many countries are ambivalent about the principle of free movement, and national laws frequently are not in harmony with regional and subregional treaties that address the issues of rights of migrants as well as the rights and obligations of the host countries.

CONCLUSION

International migration will become more important in sub-Saharan Africa for a number of reasons. The prospects of, and options for, internal migration in the region increasingly are limited as a result of generalized poverty, unemployment, and economic insecurity. Consequently, some of the migration that would otherwise have been directed internally is likely to become replacement migration in urban areas and sequentially emerge as international migration (6).

At the same time, options for legal migration are shrinking. Several countries that hosted immigrants from sub-Saharan Africa—especially the Gulf States—are facing their own need for economic restructuring. As a result, the era of importation of large numbers of African labourers to that region is likely to be over. In Europe, traditional host countries tightened both entry requirements and external border controls; immigration laws were overhauled and apparent loopholes blocked. South Africa's capacity to absorb more immigrants, likewise, is limited by its own domestic problems—unemployment top among them. In spite of these situations, unauthorized migration persists. The limited capacity of sub-Saharan Africa's labour market to absorb productively the annual cohorts of job seekers turns them into potential emigrants and the pressure to emigrate is at a peak.

Migrants are adopting more sophisticated, daring, and evasive methods to enter the countries of the north by travelling through intermediate countries and by approaching non-traditional destinations. Much of this unauthorized migration is detected and the migrants deported. Senegal and Mali established institutional mechanisms for the dissemination of information to their potential emigrants about the risks of unauthorized migration. However, migrants in other countries lack accurate information regarding regulations guiding entry, residence, and employment abroad.

Recent developments in some parts of sub-Saharan Africa give cause for guarded optimism. Namibia, South Africa, and perhaps Mozambique recorded some success in the return and reintegration of their nationals resident abroad during the years of civil struggle. Because of political and economic changes in Ghana and Uganda, some level of return migration and new immigration has been observed. If the new signals for the revival of the economic and political situation in Nigeria also hold, a wave of return migration of professionals and others who fled the dictatorial regime of the past years will grow. Other countries may follow such patterns.

In Côte d'Ivoire, Mali, Ghana, and Uganda, the removal of the marketing boards that paid farmers less than the market value for their products now results in enhanced rural incomes. The restructuring had the effect of curtailing the rural exodus and stimulating some return migration to rural areas. This budding urban-to-rural migration is expected to increase in some areas. As well, some migrants from Burkina Faso to Côte d'Ivoire are returning home or migrating to other rural areas as urban living conditions deteriorate and become intolerably expensive. This trend is likely to be seen in more countries.

Subregional and regional economic associations may facilitate intraregional labour mobility and promote self-reliant development in the region. The various protocols for the free movement of persons—operational for ECOWAS and expected to be approved for COMESA and SADC, and ultimately the African Economic Community—are likely to accelerate economic cooperation and labour migration in the region.

ENDNOTE

1. Localization and indigenization policies are post-independence policies of Africa governments designed to conserve available employment opportunities for their nationals. These policies reserve particular economic activities for nationals and others with whom they are in partnership. The policies are the fulfilment of pre-independence electoral promises to place economic management—hitherto dominated by colonial officials—in the hands of nationals and also to provide key jobs for qualified nationals. Virtually all African countries implemented these policies to varying degrees.

REFERENCES

1. Adepoju, A. (1991). South-north migration: the African experience. *International Migration,* 29(2):205-221.

2. Adepoju, A. (1995a). The politics of international migration in post-colonial Africa. In R. Cohen (Ed.), *The Cambridge Survey of World Migration.* Cambridge University Press, Cambridge.

3. Adepoju, A. (1995b). Emigration dynamics in sub-Saharan Africa. *International Migration,* 33(3/4):315-390.

4. Adepoju, A, (1996). *Population, Poverty, Structural Adjustment Programmes and Quality of Life in Sub-Saharan Africa,* Research Paper No. 1. Population, Human Resources and Development in Africa, Dakar.

5. Adepoju, A. (1997). Introduction. In A. Adepoju (Ed.), *Family Population and Development in Africa.* Zed Books, London.

6. Adepoju, A. and T. Hammar (1996). Introduction. In A. Adepoju and T. Hammar (Eds.), *International Migration to and from Africa: Dimensions, Challenges and Prospects,* Population, Human Resources and Development in Africa, Dakar, and Centre for Research in International Migration and Ethnic Relations, Stockholm.

7. Akokpari, J.K. (1998). The state, refugees and migration in sub-Saharan Africa. *International Migration,* 36(2):211-234.

8. Afolayan, A.A. (1998). *Regional integration, labour mobility, clandestine labour migration and expulsion of illegal immigrants.* Paper presented at the Regional Meeting on International Migration in Africa at the Threshold of the XXI Century. Gaborone, 2-5 June.

9. Bouillon, A. (1996). La nouvelle migration Africaine en Afrique du Sud. Immigrants d'Afrique occidentale et centrale à Johannesburg. Paper presented at Colloque Systèmes et Dynamiques des Migrations Internationales Ouest-Africaines, Institute Fondamental d'Afrique/ORSTOM, Dakar, 3-6 December.

10. Campbell, E. (1998). *Botswana: country migration profile*. Paper presented at the Regional Meeting on International Migration in Africa at the Threshold of the XXI Century. Gaborone, 2-5 June.

11. Crush, J. (1998). *Addressing the employment of migrants in an irregular situation: the case of South Africa*. Paper presented at the United Nations Technical Symposium on International Migration and Development, The Hague, Netherlands.

12. Crush, J. (Ed.) (1998b). *Beyond Control: Immigration and Human Rights in a Democratic South Africa.* Southern African Migration Project, Institute for Democracy in South Africa, Queen's University, Capetown.

13. Crush, J., (Ed.) (1997). *Covert Operations: Clandestine Migration, Temporary Work, and Immigration Policy in South Africa*, Migration Policy Series, No.1. Southern African Migration Project, Institute for Democracy in South Africa, Queen's University, Capetown.

14. deVletter, F. (1998). *Sons of Mozambique: Mozambican Miners and Post-Apartheid South Africa*, Migration Policy Series, No. 8. Southern African Migration Project, Institute for Democracy in South Africa, Queen's University, Capetown.

15. Diatta, M.A. and N. Mbow (1998). *Releasing the development potentials of return migration: the case of Senegal*. Paper presented at the United Nations Technical Symposium on International Migration and Development, The Hague, Netherlands.

16. Dodson, B. (1998). *Women on the Move: Gender and Cross-Border Migration to South Africa*, Migration Policy Series, No. 9. Southern African Migration Project, Institute for Democracy in South Africa, Queen's University, Capetown.

17. Ebin, V. (1996). *Négociations et appropriations: les revendications des migrants Sénégalais a New York*. Paper presented at Colloque Systèmes et Dynamiques des Migrations Internationales Ouest-Africaines, Institut Fondamental d'Afrique/ORSTOM, Dakar.

18. Fadayomi, T.O. (1996). Brain drain and brain gain in Africa: causes, dimensions and consequences. In A. Adepoju and T. Hammar (Eds.), *International Migration in and from Africa: Dimensions, Challenges and Prospects.* Population, Human Resources and Development in Africa, Dakar and Centre for Research in International Migration and Ethnic Relations, Stockholm.

19. Falola, T. (1997). Nigeria in the global context of refugees: historical and comparative perspectives. *Journal of Asian and African Studies,* 32(1-2).

20. Findley, S. (1997). Migration and family interactions in Africa. In A. Adepoju (Ed.), *Family, Population and Development in Africa.* Zed Books, London, England.

21. Findley, F., S. Traore, D. Ouedraogo and S. Diarra (1995). Emigration from the Sahel. *International Migration,* 33(3/4):469-520.

22. Kalunde, K.W. (1998). *International migration in Zambia: an overview*. Paper presented at the Regional Meeting on International Migration in Africa at the Threshold of the XXI Century, Gaborone, 2-5 June.

23. Le Courier (ACP) Reportage (1997). *Gabon No. 165*, September-October.

24. Lovejoy, P. and P. Williams (1997). Introduction. *Journal of Asian and African Studies*, 32(1/2).

25. Mfono, Z. N. (1998). *International migration in South Africa in the 1990s: migration country profile*. Paper presented at the Regional Meeting on International Migration in Africa at the Threshold of the XXI Century, Gaborone, 2-5 June.

26. Milazi, D. (1995). Emigration dynamics in southern Africa. *International Migration,* 33(3/4):521-556.

27. Oucho, J.O. (1998). Regional integration and labour mobility in eastern and southern Africa. In R. Appleyard (Ed.), *Emigration Dynamics in Developing Countries, Vol. I: Sub-Saharan Africa.* Ashgate for IOM/UNFPA, Aldershot, England.

28. Schmeidl, S. (1996). Hard times in countries of origin. In *Migration and Crime*. International Scientific and Professional Advisory Council, Milan.

29. Sechaba Consultants (1997). Riding the tiger: Lesotho miners and permanent residence in South Africa, Migration Policy Series, No. 2. Southern African Migration Project, Institute for Democracy in South Africa, Queen's University, Capetown.

30. South Africa. Ministry of Home Affairs, Task Team on International Migration (1999). *White paper on international migration*. **http://www.gov.za/whitepaper/1999/migrate.htm** Accessed on 23 August 1999.

31. *The Economist,* September 1995, 2 September 1996, 2 November 1996, 6 June 1998, 30 August 1998.

32. Toure, M. (1998). *Country migraton profile: Côte d'Ivoire*. Paper presented at the Regional Meeting on International Migration in Africa at the Threshold of the XXI Century, Gaborone, 2-5 June.

33. Tsietsi, M. (1998). *Migration profile for Lesotho*. Paper presented at the Regional Meeting on International Migration in Africa at the Threshold of the XXI Century, Gaborone, 2-5 June.

34. United Nations (1998). *International Migration Policies*. New York, NY.

35. UNHCR (1999). *Africa Update*. Geneva. **http://www.unhcr.ch/news/cupdates/9906afri.htm** Accessed on 25 August 1999.

36. UNHCR (1997). *The State of the World's Refugees, 1997/98: A Humanitarian Agenda*. Oxford University Press, Oxford, England.

37. US Committee for Refugees (1999). *1999 World Refugee Survey*. Washington, DC.

38. World Bank (1995). *Retaining teaching capacity in African universities: problems and prospects*. Study commissioned by the Working Group on High Education constituted under the Donors to African Education in 1993. *Findings, African Region*, No 39, May.

39. Yamuah, M. (1998). *Country migration profile: the Gambia*. Paper presented at the Regional Meeting on International Migration in Africa at the Threshold of the XXI Century, Gaborone, 2-5 June.

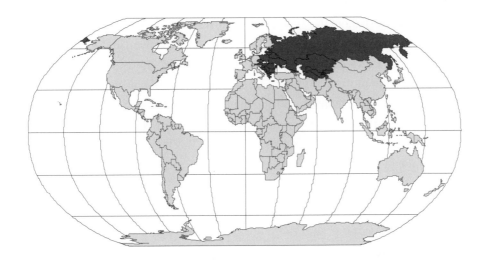

CENTRAL AND EASTERN EUROPE AND THE COMMONWEALTH OF INDEPENDENT STATES

INTRODUCTION

Central and Eastern Europe (CEE) and the Commonwealth of Independent States (CIS) comprise a vast geographical region stretching from Prague to Vladivostock with a population of more than 550 million people. In 1989, this region consisted of only nine independent countries. Today, the number of countries has increased to 27.[1] The establishment of so many new countries and the creation almost overnight of new minority groups within these countries was a major factor contributing to the tremendous increase in migration in this region at the beginning of the 1990s.

Frank Laczko, Head of Applied Research at IOM Headquarters in Geneva, Switzerland, contributed to this chapter.

When the Berlin Wall came down in November 1989, there was considerable concern in the West about the prospect of an upsurge in East-West migration. This concern increased still further when the Soviet Union dissolved in December 1991. The predicted westward mass migration never occurred, however. In the CIS, the largest population movements took place within the region as many of those living outside their home republics during the breakup of the USSR relocated. Since 1989, about 9 million people have moved within or between the countries of the CIS–one in every 30 of the region's inhabitants (7). This includes both voluntary repatriation and forced movements.

TABLE 29.

SUMMARY OF MIGRATION FLOWS AND STOCKS IN THE CIS COUNTRIES, 1997

Total population	**284,080,000**
Immigrants	25,300
Emigrants	220,600
Flows within the CIS and Baltic region	795,500
Refugees and persons in refugee-like situations from the CIS and Baltic States	1,556,000
Non-CIS refugees and asylum seekers	109,400
Internally displaced persons	1,790,000
Repatriants	482,000
Involuntarily relocating persons	100,000
Formerly deported peoples	150,000

Source: IOM (1999). *Migration in the CIS: 1997-98.*

Repatriants[2] are "persons, who for economic, social, or personal reasons, have voluntarily resettled in the country of their citizenship or origin for the purpose of permanent residence", and they constitute by far the largest migrant group in the CEE/CIS region. By 1997, the total number of repatriants within the CIS region, including Russians and other ethnic groups, was approximately 4.7 million persons. Nearly half a million repatriants migrated within the CIS and Baltic States in 1997 alone. In addition, there are about 1.5 million refugees and persons in refugee-like situations and another 1.8 million internally displaced persons.

Migration in the CEE/CIS is truly dynamic. Some population movements during the 1990s—such as the flow of persons fleeing armed conflicts—are familiar to countries in other parts of the world. Others—such as the return of formerly deported peoples, including the Crimean Tatars, Volga Germans, and Meskhetian Turks, to the areas of the CIS from which they were deported by Stalin in the 1940s—are unique to the CIS (10).

Many migration trends—trends no one would have predicted a decade ago— reflect both the region's political and economic transformations and its growing integration with the rest of Europe: the movement of skilled workers from western to eastern Europe; and the emergence of many CEE and CIS countries as transit zones for migrants from the developing world who intend to move to the west without authorization. Before 1989, hundreds of thousands of refugees from the CEE/CIS region sought asylum in western Europe and North America.

Today, the CEE and CIS countries have themselves become the target for a growing number of asylum seekers from some the major refugee-producing and poorer countries of the world. The CIS is host to a substantial number of asylum seekers, although not as many as in western Europe. More than 100,000 refugees and asylum seekers from non-CIS states were hosted in the CIS in 1997; the majority, from Afghanistan, reside mainly in Tajikistan and the Russian Federation (10).

Obtaining accurate information on migration flows in the CIS/CEE region is still quite difficult. As many governments have little interest in or need for monitoring international migration flows, migration trends in the CEE/CIS are not well documented and widely varying definitions make it extremely difficult to compare States. The most significant migration flows in the CEE/CIS region often are not fully recorded as they involve very-short-term migrants, irregular migrants, or migrants working in the informal economy. In addition, some new trends, such as the trafficking of women from central and eastern Europe, are not fully recognized by those who study international migration because of a lack of official concern and the subsequent absence of statistical data.

Further complicating the picture, many CEE and CIS countries are at one and the same time countries of immigration, emigration, and transit. While some groups within these countries are still responding to the changes brought by the fall of the Berlin Wall, others are responding to current conditions and opportunities for permanent and short-term work. Consequently, to varying degrees, flows are both outward- and inward-bound. The Russian Federation, for example, is at once *host* for the return of ethnic Russians and inflows of labour migrants and asylum seekers and *origin* for permanent outflows of ethnic Germans and other minorities and for temporary outflows of labour migrants. Further, few countries are unaffected by the outpouring of refugees from conflicts in the region. This chapter explores each of these migration situations and issues for the region as a whole.

IMMIGRATION TRENDS

The principal host countries for international migrants are the Russian Federation and the more prosperous CEE countries, the Czech Republic, Hungary, and Poland.

THE RUSSIAN FEDERATION

The most important movement into the Russian Federation since the breakup of the Soviet Union is the return of ethnic Russians and other Russian speakers. Between 1990 and 1997, some 2.7 million people repatriated to Russia from other parts of the CIS and Baltic States (10).

Russian speakers have been steadily repatriating since the late 1970s. At the end of the 1980s, this trend accelerated considerably owing to a fall in living standards and the loss of the immigrants' once privileged social status in the newly independent States. The bulk of the repatriates originate in central Asia where large Russian-speaking communities settled during the Soviet era and from the Caucasus where living conditions became intolerable after several armed conflicts.

There is some disagreement over the extent to which this movement of persons has been voluntary and the result of economic factors or the consequence of discrimination against minority groups in some of the newly independent States. The Russian authorities tend to describe these people as "forced migrants" who have had to return to the Russian Federation because of ethnic discrimination against them.

Migrants from within the CIS settle primarily in the regions bordering Kazakhstan, in the Tiumen region (which has one of the world's largest oil and gas complexes), and in the Russian Federation's central, southern and south-western regions (which have active economies). The Federal Migration Service established 73 reception centres for repatriates and "forced migrants" that host up to 25,000 people. The reception centres provide accommodation for vulnerable migrants and are responsible for facilitating their social, cultural, and economic integration. Migrants in need receive a modest grant equal to the minimum wage per family member in urban areas and twice the minimum wage in rural areas. Migrant families also may be granted interest-free loans for purchasing or building a home. These loans are available in 107 locations and benefit some 65,000 people (2).

Relatively little is known about the living conditions of the majority of repatriates as most of them resettled independently in the CIS. Some studies, however, suggest that those migrants who returned to the Russian Federation are among the hardest hit by the recent economic crisis; they are more likely to be unemployed and to have poorer quality housing (7, 10).

The Russian Federation is also a destination for labour migrants. According to data from the Federal Migration Service, in 1997, 100,000 recruitment permits were issued to hire more than 240,000 persons. The majority of these labour permits go to migrants from within the CIS, although more than 120,000 came from outside CIS borders. Foreign labour was recruited from 114 countries, with significant numbers of workers coming from the Ukraine, Turkey, China, and the former Yugoslavia. More than one-half were recruited into construction, with the remainder in agriculture, industry, trade and public catering, transport, commerce, and mining. Almost 30 per cent go to the Moscow vicinity, but labour migrants can be found throughout the Federation (10).

An additional unknown number of labour migrants in the CIS without work authorization are mainly unregistered traders and migrants who travel as tourists and often overstay their visas. The total number of unauthorized migrants is estimated at 700,000 to 1.5 million persons. They include a diverse population: former students who do not wish to return to their home countries, irregular migrants from neighbouring Chinese provinces, asylum seekers, and workers who stayed in the Russian Federation after the expiration of their work permits.

HUNGARY, POLAND, AND THE CZECH REPUBLIC

Foreign citizens represent less than 1 to 2 per cent of the total population in most CEE countries. Even in such relatively richer countries in the region as Hungary (1.4 per cent) and the Czech Republic (2 per cent), the percentage of foreign population is still low (16). In most CEE countries, with the notable exception of the Czech Republic,[3] the stock of foreign population and the officially recorded inflow of migrants has remained stable since 1995 (13).

However, it is likely that official figures considerably underestimate the real number of foreigners and migrants living and working in the CEE because of the large number of foreign workers from eastern Europe who work in the informal economy. It is also difficult for the authorities to record these flows when many migrants move back and forth between their country and the country in which they are working.

TABLE 30.
TOTAL AND FOREIGN POPULATION STOCKS IN SELECTED CEE COUNTRIES, 1997

	Total population stocks	Total foreign population stocks
Bulgaria	8,409,000	73,300[1]
Croatia	4,493,350	38,300
Czech Rep.	10,315,000	209,800
Estonia	1,462,130	320,400
Hungary	10,246,000	143,000
Latvia	2,458,000	686,200
Lithuania	3,704,800	28,000
FYROM[2]	1,991,400	600
Poland	38,660,000	36,300
Romania	22,760,450	60,300
Slovakia	5,387,650	24,763
Slovenia	1,992,000	42,500

Notes: [1]As of 1996; [2]FYROM = The former Yugoslav Republic of Macedonia.
Sources: 1997 International Centre for Migration Policy Development annual questionnaires.
OECD (1998, 1997). *Trends in International Migration: Sopemi Annual Report.* Paris.
Latvia: Annual demographic yearbooks.
Slovenia: Council of Europe (1999). *Recent Demographic Developments in Europe 1999.* Strasbourg.

TABLE 31.

IMMIGRATION AND EMIGRATION FLOWS IN SELECTED CEE COUNTRIES, 1995-1997

	Immigrated persons[1] Flows			Emigrated persons[2] Flows		
	1995	1996	1997	1995	1996	1997
Bulgaria	na	na	25,285	53,000	62,000	na
Croatia	42,000	44,600	na	15,413	10,027	na
Czech Rep.	10,540	10,857	12,880	541	758	805
Estonia	1,616	1,574	1,583	9,786	7,235	4,081
Hungary	13,185	12,537	na	na	na	na
Latvia	2,799	2,747	2,913	13,346	9,999	9,677
Lithuania	2,020	3,025	2,536	3,773	3,940	2,457
FYROM	960	639	556	392	247	282
Poland	8,121	8,186	8,426	26,344	21,297	20,222
Romania	na	na	37,794	25,675	21,526	21,635
Slovakia	4,493	4,039	4,318	4,100	3,600	572
Slovenia	5,873	8,003	na	766	na	na

Notes: In general, three types of residence permits are issued in the CEE countries: short-term temporary, long-term, and permanent. Temporary residence permits are granted for a maximum of one year. Long-term permits (more than one year) are renewable annually and cover the period of activity justifying residence in the country (work or study). Permanent permits are most often granted following a marriage to a citizen of the host country, the repatriation of members of an ethnic group originating from the country concerned, or for humanitarian reasons.

[1] These figures refer to permanent immigration, i.e., the number of foreigners who were granted permanent residence permits during the year, and/or registered as permanent residents in population registers during the year. For Bulgaria, Croatia, Romania, Slovakia, and Slovenia, the figures refer to the total number of long-term and permanent resident permits issued during the year. For Hungary, the figure refers to the number of long-term resident permit holders registering in the given year.

[2] These figures refer to permanent emigration flows, i.e., the number of persons leaving the country permanently and registered according to national regulations and requirement in national population registers during the year. For Bulgaria, Hungary, Romania, and Slovakia, long-term temporary emigration is also included. In general, these figures are under-reported as the people leaving the country are requested, but not required, to report their departure.

Sources: International Centre for Migration Policy Development annual questionnaires.
OCED (1998, 1997). *Trends in International Migration: Sopemi Annual Report*. Paris.

Some of the relatively more affluent countries of central Europe, such as Hungary, Poland, and the Czech Republic, increasingly have become target countries for workers in neighbouring eastern countries, mainly for seasonal, cross-border, individual, or contract-based employment. In the Czech Republic, migrants are primarily Slovak citizens who settled in the country after the dissolution of Czechoslovakia, as well as Ukrainian and Polish temporary migrants. In Hungary,

TABLE 32.
IMMIGRANTS WITH WORK PERMITS IN SELECTED CEE COUNTRIES, 1995-1997

	Stocks 1995	1996	1997
Albania		310	
Bulgaria	331	300	779
Croatia		4,752	5,978
Czech Rep.	52,559	71,046	69,367
Hungary	26,085	20,296	20,238
Latvia	598	855	849
Lithuania	410	535	754
Poland	10,500	13,668	
Romania	694	678	1,031
Slovakia	2,686	3,686	6,652
Slovenia	22,642	25,232	26,236

Sources: International Centre for Migration Policy Development annual questionnaires.
OECD (1998, 1997). *Trends in International Migration: Sopemi Annual Report*. Paris.

migrant workers are predominantly ethnic Hungarians from Romania. Ukrainians, Russians, and Belarussians comprise much of the migrant labour force in Poland (13). Many of these migrant workers have strong links to their home country, often maintaining a household there. One study reported circular migration in which the majority of Ukrainians in the Czech Republic return to the Ukraine on average every second or third month (3).

It is relatively easy for migrant workers from poorer neighbouring countries in eastern Europe and the CIS to seek employment—often on a temporary basis—in one of the wealthier central European countries. No visas are required for entry to these countries. The relatively large shadow economy and the lack of regulation make it relatively easy to employ foreigners illegally. There are few reliable statistics regarding the likely number of migrants working illegally in CEE and CIS countries, but it is suspected that the numbers are huge. For example, the Polish Ministry of Labour and Social Policy estimates that 100,000 to 150,000 illegal foreign workers come to Poland each year (14).

As a result of the establishment of new asylum systems in central and eastern Europe and of the recent Kosovo crisis, asylum applications in the CEE region have risen sharply. In 1997, there were nearly 10,000 asylum applications in the

10 associated CEE countries—more than a 35 per cent increase compared to 1996. By 1998, the number of asylum applications was already higher in the Czech Republic (4,806) and Hungary (7,386) than the total figure for all associated countries in 1997. The number of applications in 1998 in the Czech Republic and Hungary was higher than in EU states such as Finland (1,272) and Greece (2,953). This trend continued in 1999, with sharp increases in asylum applications reported during the first nine months of the year, compared to the same period in the previous year in Slovakia (246 per cent), the Czech Republic (238 per cent), Hungary (112 per cent), and Bulgaria (82 per cent) (18). Although the bulk of asylum seekers originate in developing countries and the successor States of former Yugoslavia, in some countries significant numbers of migrants from CEE and CIS States make asylum applications. For example, one-third of claimants in the Czech Republic in 1997 were Bulgarian, and 15 per cent of asylum applicants in Poland in 1998 were from Armenians (12).

Relatively little attention has been paid to the integration of migrants in the CEE countries in recent years because most of these countries still tend to perceive themselves as transit countries. This is likely to change as some of the more affluent CEE countries are target countries for immigrants. Many are also attracting a rising number of asylum seekers whose claims are usually rejected but who cannot often be returned to their country of origin.

One study on the integration of persons in need of international protection in the Czech and Slovak Republics and in Poland found that authorities in these three countries have a relatively limited involvement in promoting integration (5). In a Council of Europe survey seeking CEE Government information on their integration programmes and measures for migrants (2), relatively few Governments provided information on specific programmes and, where such measures did exist, they often were rather modest and targeted only asylum seekers.

EMIGRATION TRENDS

Although the massive East to West outflow never occurred on the scale predicted, approximately 2.5 million people did emigrate to the West from the CEE/CIS region during the first half of the 1990s (17). Most of this emigration involved minority ethnic groups, but there was also significant migration for purely eco-

TABLE 33.
PERMANENT AND LONG-TERM EMIGRATION FLOWS FROM SELECTED CEE COUNTRIES BY COUNTRY OF DESTINATION, 1997

Romania permanent and long-term emigration

Total	21,635	
Germany	5,362	24.8 %
USA	2,920	13.5 %
Canada	2,416	11.2 %
Italy	1,958	9.1 %

Poland permanent emigration

Total	20,222	
Germany	14,202	70.2 %
USA	2,229	11.0 %
Canada	1,336	6.6 %
Austria	631	3.1 %
Sweden	268	1.3 %

Czech Republic permanent emigration

Total	805	
Slovakia	260	32.3 %
Germany	237	29.4 %
Austria	59	7.3 %
Switzerland	49	6.1 %
USA	40	5.0 %

Latvia permanent emigration

Total	9,677	
Russian Fed.	5,064	57.9 %
Belarus	916	9.5 %
Ukraine	876	9.1 %
Germany	674	7.0 %
USA	511	5.3 %

Lithuania permanent emigration

Total	2,457	
Russian Fed.	1,645	67.0 %
Belarus	279	11.4 %
Israel	271	11.0 %
Ukraine	130	5.3 %
Germany	130	5.3 %

Estonia permanent emigration

Total	4,081	
Russian Fed.	2,333	57.2 %
Finland	550	13.5 %
Germany	322	7.9 %
USA	262	6.4 %
Ukraine	156	3.8 %

Source: 1997 International Centre for Migration Policy Development annual questionnaires.

nomic reasons. Following the collapse of the communist regimes in 1989, some 1.2 million people left the region. More than one-half of those who left the region (720,000 people) were ethnic Germans; approximately 320,000 were Bulgarian Turks, of whom about half later returned to Bulgaria.[4] Albania was perhaps the most affected by emigration: an estimated 300,000-450,000 Albanians (10 to 14 per cent of the population) left the country in the early 1990s when removal of prior exit controls coincided with recurrent economic and political crises (17).

Although the number of persons emigrating from the CEE to the West has fallen substantially since the early 1990s, emigration from the CEE region remains significant, especially from Poland and Romania. In both of these countries there were more than 20,000 officially recorded emigrants in 1997 (13). As individuals leaving their country often are not required to report their departure, the true level of emigration is likely to be greater than official figures indicate. Increasingly, individuals migrating from CEE countries appear to be moving to neighbouring

CEE countries. For the most part this more recent intraregional movement is more likely to be short-term migration for work than permanent emigration for ethnic reasons (12, 14, 16).

Permanent emigration to western European countries is declining, but the same cannot be said of temporary migration of workers for seasonal, cross-border, individual, or contract-based employment. Temporary labour migration chiefly involves Polish citizens moving mainly to Germany and Austria, but also to France, the Czech Republic, and Sweden. On a smaller scale, Albanians typically migrate for work to Italy or Greece, Estonians to Finland, Romanians to Israel, Bulgarians to Germany, Czechs to Austria and Germany, and Hungarians to Austria and Germany (15). Germany remains the main host country for permanent and long-term migrants from the CEE.

No single explanation lies behind migrants' desire to move to other countries (8). Emigration pressures vary by country and involve a combination of factors. For the Czech Republic, Poland, and Hungary, for example, the lure of higher wages and better living conditions pulls workers into the migration stream. Their geographic proximity to Germany and Austria, the main destination countries, ensures low costs associated with migration that maximize their earnings. Migrants are drawn by the knowledge that they can earn two to three times the wages they would earn at home. However, economic factors alone do not explain CEE migration trends, as migration from Poland is much greater than from Hungary or the Czech Republic despite similar economic conditions in these countries (14). In most cases, the greater the network of contacts in the destination, the greater the migration.

For other countries in the region, worsening conditions for ethnic minorities are more important push factors. The largest numbers of people on the move in the CEE and CIS region are refugees or internally displaced persons resulting from armed conflicts in the successor States of the former Yugoslavia, the Caucasus, the Republic of Moldova, Tajikistan, and parts of the Russian Federation. By mid-1999, the Kosovo conflict in Yugoslavia resulted in nearly 2 million persons being displaced or seeking refuge outside the country (see box on the Kosovo crisis). As a result of conflicts since 1989 in Armenia, Azerbaijan, Georgia, Tajikistan, the Republic of Moldova, and Chechnya, some 870,000 persons became refugees and a further 1.1 million persons were internally displaced (7).

In 1999, there were 173,000 internally displaced persons in the Russian Federation, of whom 150,000 were from Chechnya (18). After Russia began bombing and shelling Chechnya in September 1999, an estimated 300,000 people fled their homes. An estimated 200,000 internally displaced persons were forced to seek refuge in neighbouring Ingushetia, placing an enormous strain on the resources of this tiny republic of 347,000 people.

KOSOVO CRISIS:
MAIN FACTS AND STATISTICS

Kosovo is located in the southern part of the republic of Serbia, which remains part of Yugoslavia. Its ethnically diverse population is composed of Albanians, Serbs, Hungarians, and Roma. Although ethnic Albanians traditionally have been in the majority, Serbs had held political control since the abolition of Kosovo's autonomous status in 1989. At that time, some 350,000 ethnic Albanians left Kosovo and applied for asylum in Europe.

Beginning in 1998, when the recent conflict began, until March 1999 when the North Atlantic Treaty Organization (NATO) intervened, some 400,000 Kosovo Albanians were displaced from their homes in what is alleged to have been a deliberate campaign of ethnic cleansing. Approximately one-quarter (89,000) of those displaced sought asylum in central and western Europe, bringing the total population of Kosovo Albanians living in western Europe to 500,000. About 85 per cent of this population resides in Germany, Sweden, and Switzerland.

Once the bombing campaign was in full swing, a total of 848,100 ethnic Albanians fled or were expelled from Kosovo, including 444,600 refugees to Albania, 244,500 to the former Yugoslav Republic of Macedonia, and 69,900 to Montenegro. Some 91,057 refugees were airlifted from Macedonia to 29 countries as part of the Humanitarian Evacuation Programme.

Most of the 860,000 Kosovars who fled to Albania and Macedonia returned to Kosovo by the end of July 1999, in one of the fastest returns in modern refugee history. About 23,000 Kosovars (of whom 8,000 are in camps), remain in Macedonia, where they were expected to spend the winter of 1999-2000.

After the peace accord, an estimated 180,000 Serbs and Roma fled Kosovo, mainly to Serbia.

An estimated 30,000 ethnic Hungarians, most of whom were from Vojvodina in Kosovo, moved to Hungary between March and July 1999.

As the most significant source countries of migration (particularly to countries outside the region) are the Russian Federation, the successor States of the former Yugoslavia, and Albania, trends in these countries are detailed below.

THE RUSSIAN FEDERATION

More than 1 million people from the CIS emigrated to the West after 1989 (7). While most emigrated from the Russian Federation, only a minority were ethnic Russians. In 1996, for example, 44 per cent of emigrants were ethnic Germans and 14 per cent were officially classified as Jews. Germany, Israel, and the United States were the main destination countries for emigrants from the CIS. Many of those who emigrated to the West were formerly deported peoples who were expelled to Central Asia during the Second World War. In 1997, approximately 120,000 ethnic Germans from the CIS emigrated to Germany, mainly from Kazakhstan and the Russian Federation (10).

Other than permanent emigration, Russians have few legal avenues for migration. Russians who do seek temporary work abroad are more likely to move to countries such as Poland where no visas are required for entry and where it is easier to trade and work in the informal economy than in western countries.

SUCCESSOR STATES OF THE FORMER YUGOSLAVIA

Between 1991 and 1998, more than 1 million persons from the countries in the former Yugoslavia sought refuge in western Europe, including about 600,000 persons from Bosnia and Herzegovina and approximately 400,000 from Croatia and other successor States of the former Yugoslavia. As of September 1998, about 40 per cent of Bosnian refugees in western Europe had returned to the Federation area of Bosnia and Herzegovina. However, as of that time, only 10 per cent of the 520,000 refugees and displaced persons who returned to the Federation returned to an area in which their ethnic group is a minority (13).

Details of the numbers of persons displaced as a result of the Kosovo conflict are presented in the box on the Kosovo crisis. Annual remittances to Kosovo prior to the war were estimated at more than US$ 1 billion and represented 70 per cent of economic activity in the province, obviously its most important income source.

ALBANIA

Albania, the poorest country in Europe, has bad security conditions and widespread crime and corruption—factors that contribute to and facilitate unauthorized migration from the country. Emigration peaked in 1992, but has continued at a significant rate throughout the 1990s. In March 1997, for example, some 17,000 Albanians arrived in Italy (13). Albanians represent the highest share of third-country nationals legally resident in Greece and Italy. Many more Albanians work in these countries clandestinely. For example, the number of unauthorized foreign workers in Greece is estimated at 250,000-500,000, about one-half of them Albanian (3 to 6 per cent of the Greek labour force) (14).

The Albanian economy relies enormously on migrant remittances. A 1992 study showed that 23.3 per cent of total family income is derived from remittances from international migrants (17). Families with members working abroad were calculated to have incomes 2.5 times higher than the average Albanian family. In 1994 remittances from Albanian migrant workers in Greece and Italy were officially estimated at US$ 266 million, equivalent to around 16 percent of GDP (4).

REGIONAL MIGRATION ISSUES

Three regional migration issues interconnect: the implications of enlargement of the EU; the growth in the number of extraregional migrants transiting the CEE and CIS countries to reach western nations; and migrant trafficking and people smuggling.

EASTWARD ENLARGEMENT OF THE EUROPEAN UNION

In March 1998, negotiations on EU accession were opened with 10 CEE countries (Bulgaria, the Czech Republic, Estonia, Hungary, Latvia, Lithuania, Poland, Romania, Slovakia, and Slovenia). All these "associated" countries are expected to adapt their migration regimes in line with EU practice and the EU is closely monitoring their progress. All countries neighbouring the EU and newly associated countries will unavoidably have to take these new cooperation structures into account by adapting to the new EU entry control and visa regime. The process of adaptation will involve, among other things, introducing visa policies in line with EU norms, something which some western countries already are calling for in response to unauthorized transit migration through Central Europe. In 1997, the European Commission highlighted the lack of effective border management in the associated countries as one of the most important gaps in migration policy that will need to be closed prior to accession (13).

Responding to such concerns, however, may create new difficulties for the associated countries. When Hungary and Poland enter the EU, for example, they may need to require Ukrainians and Romanians to have entry visas. Imposition of such restrictions would not be welcome to the large ethnic Hungarian minority in Romania, nor would such restrictions facilitate Poland's existing economic and trade links with the Ukraine.

The extension of cooperation on immigration and asylum policy, among other issues, was specifically noted as a priority in the EU's preaccession strategy. Having signed the Amsterdam Treaty in 1997, EU member countries were allotted five years in which to adopt common standards and procedures in the control of the external borders of the EU. Thus, even countries awaiting membership are now required to make changes in their immigration and border control policies that previously might have been considered optional.

To help the associated countries meet these new migration challenges in preparation for membership, the EU took some advance steps. In 1998, the European Commission approved partnerships between each of the 10 CEE applicants and an existing EU member that will help set priority areas for further work and provide financial assistance. The EU in recent years set aside increased financial support for migration programmes, some tailored to support its preaccession strategy (13).

In 1998, the European Commission cited the following progress in the area of immigration and border controls. A number of countries, including Estonia, Hungary, and Poland, passed new legislation or amended existing legislation on alien and asylum issues in line with EU practice in 1997-1998. In Bulgaria, Latvia and Hungary, the Border Guard service is in the process of being fully professionalized, with less reliance on conscripts or military personnel. Many of the associated countries expect to increase the number of border guards employed over the next few years. In Estonia and Lithuania, countries that did not have an international border with CIS countries until recently, the planned increase in the number of border guards is substantial, rising from 2,185 to 3,500 in Estonia and from 4,300 to 6,000 in Lithuania.

According to the European Commission, however, border management is still weak in the CEE. Most countries still lack the necessary financial, technical, and human resources for adequate border controls. Some countries also are being required do more to improve the training of border guards and improve the way in which the service is organized. The CEE countries, for their part, argue that they need much greater financial assistance from the EU if they are to meet requirements of EU membership (13).

There are expression of concern about the extent to which eastward EU expansion might contribute to a new wave of East-West migration. A 1998 IOM survey suggests that the percentage of people in the CEE/CIS who wished to emigrate permanently was fairly low (7 to 26 per cent) and that these potential emigrants were more interested in moving overseas to the United States, Canada, Australia, and New Zealand than to the EU.[5] Potential migrants indicated interest in moving to western Europe only for short-term labour migration (for a few weeks or months), including cross-border commuting and seasonal work. Countries with by far the greatest migration potential, such as Croatia and Yugoslavia, are not among those likely to join the EU in the near future.

The CEE/CIS countries were divided into three main groups on the basis of the survey results. The first group—countries with both permanent and temporary high migration potential in which some two-thirds of respondents expressed an interest in leaving—not surprisingly were Yugoslavia and Croatia. The second group—where a strong preference for short-term labour migration was found included the Czech and Slovak Republics, Hungary and Poland. The third group— where generally low general migration potential was found—included Belarus, Bulgaria and Slovenia, countries quite different from each other. Slovenia is among the most prosperous of the post-communist countries; Bulgaria and Belarus are among the least prosperous. Further research is necessary to explain such country-to-country variances in migration potential.

TRANSIT MIGRATION

Border traffic has grown enormously throughout the CEE/CIS region. Because there were no border controls between the republics of the former Soviet Union, long sections of the CIS borders today remain poorly guarded. For the first time, the region is witnessing unauthorized transit migration to the West and to certain central European countries. In the Russian Federation, the number of unauthorized migrants from countries outside the CIS is estimated at 700 thousand to 1 million persons (10). Countries of the CIS have become a significant stepping-stone to the West especially for migrants from developing countries. Nevertheless, only a fraction of migrants trying to cross CIS borders without authorization are caught. In Ukraine, for example, only 10,800 migrants were apprehended in 1997, which was about the average annual apprehension rate between 1993 and 1997 (10). Yet the State Border Committee recently estimated that there were 600,000 unauthorized migrants in Ukraine, most from Afghanistan, Sri Lanka, Bangladesh, and Pakistan. There is an urgent need to develop Ukraine's institutional and operational capacity to combat migrant trafficking in view of the planned accession of several of its neighbours to the European Union. When the western borders of Ukraine become the EU's new external borders, migrant trafficking is likely to increase in the absence of strong and effective countermeasures.

As in the CIS, few migrants are caught actually crossing the borders of eastern European countries without authorization, but in central European States such as the Czech Republic and Hungary the situation is quite different. In these important transit and target countries that have improved their border controls in recent years, border apprehensions are higher than in many EU States. Other CEE countries, however, such as Bulgaria and Romania, which continue to be major source countries for unauthorized migrants seeking to enter EU countries without authorization, apprehend relatively few unauthorized migrants at their borders (11).

Throughout the CEE, official statistics suggest that the number of attempted unauthorized border crossings increased little between 1995 and 1997, but increased sharply in 1998 owing to the conflict in Kosovo (13). For example, in Poland, the number of unauthorized crossing attempts in 1997 was 16,438, a little higher than the 1996 total of 15,345 and a bit lower than the 1995 total of 16,535. Moreover, the number of attempted unauthorized border crossings was generally lower than in the first half of the 1990s. In the Czech Republic, for example, slightly more than 43,000 crossings ended in apprehensions in 1993, as compared to just under 24,000 in 1997.

Unauthorized transit migration to the West and to certain central European countries was almost unknown prior to 1989. In addition to migrants from developing countries, unauthorized migrants from other East European countries not directly bordering the West now find their way through this central European transit route. The region is attractive to unauthorized and transit migrants because of the lack of visa requirements and the weakness of border controls.

Most unauthorized attempts at border crossing in CEE countries occur on western borders and in countries that border Germany and Austria, such as the Czech Republic, Hungary, and Poland. The highest number of unauthorized migrants is apprehended in the Czech Republic attempting to enter Germany. In 1998, there were 44,000 border apprehensions, a figure higher than for any other European country.[6] The respective figures for Hungary and Slovakia were 18,107 and 8,187 (11). Assuming border enforcement is uniform on all borders, this finding suggests migrants are heading for the West.

However, not all CEE countries that share a border with a country in the EU report large-scale apprehension of unauthorized migrants at the border. Slovenia and Bulgaria both share borders with EU countries but report a low apprehension rate of approximately 2,000-3,000 per year (13). In Romania, the number of apprehensions was even lower, only 1,160 in 1997.

The overall decline in the number of attempted unauthorized border crossings to the CEE countries since 1993 probably is related more to the change in the nature of migration pressures in the region than to major improvements in the capacity of authorities to detect unauthorized movements, although the number of border guards and investment in border management have increased in many CEE countries in recent years. Unauthorized migration from East to West increased to a large extent in 1998 and 1999 because of the conflict in Kosovo. Beginning in 1998, the number of Kosovo Albanians without documents who were apprehended trying to cross into western European countries greatly increased. At the German-Czech border, the number of Kosovo migrants was more than three times higher in the first half of 1998 than it was during the same period the year before.

According to the Czech Border Guard, nearly 9,500 citizens of Yugoslavia were detained for attempted unauthorized border crossings, accounting for 31 per cent of the total number of unauthorized border crossings during that period. Between January and the end of August 1998, another 4,700 persons from that country were caught trying to enter Austria without authorization. This figure represented 44.6 per cent of border apprehensions during the period.

TRAFFICKING OF MIGRANTS

Trafficking and smuggling of migrants are terms that often are used interchangeably, but that can refer to quite different acts. Migrant smuggling, or people smuggling, are terms that usually refer to the facilitation of unauthorized border crossings by a smuggler who usually is paid for this service. Although this is also a common method used to traffic migrants, trafficking refers to a set of practices that go beyond the facilitation of unauthorized border crossings, where legal means may in fact be used to bring migrants into a country in order to exploit their labour. Most CEE/CIS countries collect relatively little information on trafficking in migrants specifically; most of the data refer to smuggling or to cases in which an individual is apprehended at the border with a smuggler. Official figures most likely underestimate the scale of the problem. In Hungary, for example, the number of migrants apprehended trying to cross Hungary's borders with the assistance of a smuggler has increased substantially, rising from an average of 1,000-1,500 persons per year between 1995 and 1997 to 3,200 in 1998. The latter figure, however, accounts for only one-quarter of the migrants apprehended (12). In the Czech Republic, the situation seems to be similar; 22 per cent of the 24,000 persons apprehended for unauthorized crossing during the first 10 months of 1997 reportedly were assisted by a smuggler (13).

There are other indicators of a growth in East-West people smuggling. In Hungary, for example, the number of migrants apprehended in groups of 10 persons or more has been increasing. Clearly such attempts at unauthorized crossing must be organized (12). In Hungary, migrants who are not from the CEE region are much more likely to be apprehended in large groups. Approximately 60 per cent of apprehensions for unauthorized crossing of persons from Asia involved large groups in 1998, compared to only 10 to 20 per cent of apprehensions involving East European migrants.

Some of those who turn to traffickers for assistance in unauthorized travel to the West face considerable risks, as many are exploited en route or face hazardous journeys. During 1998 and 1999, numerous cases of this kind were reported involving Kosovo Albanians. For example, in July 1998, seven Kosovo Albanians were killed and 21 injured when the driver of their van, a suspected Czech smuggler, tried to evade German border guards and crashed the vehicle. In October 1998, police near Munich deported 75 Kosovo Albanians who had entered the country without authorization, some of whom nearly suffocated after being packed too tightly into a truck. Some 19 individuals, including five pregnant women, were taken to the hospital suffering from exhaustion and oxygen deprivation (11).

Most flows of unauthorized migrants involve men. More than 80 per cent of migrants detected trying to cross Czech and Hungarian borders, for example, are male (11). This statistic may partly explain why the trafficking of women from the CEE/CIS region for the purpose of sexual exploitation is almost completely ignored in current reports on CEE country migration trends (14). Such trafficking in women has been of increasing concern to European governments. The EU launched the 1996-2000 five-year Programme to Combat the Sexual Trafficking of Persons (STOP) to prevent it. Both the European Union and the United States supported information programmes to prevent the trafficking of women in Poland and Ukraine in 1998. In 1999, the EU and the United States supported new information campaigns implemented by IOM in Bulgaria, the Czech Republic, and Hungary.

Although it is difficult to obtain accurate statistics, there is little doubt that a considerable increase in trafficking of CEE/CIS women for purposes of sexual exploitation occurred during the 1990s (6, 13). In 1997, the US Government estimated that such trafficking involved 175,000 women and girls from central and eastern Europe and the newly independent States, representing one-quarter of all women involved in this trade worldwide (21). One of the leading nongovernmental organizations dealing with this problem in Europe, the Foundation Against the Trafficking in Women in the Netherlands, reported that the majority of victims of this form of trafficking now come from the CEE/CIS region, whereas in 1990 most of the women came from developing countries (6). Generally, the profile of women involved in trafficking from the CEE is younger, better educated, unmarried, and without children, compared to women from other parts of the world (12). According to official statistics in Germany in 1996, 80 per cent of the 1,500 victims of trafficking in women were from the CEE/CIS region (13)—nearly 40 per cent from the CIS, and slightly more than 30 per cent from Poland, the Czech Republic, and Slovakia.

There appears to be an emerging trend: trafficking of refugee women. Women from Kosovo were recruited from refugee camps in Albania and forced into prostitution abroad, mainly in Italy and the United Kingdom (12). Reports from Italy, Germany, Belgium, and the United Kingdom suggest this trade also involves growing numbers of Albanian women, especially from rural areas.

There are several causes of this increased trafficking of women from the CEE/CIS. The high level of poverty and unemployment among women as well as the tighter western European immigration controls probably provide only part of the explanation. The main factor is more likely the existence of organized networks of traffickers and criminals who for huge profits at relatively little risk recruit, transport and then exploit these women (6). Penalties for trafficking in women are not severe and convictions are rare. It is easier and less expensive to bring women from the CEE/CIS region to western Europe than to recruit women from developing countries: these women do not have to travel as far and, as visa restrictions no longer apply to many CEE citizens, authorized entry on a tourist visa is relatively easy.

The majority of women involved in trafficking are sexually exploited for prostitution; a minority are engaged as domestic help, usually with little or no pay and no contract.

In 1997, a survey on the availability of statistics on trafficking in women and children was conducted in 25 countries, including all EU countries and five candidate countries (9). Although many countries were unable to produce reliable statistics specifically on the scale of trafficking in women, the majority of surveyed countries reported this form of trafficking to be a growing problem, especially involving women from the CEE. However, because victims fear turning to authorities for help, much underreporting is suspected. Law enforcement agencies often do not give sufficient priority to combating trafficking in women because the crime is poorly defined in national legislation, when it is defined at all.

CONCLUSION

The post-communist transformation in the CEE/CIS region is without precedent in world history. Countries, many of which did not exist 10 years ago, have been forced to adapt quickly to a new range of population movements during a difficult transition period and with limited resources.

Current migration trends in the region present several challenges for the CEE/CIS region and for Europe as a whole. Western European countries and the EU have tried to restrict irregular migration from CEE/CIS as much as possible but have not completely closed the door to legal migration from the East. In 1997, as in previous years, Germany allowed more than 100,000 ethnic Germans from the CIS to immigrate to Germany, a figure that is higher than the total number of persons apprehended trying to cross without authorization from East to West in that year.

CEE countries, and to a lesser extent the CIS (with the notable exception of the Russian Federation), tend not to think of themselves as target countries for immigrants despite substantial interregional migration. Even given recent concern about the prospects for a large-scale emigration from Russia, it is likely that the rate of immigration to Russia will continue to be much greater than the rate of emigration. Repatriation continues to be the major migration trend affecting the CIS. In 1999, renewed fighting in Chechnya, in the Russian Federation, added hundreds of thousands of new migrants to the already high number of refugees and internally displaced persons in the CIS. The major migration challenge for the CIS— and for the Russian Federation in particular—over the next few years will be how to promote the integration of those who return to their home republics and how to find durable solutions for those who are displaced.

Finally, less than 10 years after the fall of the Berlin Wall, new dividing lines may be forming in the CEE/CIS. Although the purpose of EU enlargement is to take a step towards unifying Europe, concerns abound among some countries in the CIS— and other countries not included in the EU membership negotiations—that new divisions are being created between the peoples of the CEE/CIS region. Ironically, at a time when frontier controls are being abolished in the EU, the CEE and CIS states are being encouraged to develop tougher border controls. Thus, the enlargement of the EU may have the unintended result of creating new distinctions between the populations of CEE and CIS countries even as it bridges other divisions.

ENDNOTES

1. The countries of Central and Eastern Europe include Albania, Bosnia and Herzegovina, Bulgaria, Croatia, The Czech Republic, Estonia, Hungary, Latvia, Lithuania, Poland, Romania, Slovakia, Slovenia, The Former Yugoslav Republic of Macedonia, and Yugoslavia. The Commonwealth of Independent States refers to Armenia, Azerbaijan, Belarus, Georgia, Kazakhstan, Kyrgyzstan, The Republic of Moldova, The Russian Federation, Tajikistan, Turkmenistan, Ukraine, and Uzbekistan. These two categories overlap; some countries that belong to the political grouping of the CIS, such as Ukraine, are also located in the geographical region of Central and Eastern Europe.

2. The definition of a repatriant was agreed upon at the May 1996 CIS Conference, held in Geneva under the auspices of UNHCR, IOM, and the Organization for Security and Cooperation in Europe [OSCE] to address the problems of refugees, displaced persons, other forms of involuntary displacement, and returnees in the countries of the CIS and relevant neighbouring States.

3. In the Czech Republic the total foreign population rose from 158,700 in 1995 to 209,800 in 1997 (11).

4. The Bulgarian Turks left during the spring/summer of 1989 just before the communist Government collapsed in November of the same year.

5. During the spring and early summer of 1998, under the sponsorship of IOM, a representative sample of 1,000 persons was surveyed in Belarus, Bulgaria, Croatia, the Czech Republic, Hungary, Poland, Romania, Slovakia, Slovenia, Ukraine, and Yugoslavia (7).

6. These figures refer to the number of apprehensions and not to the number of migrants trying to cross borders illegally. At some borders the same person may have been apprehended on more than one occasion. Therefore, the high Czech figure may be partly because many migrants make several attempts to cross the border illegally. Under Germany's readmission agreement with the Czech Republic, approximately 17,000 people were returned to the Czech Republic in 1998, most of whom were third-country nationals (10).

REFERENCES

1. Cole, D. (1998). Germany fights wave of immigrant smuggling. Reuters News Service, 9 November.

2. Council of Europe, European Committee on Migration (1999). *Recent Developments and Policies Relating to Migration and Migrants*, 97/17/rev.1. Strasbourg.

3. Drbohlav (1997). *Labour migration in central Europe with special respect to Poland, the Czech Republic, Slovakia and Hungary: contemporary trends.* Paper presented at European Science Foundation International Seminar on Transnational Processes and Dependencies of Central and Eastern European Societies, Prague, February.

4. Economist Intelligence Unit (1997). *Albania, Country Profile.* London.

5. Giorgi, L. (1996). *Integration of persons in need of international protection in the Czech and Slovak Republics and Poland, 1996.*

6. IOM (1995). *Trafficking and Prostitution: The Growing Exploitation of Migrant Women from Central and Eastern Europe.* Geneva.

7. IOM (1997). *The CIS Migration Report.* Geneva.

8. IOM (1998a). *Migration Potential in Central and Eastern Europe.* Geneva.

9. IOM (1998b). *Information Campaign Against Trafficking in Women from Ukraine.* Geneva.

10. IOM (1999a). *Migration in the CIS 1997-98.* Geneva.

11. IOM Technical Cooperation Centre for Europe and Central Asia (1999b). *Return of Irregular Migrants: The Challenge for Central and Eastern Europe.* Vienna.

12. IOM (2000 forthcoming). *Migrant Trafficking and Human Smuggling in Europe: A Review of the Evidence with Case Studies from Hungary, Poland and Ukraine.* Geneva.

13. IOM/International Centre for Migration Policy Development (1999). *Migration in Central and Eastern Europe: 1999 Review.* Geneva.

14. OECD (1998). *Trends in International Migration: SOPEMI Annual Report.* Paris.

15. Okolski, M. (1998). *Regional dimension of international migration in central and eastern Europe.* Paper presented at UNESCO Conference on Migration in Central and Eastern Europe, Moscow, 6-9 September 1998.

16. Salt, J. (1998). *International migration in the UNECE region: patterns, trends, policies.* Paper presented at the Regional Population Meeting, Budapest, 7-9 December 1998.

17. United Nations Ecomonic Commission for Europe and United Nations Fund for Population Activities (1996). *International Migration in Central and Eastern Europe and the Commonwealth of Independent States.* Geneva.

18. UNHCR (1999a). *Asylum Application Statistics in Europe, Third Quarter.* Geneva.

19. UNHCR (1999b). *UNHCR Country Profiles, Russian Federation.* **http://www.unhcr.ch/world/ euro/russia.htm** and **http://www.unhcr.ch/fdrs/ga99/rus.htm**

20. UNHCR (1999c). *Refugees,* 3(116).

21. US Department of State, Bureau of Intelligence and Research (November 1997). *International Trafficking in Women from Central Europe and the NIS.* Washington, DC.

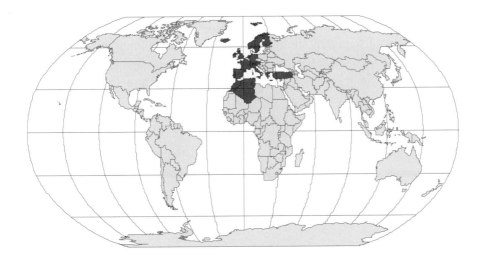

WESTERN EUROPE AND THE MEDITERRANEAN

INTRODUCTION

Western Europe remains an important centre of intra- and inter-regional migration. No single type of population movement, country, or even continent-of-origin dominates; a variety of economic, social, and political processes and events generates a range of population movements into and out of the region, back and forth across the Mediterranean, from central and eastern Europe, and from further afield in sub-Saharan Africa, Asia, Latin America, and the former Soviet Union.

Some 18 million non-nationals reside in the 15 member States of the EU, with a total population of approximately 375 million persons (Table 34). While much of this migration follows former colonial and other historical and cultural ties, it is also shaped by new and diversifying regional and global communication links that include expanding worldwide transport, business, information, and migrant trafficking networks. As a result, migration to and from the region—whether family reunification, skilled or unskilled, legal or unauthorized, temporary or

Sarah Collinson, Senior Policy and Research Coordinator, Action Aid, London, United Kingdom, contributed to this chapter.

permanent—is becoming increasingly cosmopolitan or "globalized", involving flows of migrants from every continent and almost every country. At the same time, a number of important immigration routes are becoming more entrenched, including those between North Africa and southern Europe; between the eastern Mediterranean as well as central and eastern Europe and Germany; and among the Baltic and Nordic States. Thus, the globalization of migration is taking place alongside a significant regionalization of flows.

TABLE 34.
NON-NATIONALS IN EUROPEAN UNION MEMBER STATES, 1997

Country	Total population	Non-nationals
Austria	7,795,800	517,700
Belgium	10,170,200	890,400
Denmark	5,037,400	237,600
Finland	5,132,300	73,000
France	56,652,000	3,596,600
Germany	82,012,200	7,314,000
Greece	10,486,600	161,100
Ireland	3,660,600	114,400
Italy	57,461,000	884,600
Luxembourg	418,300	142,900
Netherlands	15,567,100	679,900
Portugal	9,934,100	172,900
Spain	39,298,600	550,700
Sweden	8,844,500	526,600
United Kingdom	58,185,000	2,121,000
TOTAL	**370,655,700**	**17,983,400**

Source: Eurostat, *Demographic Statistics, 1999.*

Countries in western Europe differ considerably in terms of the size and profile of their migration flows and their resident migrant populations and in terms of the challenges posed by migration. The case of Germany stands out because of the sheer volume of migration it has experienced in recent years. Throughout the 1990s, Germany was Europe's most important country of migration, the annual registered in-migration of foreign nationals consistently exceeding inflows into the rest of western Europe combined. Recent migration into Italy, by contrast, is dominated by unauthorized arrivals of migrants (mainly young males) from Morocco, Albania, and other Mediterranean and African countries who are seeking work in Italy's flourishing informal economy. Fundamentally different again from these cases is migration into the United Kingdom. Here, the larger part of non-EU immigration is accounted for by family reunification and marriage migration (particularly from the Indian subcontinent) and the legal immigration of skilled and managerial workers and their families from the United States and other advanced industrial countries.

While numbers of migrants were significant throughout the decade of the 1990s, migration patterns ebbed and flowed (Table 35). The fall of the Berlin Wall and the subsequent outbreak of conflict in Bosnia and Herzegovina fuelled a sharp increase in net immigration in the EU as a whole at the end of the 1980s and early 1990s. In-migration reached an annual figure of between 1 and 1.5 million from 1989 to 1993 (compared to less than 200,000 in the mid-1980s). Despite large increases in immigration, the feared immigration crisis from Central and Eastern Europe and the former Soviet Union following the collapse of the Eastern bloc never happened.

TABLE 35.
NET MIGRATION INTO THE EUROPEAN UNION, 1990-1998

1990	1,008,251
1991	1,078,441
1992	1,350,132
1993	1,062,116
1994	782,855
1995	805,363
1996	734,596
1997	512,208
1998	378,687

Source: Eurostat, *Demographic Statistics, 1999.*

In most countries of western Europe, authorized immigration either levelled off or declined by the mid-1990s, mainly as governments introduced tighter immigration controls and more restrictive entry policies. By 1994, migration into the EU fell to less than 800,000, and continued to fall as large numbers of persons returned to the former Yugoslavia after the war in Bosnia and Herzegovina. By the end of the decade, however, western European States saw a modest upturn in legal immigration flows (11). Movement rose sharply in 1999 when nearly 1 million ethnic Albanians were driven out of Kosovo in Yugoslavia.

Much of the immigration to western Europe originates from Mediterranean countries. While other chapters in this report focus on the flows and characteristics of migrants from central and eastern Europe and from other parts of the world, this chapter highlights a few countries in the southern and eastern Mediterranean whose outbound flows are directed almost wholly to western Europe.

Public attention tends to focus on migration *into* western Europe from outside. This is partly because migration *within* western Europe itself remains at relatively low levels, despite the right of citizens of the member countries of the EU to move and take up jobs in other member States.

Recent efforts by EU States to develop a common migration policy have not come easily. States are reluctant to relinquish national control over immigration, especially over citizenship issues. Their main immigration concern is restricting the entry of groups from the developing world whose socio-economic and/or political integration they see as problematic. Nevertheless, in moves far ahead of other geographic regions, European States forged agreements to open "internal" borders among member States. And, while concerns about management of non-EU migration flows continue to dominate discussions of immigration within western Europe, the demographic realities of an ageing population—as well as the economic demands of a global marketplace—are of increasing importance.

IMMIGRATION TRENDS

In immigration terms, western European countries falls very roughly into two groups: north-western Europe and southern Europe. Countries in the former have been immigration host countries over several decades; the latter countries experienced emigration until they too recently became net immigration countries. Earlier distinctions in migration between the northern and southern groups of countries diminished over time.

LEGAL ADMISSIONS

Family reunification and marriage immigration, including families of migrants, comprises the largest share of authorized foreign (non-EU) migration. In France and Sweden, for example, it accounts for at least half of new admissions (11). Family migration is dominated by the nationalities of already-established immigrant communities in Europe, including Turkish and former Yugoslav nationals in Germany and Switzerland, migrants from the Maghreb in France (and, to a lesser extent, the Netherlands and Belgium), and Indian, Pakistani, and Bangladeshi nationals in the United Kingdom.

Labour migration intakes occupy smaller proportions of the total. On the one hand, temporary labour migration appears to be making a significant comeback, —although in the 1990s it is highly skilled and managerial workers and investing entrepreneurs who are of growing importance. On the other hand, permanent labour immigration appears to be declining. The profile of temporary economic migration is more mixed than that of family reunification. Most skilled workers move back and forth between European countries, North America, Japan, and other rich countries, but many skilled workers and managers also move from less developed and middle-income countries in Asia, Africa, and Latin America. Most immigrant workers entering the United Kingdom from sub-Saharan Africa, for example, are skilled workers. In France, meanwhile, approximately 18 per cent of non-western European citizens admitted for work are low-skilled. By contrast, 40 per cent of western European nationals are lower-skilled, largely Portuguese workers in construction and the service sector (12).

Migrants working in high-skilled positions in the labour market are usually recruited by companies before they move, and many make successive moves from one country to another within the structure (and with the assistance) of a single transnational company or international organization. Indeed, in the European (and worldwide) growing and highly dynamic transnational or globalizing high-skilled labour market, both companies and countries compete for the best human resources in such sectors such as high-tech industry, information technology, and financial services. Therefore, while tightening up on other types of immigration, some governments are making new efforts to encourage or facilitate the entry of people with skills and experience useful to the economy. In France, for example, labour market access and employment eligibility requirements were relaxed for highly skilled foreigners; in Switzerland, rules on the entry of family members and service providers were recently relaxed (12).

Meanwhile, various channels remain open for the legal migration of non-EU workers into *un*skilled jobs in various sectors of the labour markets of north-western Europe. Economic migration into Germany, Switzerland, France and other countries has included significant numbers of unskilled workers (usually on a temporary or seasonal basis) for work in agriculture, construction, services, and manufacturing. New migrants from the Maghreb and eastern Mediterranean countries are still very important for these sectors in north-western Europe. For example, as many Moroccans now migrate to Germany as to Spain. An increasing share of unskilled labour migration—particularly in Germany—originates in central and eastern Europe.

Germany recruits large numbers of temporary contract and guest-workers under bilateral quota agreements with some 13 countries in central, eastern, and south-eastern Europe. Quotas have been lowered over the last few years as a result of a downturn in the German economy, but in the late 1990s there were still more than 40 thousand contract workers registered in Germany, mostly from Poland (11). Although defined in terms of development cooperation and skill transfer between Germany and its neighbours, these recruitment agreements also benefit the German economy.

Seasonal workers are allowed to enter and work in a number of countries in the region (11), including Germany, Switzerland, and, in smaller numbers, France. In all three countries, the admission of seasonal workers is governed by national legislation as well as bilateral agreements with particular countries of origin that often put a cap on the numbers. Switzerland, for instance, has agreements with Italy, Spain, and Portugal; France has ones with Morocco, Poland, Senegal, and Tunisia. In 1997, more than 45,000 seasonal workers were permitted to enter Switzerland to work in a number of sectors, including hotels and catering. Germany recruits even larger numbers of seasonal workers—more than 226,000 in 1997—who are restricted to working in particular sectors, including agriculture and forestry, hotels and catering, and fruit and vegetable processing. Seasonal workers generally are not allowed to stay for more than six months; they cannot bring family members with them; and they are usually restricted to work in a single sector and geographical area, and/or with a single employer.

A uniquely German phenomenon is the admission of ethnic Germans from outside the country. Migration from central and eastern Europe and the CIS to Germany since 1989 has been dominated by the movement of ethnic Germans (*Aussiedler*) invoking their right to German citizenship. The numbers of *Aussiedler* migrating to Germany has declined progressively during the last few years (from nearly 220,000 in 1993 to fewer than 135,000 in 1997), largely as a result of new entry restrictions introduced by Germany in 1993. In recent years, more than 90 per cent of these movements have been from the former Soviet Union (11).

With the reduction in inflows and increase in emigration in the late 1990s, the net migration of foreigners into Germany declined substantially during the decade—from more than 500,000 in 1992 to around 150,000 in the space of two years. Nevertheless, in 1994, net foreign migration into Germany still counted for more than one-third of the total for the EU as a whole. In 1997, for the first time in more than a decade, the number of foreigners who left Germany (some 637,000) exceeded the number who arrived (around 615,000) (11).

Citizens of non-EU Mediterranean countries account for roughly 2 to 3 per cent of total populations in the main EU receiving States (Germany, Belgium, France, and the Netherlands) (7). The data recording methods exclude all immigrants and descendants of immigrants who have naturalized and/or opted for the nationality of their State of residence. The majority of registered non-EU citizens living in the EU (a total of more than 11 million) are in Germany (just over 5 million), France (2.25 million), the United Kingdom (more than 1 million), the Netherlands (more than 500,000), Italy (more than 500,000) and Belgium (nearly 400,000). Apart from migrants in the United Kingdom (where the majority of non-EU citizens are from the Asian subcontinent, North America, and Africa), the majority of non-EU nationals in western Europe come from non-EU Mediterranean countries, most notably Algeria, Morocco, Turkey, and the former Yugoslavia. In Germany, Turkish nationals form the largest contingent (nearly 2 million), followed by former Yugoslavs (more than 1 million). However, a large proportion of these communities are second- (or third-) generation descendants of immigrants, who are not strictly speaking migrants, but who have kept their parents' nationality because of Germany's relatively restrictive naturalization laws. In France, Algerians and Moroccans are the largest non-EU groups (each community numbering about 600,000).

The exclusion of EU nationals from the overall migration figures hides both France's and Germany's substantial minority populations originating from Mediterranean countries now within the EU. In France, the Portuguese community is the largest foreign minority by citizenship (650,000 in 1990), while Spaniards and Italians also contribute large numbers. Italians are the third largest group in Germany (more than 500,000), followed by roughly 350,000 Greeks.

Although Italy, Spain, Portugal, and Greece traditionally have sent migrants abroad, they are now important countries of immigration, particularly for migrants from non-EU Mediterranean countries. For example, the majority of Italy's million or so registered immigrants come from Morocco, the former Yugoslavia, and Albania. The Egyptian populations in Italy and Greece account for one-third of all Egyptians living in the EU. And Moroccans represent the largest single nationality group among registered immigrants in Spain (11).

Unlike migration to north-western Europe, these migration flows took on significant proportions only within the last decade. The combined registered Moroccan population of Spain and Italy, for example, increased more than 10 times from less than 10,000 in the mid-1980s to more than 150,000 in 1994 (14). As a result, migrant populations in southern Europe tend to be younger and less gender-balanced in their demographic profiles than those in the longer-standing immigration countries of north-western Europe. Moroccan communities in the Netherlands, France, and Germany in 1990, for example, reflected gender ratios of between 650 and 800 women per 1,000 men, whereas in Italy the ratio was only around 100 women per 1,000 men. The differences between migrants to southern and north-western Europe are not clear-cut, however. As migrant populations in southern Europe have become more established, for instance, so family-based immigration has started to become more important. The migration of highly skilled professionals and managers also has increased in southern Europe—just as it has elsewhere in western Europe during recent years.

ASYLUM SEEKERS

Another type of immigration includes asylum seekers and persons granted temporary protection. As with net migration in general, the number of asylum seekers has ebbed and flowed during the 1990s, from a high of more than 670,000 applicants in 1992 to a low of 226,000 in 1996 (Table 36). According to UNHCR, about 430,000 persons applied for asylum in Europe in 1999, significantly more than during the previous five years. Germany received the largest number (95,000)[1] followed by the United Kingdom (88,000), Switzerland (46,000), and the Netherlands (40,000). Residents of Kosovo constituted the largest number of asylum seekers.

TABLE 36.
ASYLUM SEEKERS IN THE EU, 1990-1999

1990	397,027
1991	511,184
1992	672,381
1993	516,710
1994	300,232
1995	263,655
1996	226,850
1997	240,483
1998	288,757
1999	430,000

Sources: Eurostat, *Demographic Statistics, 1999;* UNHCR (1999) statistics.

In addition to asylum seekers, Europe continues to see admission of persons granted temporary protection. Temporary protection—used extensively when Bosnians fled the conflict in the former Yugoslavia—has been invoked to deal with mass migration emergencies and to provide status to persons who do not qualify as refugees but who cannot return to their countries of origin because of unsafe conditions. In 1999, thousands of Kosovars, including those evacuated from The former Yugoslav Republic of Macedonia, received temporary protection. European countries differ in their approaches to temporary protection. For example, in some countries Bosnians given temporary protection were later granted asylum or another permanent status. Other countries, most notably Germany and Switzerland, mandated repatriation after the Dayton Peace Accords were signed.

UNAUTHORIZED MIGRATION

Unauthorized immigration is perceived as a particular problem throughout western Europe. Although push factors such as poverty and unemployment in the countries of origin often are perceived as the principal reason for such migration, equally, if not more, significant is the persistent demand for cheap, exploitable labour within many sectors—including agriculture, services, construction and manufacturing—of the economies of western Europe.

Information on unauthorized migration is, by its nature, very sketchy. Estimates placed the upper limit of unauthorized migrants in Europe at 3 million in 1998, as compared to just less than 2 million in 1991. Guesses as to the number of unauthorized migrants in France run as high as 500,000. In Germany, almost 40,000 foreign nationals were apprehended in 1998 after entering illegally, usually across the Polish or Czech border (11). Unauthorized migration into Germany—as throughout Europe—has diversified; unauthorized migrants arrive from the Mediterranean, eastern Europe (including Romania and Bulgaria), the former Soviet Union, Asia, and sub-Saharan Africa.

In Italy, the number of unauthorized migrants is estimated at nearly 235,000 (11). Thousands of unauthorized migrants enter the country along the Adriatic coasts or through Sicily. Many enter Italy with a view to travelling on into Switzerland, France, Germany, and other countries further north. As many as 150,000 unauthorized immigrants are believed to be residing in Spain, while 9,000 migrants reportedly were expelled from the country in the first half of 1998; a total of some 50,000 unauthorized entries were expected for 1998.

Moroccans figure as the largest nationality group among those apprehended in Italy and Spain, significantly outnumbering those arriving from Tunisia and Algeria. Other nationalities without authorization in Italy include nationals of Romania, Poland, and Brazil (11). Migrants from sub-Saharan Africa and Asia enter in smaller numbers, but from an increasing variety of different countries. While many of these migrants will probably try to stay in southern Europe, at least as many again would be expected to try to migrate on to other countries in western Europe, including France and Germany.

One response to unauthorized migration has been regularization programmes. During the 1990s, Spain, Italy, Portugal, Greece, and France all enacted amnesty programmes for unauthorized migrants. In addition, quotas are in force or planned for migrant workers entering a number of countries, including Germany, Italy, Switzerland, and Spain (where, in practice, quotas provide a mechanism for legalizing the status of those already in the country). These policies attempt to bring otherwise unauthorized flows, if not under government control, then at least into the official statistics.

Policy-makers increasingly are focusing on the problem of migrant smuggling and trafficking. As governments in the region introduced new visa and other policy restrictions on the legal entry of foreigners and tightened up immigration controls at airports and border crossings, so organized traffickers managed to expand their control over unauthorized border crossing. With official controls so much stricter in western Europe than in the past, it is increasingly difficult for unauthorized migrants to reach the region without the assistance of traffickers. Ironically, therefore, stricter immigration controls in western Europe appear to play into the hands of organized crime networks. During the first half of 1998, for instance, more than one-half of the 5,000 or so unauthorized migrants from the former Yugoslavia apprehended in Germany were reported to have used traffickers.

The use of smugglers and traffickers has a number of implications, the most tragic of which is the human consequences for many of the migrants involved. Many trafficked migrants find themselves forced into prostitution and/or effective slavery to pay off their debt to the traffickers or otherwise dependent on jobs where they suffer severe exploitation and abominable working conditions. Newspapers report people drowning in the Straits of Gibraltar as traffickers try to bring them across from Morocco to Spain in small boats or *pateras*, immigrants being abandoned in unseaworthy ships before reaching the coast of Italy, or others being found suffocated or dead from hypothermia as a result of traffickers using cargo containers to bring them in across land borders.

While smugglers and traffickers strengthened their control over unauthorized border crossing, governments introduced a range of policies during the last decade or so designed to restrict asylum seekers' access to western Europe. As a result, asylum seekers attempting to reach western Europe often have little choice but to turn to traffickers; and thus, arrivals of asylum seekers fleeing conflict and human rights abuse increasingly intermix with the entry of unauthorized economic migrants. As a result, large numbers of ethnic Albanians from Kosovo, Kurds from Iraq, and Roma from eastern Europe—among other asylum seekers—are labelled and treated as unauthorized immigrants, or (a relatively new term) illegal refugees.

Like the more general migration flow, organized trafficking networks appear increasingly globalized, extending to countries all over the world and thus contributing to the recently witnessed diverse immigration flows into Europe. Spanish authorities, for instance, identified trafficking networks linking Mali, Senegal, and other sub-Saharan countries with Spain via Morocco (4). It is not unusual for single groups of unauthorized migrants—both refugees and economic migrants—arriving in Germany and other destination countries in western Europe to include a whole variety of nationalities from different countries and different continents,

FACTORS INFLUENCING MIGRATION PATTERNS

Why migrants go to Europe has as much to do with history as with current market forces. The countries in Europe that are most prominent in terms of the volume and diversity of their immigration (most notably Germany, France, the United Kingdom, the Netherlands, Belgium, and Switzerland) generally are the same countries that recruited large numbers of migrant workers from abroad from the 1950s through the early 1970s. These countries already have significant and established "foreign" or immigrant minority communities of at least 30 years' standing, originating mainly from non-EU Mediterranean labour-sending countries (Turkey, the former Yugoslavia, and countries in North Africa) and from former colonies.

Reflecting the pull of these large immigrant minority communities, migration into Europe today includes relatively high levels of family reunion and marriage immigration from the countries of origin that dominated labour immigration during the 1960s and 1970s. This immigration is complemented—and often substantially balanced—by sustained levels of movement back to the countries of origin for both short visits and more permanent return migration. At the same time, improved international communications and increased mobility and contacts means more and more people are migrating to Europe as foreign spouses and foreign-born children of native-born residents.

With structural unemployment having largely supplanted labour shortages as the key labour market challenge in north-western Europe, former recruitment countries now greatly restrict the permanent entry of foreign workers. Thus, family immigration involving minority and majority populations is now the most important channel for permanent immigration into this part of Europe. Governments attempted to reduce further permanent immigration by introducing new restrictions on family immigration. The reductions in permanent labour immigration reflect, in part, governments' preference for temporary migration that carries minimum social costs in terms, for example, of possible future family immigration or future demands on the welfare state.

The impulse to introduce significant restrictions on family reunification is held in check, however, by international and regional human rights norms that protect the right to family life. In addition, a more general concern in these countries with protecting civil liberties, upholding social justice, and securing the successful integration of immigrant minority groups fosters a more generous approach to family reunification. For example, the United Kingdom recently relaxed the administrative rules governing marriage immigration because of concern for the dignity and rights of the individuals affected.

The profile of immigration suggests that changing labour markets and the new demands of the international economy—not just government policy—are key factors in the migration shift. Albeit on a far smaller scale, this new migration is no less responsive to economic demand in Europe than were the major labour recruitment inflows of earlier decades. Further, recent years witnessed a progressive and substantial "privatization" of migration flows in western Europe. Within the EU, the suppression of internal border controls means that migration patterns are almost entirely determined by individual, private, and company decisions and by economic factors. The scope and pattern of authorized labour migration from outside the EU—increasingly dominated by highly skilled, technical and managerial workers—is determined more and more by the investment and human resource decisions of private companies. Meanwhile, a variety of traffickers and other private agents allow an increasing number of migrants to enter without authorization, bypassing government controls.

Demographic trends also influence responses to migration. While population growth is still positive in the EU countries, the current level is one-third of that recorded 40 years ago (5). Fertility rates have declined so greatly in a number of countries—Italy, Sweden, and Greece, for example—that loss of population would be expected in the absence of immigration (5).

EUROPEAN UNION HARMONIZATION

Efforts by the EU to create a border-free internal market have meant greater cooperation among member States in the area of internal and external border controls. This cooperation has, in turn, created pressure for closer cooperation in all other areas of migration policy. Since the late 1980s, member governments have been involved in a complex process of harmonizing their policies in a number of areas, including admission policies, control of unauthorized migration, labour migration, and the status and rights of resident non-EU nationals. International cooperation to manage international migration flows and to address emigration dynamics in some countries of origin is also on the agenda.

This harmonization process has proved extremely cumbersome and difficult. Not only do national policies differ considerably across the region, but governments are very reluctant to relinquish their control to the EU institutions and the normal processes of regional policy-making. In a number of areas, it is not only the particular procedures that vary, but also the capacity to implement or effect particular policy goals and/or the more fundamental or substantive bases and aims of policy. In these respects harmonization—or even a less ambitious "alignment" of policies—has proved most problematic.

These difficulties primarily reflect countries' differing migration challenges—for example, the relative importance of unauthorized migration. But in other areas, such as the status and integration of third-country nationals, the lack of consensus reflects deeper differences in national political and cultural histories that shape and define concepts of membership and identity in European societies. In still other areas, such as the control of economic immigration and the employment of immigrants, the different concerns and orientation of the different governments reflect important variations in their economies and labour market structures.

Despite more than 10 years of effort, it is still not possible to talk of a common *European* migration policy. What has been achieved is a relatively complex mosaic of cooperative arrangements between countries within and outside the EU. The greatest policy integration has taken place in those areas connected most directly with the completion of the internal market. Progress by the members of the "Schengen Group" (Austria, Belgium, France, Germany, Greece, Italy,

Luxembourg, the Netherlands, Portugal, Spain, and new EU member countries Sweden and Finland) includes the suppression of internal border controls, strengthening of external border controls, harmonization of visa arrangements, and free movement of citizens.

At the institutional level, there are a number of spheres of cooperation. These include an inner and outer core of Schengen States (defined by whether or not these countries are able or are perceived to control their external borders to the satisfaction of the other member States); an associated group of countries remaining outside the EU but associated with the Schengen grouping (Norway and Iceland); EU member States remaining outside the Schengen group (the United Kingdom, Ireland, and Denmark); future EU member States "in transition"; and cooperating third countries in eastern Europe and non-EU Mediterranean countries that, for the time being at least, are set to remain outside the EU.

Perhaps partly for this reason, and despite their many differences, governments in the region share a clear, overarching concern with security and control, as reflected in a January 1998 Action Plan agreed upon by the EU foreign ministers aimed at curbing the arrival of Turkish and Iraqi Kurds. Of the 46 points that could be agreed upon by ministers, no less than 20 were listed under the heading of combating unauthorized immigration. The concentration on unauthorized migration is illustrative of the focus of EU policy-makers, as are the number of items under other headings: tackling the involvement of organized crime, four items; preventing abuse of asylum procedures, six; effective application of asylum procedures, six; and improved analysis of the causes and origins of the influx, only one.

More recently, the 1999 summit meeting of European leaders in Tampere, Finland reflected a broader view of the migration challenges facing the EU. The summit addressed a wide range of migration issues, concluding that the European Union must:

> . . . develop common policies on asylum and immigration, while taking into account the need for a consistent control of external borders to stop illegal immigration and to combat those who organize it and commit related international crimes. These common policies must be based on principles which

are both clear to our own citizens and also offer guarantees to those who seek protection in or access to the European Union.

The Tampere summit called for further harmonization of policies as well as improved management of migration flows. The European leaders also reiterated the need for their countries to work more effectively with source countries of immigration to reduce emigration pressures while, at the same time, attending to the integration of legal immigrants into European society. Difficulties in achieving full control over migration flows forced a *de facto* shift in policies away from the straightforward goal of restricting entries towards more pragmatic migration *management* policies.

INTEGRATION OF IMMIGRANTS

Throughout western Europe, governments are pursuing a dual policy of trying to restrict immigration while at the same time promoting the economic and social integration of immigrants and their descendants. It is not all immigration that is viewed as problematic; rather, immigration from developing countries causes the most concern. Few people in the United Kingdom, for example, would be aware that net immigration from the USA and Australia is at more or less the same level as immigration from Africa and approximately five times that from central and eastern Europe; nor would they usually think of the large Irish population in the United Kingdom as one of the country's main immigrant groups (representing, by nationality, its largest single immigrant group). Yet, even in countries in which EU nationals account for about 50 per cent or more of the resident foreign population—Belgium (48 per cent), Ireland (72 per cent) and Luxembourg (78 per cent)—political concerns focus almost entirely on immigration from less developed and less stable countries outside western Europe. Although less explosive politically than during the early 1990s, immigration remains a sensitive political and social issue throughout the region, as illustrated by its prominence in election campaigns in Austria, France, Germany, and the Netherlands.

Most migrant groups suffer a degree of social and economic marginalization in western Europe, as illustrated by employment figures that consistently report high levels of unemployment. In the Netherlands, for instance, a foreign member of the labour force is three times more likely to be unemployed than a national. The situation is also critical in Denmark, Sweden, and Belgium (12). In most countries, foreign women are particularly susceptible to unemployment.

Moreover, immigrants and their descendants who are working tend to be overrepresented in the lower paid, less skilled, and less secure sectors of the labour market, such as unskilled manufacturing work, including employment in declining industries (e.g., textiles), hotels and catering, and agriculture. Levels of achievement in education vary considerably from group to group (with some, such as the Indian ethnic minority in the United Kingdom, doing better in education than the majority population). Nevertheless, many immigrant groups are overrepresented in the slowest tracks of the education system and underrepresented in secondary and tertiary education.

In southern Europe—particularly in Italy, Spain, and Greece—labour migration far outweighs family immigration and is dominated by the arrival of young workers from southern and eastern Mediterranean countries (particularly from North Africa), and, to a lesser extent, from a variety of countries in sub-Saharan Africa, Asia, and Latin America. These people move to seek out unskilled jobs in particular areas of the informal economy where there is significant demand for cheap—and often temporary or seasonal—labour, typically in agriculture, services, construction, or manufacturing. The majority initially enter, reside and/or work without documentation, and many suffer severe exploitation, poor working conditions, and high levels of insecurity as a result of their vulnerability. However, successive regularization programmes have allowed large numbers of migrants to obtain legal status. These programmes, in turn, have accorded migrants important socio-economic and political rights and have brought them into the official migration statistics.

Since the mid-1980s, there has been a growing recognition among governments, as well as nongovernmental organizations, that more needs to be done to strengthen and improve immigrant minorities' social and economic rights and opportunities. An issue that attracts particular attention is the integration of so-called second- and third-generation immigrants, as it is common for immigrants' marginal position in housing, employment, and public life to be perpetuated among their children.

Approaches to immigrants' socio-economic integration vary considerably, but most aim at either helping immigrants compete better with the majority population (particularly through education and training policies) or at removing obstacles to immigrants' integration (for example, through housing and employment schemes, and, increasingly, through anti-discrimination policies). Many countries have made some progress in advancing immigrants' political integration by extending the right to vote in local and/or, less commonly, national elections.

Immigrant minorities suffered over the last decade from an upsurge in racism and xenophobia across the continent, resulting, at least in part, from the rapid economic and political changes that took place after the fall of the Berlin Wall and from the insecurity and uncertainty resulting from economic recession and accelerating globalization. In many countries, reaction to these events translated into increased levels of support for extreme anti-immigrant political parties (e.g., France, Austria, Belgium, Italy, and Germany) and in many cases spilled over into overt racial violence and harassment. It should not be forgotten, however, that European societies also have powerful anti-racist impulses with deep roots in European liberal traditions, illustrated by such movements as the Anti-Nazi League in the United Kingdom and *SOS Racisme* in France. This impulse is in constant tension with nationalistic, xenophobic, and exclusionist tendencies in western European societies.

Naturalization of immigrants and citizenship for their children born in host countries galvanized attention in western Europe, particularly Germany. In 1999, the German Government adopted new legislation that facilitates naturalization and provides citizenship based on birth in Germany (*jus solis*) to certain children born of immigrant parents. Adult foreigners now qualify for naturalization after eight—instead of 15—years of legal residence. Children born in Germany to foreign parents, at least one of whom was born in Germany or settled there before the age of 14 years, automatically qualify for citizenship. Dual citizenship is permitted until the age of 23, when a dual national must decide which citizenship to adopt. One reason for the change was to enhance opportunities for the integration of long-term residents (11).

Naturalization rates vary greatly from one European country to another. The Netherlands and Scandinavian countries tend to have higher rates of naturalization

(4.5 to 6 per cent of the total foreign population each year for the Netherlands, Sweden, and Norway), southern European countries lower rates of naturalization (less than 1 percent for Italy). This variation reflects, in part, differences in the length of residence and legal status of the resident immigrant population.

EMIGRATION TRENDS

Despite the diversification in international migration flows during the last 10 years or so, only certain countries in the southern and eastern Mediterranean have strong migration links with western Europe. Migration patterns in the Mediterranean were heavily influenced by economic and former colonial and other political ties between particular countries on each side of the Mediterranean.

MAHGREB

Morocco, Algeria, and to a lesser extent Tunisia and Egypt, dominate flows from the southern Mediterranean. Migration from this region has long been comprised of economic and family migration flows, particularly from Morocco and Algeria. The labour recruitment tradition in the Mediterranean can be traced to the First World War, when France brought workers from its colonies in North Africa to help cover its domestic labour needs. At the time of Algerian independence from France in 1962, some 350,000 Algerians were registered in France. Modern labour recruitment of migrants from the Maghreb began in the 1960s and continued until the petroleum crisis in the early 1970s (13). Germany, France, Belgium, and the Netherlands signed bilateral agreements for workers during this period of economic boom in western Europe. Migration did not stop with the end of official recruitment, however.

In 1975, some 388,000 Moroccans—mostly unskilled men—were registered in Europe. By 1992, this figure tripled to 1.3 million, only 60 per cent of whom were male and an increasing number of whom were skilled labourers. Family reunion was significant in the intervening years, with the result that only one in four Moroccan immigrants was actually on the European labour market by 1992 (13).

France remains the principal destination in western Europe for migrants from the Maghreb. Algerian migration in particular is still directed to France almost exclusively, although a minority of individuals migrates to Belgium. By 1994, there were an estimated 620,000 Algerians in France. These figures hardly capture the increase in migration, however, because they do not include the sizeable number of Algerian-born individuals who naturalized in France and, thus, are not captured in data on foreigners. Moroccan migration, now the most important flow of migrants from North Africa, is directed not only to France and the other former recruitment countries in north-western Europe, but increasingly to Spain and Italy.

Today, strong emigration pressures continue in both Morocco and Algeria, given the lack of opportunities due to persistent economic crises in North Africa, on the one side, and the attraction of large numbers of compatriots settled in Europe, on the other. Compared to their sub-Saharan neighbours, both Morocco and Algeria are experiencing declining fertility levels that reduce demographic pressures to migrate. Still, the migration tradition is now entrenched. From a localized phenomenon in rural Morocco, for example, migration now originates throughout the country and involves increasingly more urban and educated migrants.

The character of emigration from Algeria changed recently as a result of civil war. More people trying to leave Algeria are seeking asylum in Europe and elsewhere; meanwhile, overall emigration from Algeria is constrained by visa restrictions in France and other countries designed to reduce the number of arriving asylum seekers. Whereas Algerians previously migrated almost exclusively to France and Belgium, many have recently headed for Germany in the hope of finding asylum there. Migration patterns between North African States also changed as a consequence of border closures and refugee flight caused by the war. Today, migration across the Mediterranean includes significant numbers of people from sub-Saharan Africa, reflecting, among other things, the emergence of interregional asylum flows as an enduring feature of migration to western Europe.

The discrepancies remain great between the profiles of foreign labour migrants and European workers, despite relatively more educated and skilled migrants in recent flows. Concern with the build-up of migration pressures in non-EU Mediterranean countries led the EU to attempt to stem migration at its source. Levels of official development aid to countries in the southern and eastern Mediterranean increased as part of the EU's "Mediterranean Policy" during the past two decades. The policy aimed to provide economic and social transfers to the countries of origin, but met with limited success. Only Morocco received significant transfers for investment and development, while private direct investment in Africa is negative (13).

Ongoing concern for the rights and working conditions of migrants was addressed in a series of agreements with the Maghreb governments. Agreements concluded in 1995 between the EU and Morocco and Tunisia, respectively, (and still under negotiation with Algeria) reiterate these concerns and place priority on the reintegration of unauthorized migrants who are returned to their home countries (12). Throughout the last decade, migration figured as a prominent political issue in the region, largely because of the mutual sensitivity of societies on both sides to a variety of cultural, social, and political concerns that arise with migration. Among key concerns are the place of Islam in western European societies and the perceived closure of western European societies to people from the southern and eastern Mediterranean as reflected in restrictive visa policies.

As in the past, migration continues to have a profound impact on political, social, and economic relations between countries on all sides of the Mediterranean. For both host countries and countries of origin, migration remains an important economic resource. For southern Europe, largely unskilled immigrant labour ensures the continued profitability of a number of sectors and companies that would otherwise not be competitive. For the countries of origin in North Africa, remittances sent back by migrants living in western Europe remain a crucial source of foreign currency. Indeed, in Morocco, remittances represented as much as one-quarter of foreign exchange receipts in recent years (about US$ 2 billion in 1997), above the country's earnings from phosphate exports and from tourism, and consistently above inflows of foreign direct investment (1, 15). While Algeria reports much lower remittance levels on average, it is believed that much of workers' returns are channelled informally and often as goods and services that the data cannot fully capture (13).

TURKEY AND THE EASTERN MEDITERRANEAN

Turkish migrant communities are still the most numerous in Europe, although current flows are much diminished; Germany remains their top destination in western Europe. However, in the 1990s, most Turkish migrants headed in larger numbers to Russia and the newly independent States, followed distantly by Saudi Arabia and Israel before Germany. Official labour migration programmes dropped from roughly 60,000 in the early 1990s to approximately 40,000, owing to a reduction in demand in the Middle East especially. Approximately 5 per cent of Turkey's population is estimated to live abroad, however, and this number continues to increase (12).

Few migrants are believed to return to Turkey after their contracts, for a number of reasons: changes in policy permit family accompaniment; migrant children who have been educated in and speak the language of the host country do not want to return; access to health services is not available to migrants at home; and scant prospects for employment upon return further impede repatriation. This is not to imply that integration in the host society is easy. Turkish unemployment among foreign workers in the EU is high, given the discriminatory environment they face in many European countries, the advancing age and ill health of workers who came early into the programme, and their relative lack of education and skills.

While naturalization has not always been an option for foreigners in Europe, naturalizations among Turks in Germany increased after Germany eased some requirements. A 1993 law in Turkey that permitted individuals to retain property rights even if they renounced their Turkish citizenship (required for German citizenship) lifted further stumbling blocks to German citizenship. Only 36,000 Turks naturalized between 1981 and 1993; in 1995, after the law change, some 42,000 Turks did so in one year.

INTERREGIONAL COOPERATION

The emphasis on migration control and restriction in western Europe has a powerful effect on the migration policies of neighbouring countries in central and eastern Europe and the Mediterranean and on the nature of broader cooperative relations between these countries and the EU. Thus, countries of origin and transit are viewed by western European States not only as sources of unwanted immigration, but also as important partners in migration control, i.e., as migration buffer States. Capacity-building and technical assistance are seen as important mechanisms for achieving greater cooperation. Source and transit governments also entered into numerous bilateral readmission agreements under which they undertook to accept apprehended, unauthorized migrants who travelled through or originated in their country. In practice, the difficulty in proving the transit route and true nationality of unauthorized migrants, governments' reluctance to accept back large numbers of migrants, and the costs involved in physically returning migrants, make the implementation of these agreements difficult. But, at the very least, they are effective in exerting political pressure on neighbouring countries to strengthen their migration controls (3).

The incentive to cooperate is greatest among those countries, particularly in central Europe, that are experiencing higher levels of immigration than they would like and/or that have a prospect of becoming members of the EU in the foreseeable future (e.g., Poland and the Czech Republic). No country can now join the EU without being able to sign up fully to and apply the EU's border control and related policies. For other countries with little prospect of joining the EU—and particularly those, such as Morocco and Tunisia, that benefit economically from continuing presence of their citizens in western Europe—the incentive to cooperate stems from a more general concern not to jeopardize their commercial, financial, and political standing with the EU.

In June 1998, migration ministers from more than 30 countries met in Budapest for a special meeting on unauthorized migration through south-eastern Europe. At that time, ministers agreed to pursue a number of measures described as being "of particular urgency to prevent illegal immigration" and which placed greater pressure on countries surrounding western Europe to impose stricter controls at their borders. In September 1998, the EU's Schengen members announced a plan to tighten border controls, fingerprint all unauthorized foreigners detained, and increase penalties on employers who hire unauthorized migrants. Also in the last quarter of 1998, the EU launched Operation Odysseus to combat unauthorized immigration and, among other things, to finance a number of new control initiatives both within and outside the EU, support training, and promote police cooperation throughout the EU.

Politicians in Italy, Spain, and Germany recently advocated that the granting of official development aid be made conditional upon recipient governments' cooperation in the area of migration control. This requirement reflects the degree to which the entire landscape of economic and political relations between western Europe and countries of origin and transit in central and eastern Europe and the Mediterranean is affected by migration (4).

The increase in the proportion of EU development assistance going to recipient countries in Europe, the Maghreb, and the Middle East in recent years—from 14 per cent of total EU aid in 1986-1987 to 30 per cent in 1996-1997 (10)—is at least in part attributable to concerns about addressing the root causes of migration in these countries. A substantial increase in EU aid to non-EU Mediterranean countries announced in December 1995 was deemed necessary to accelerate sustainable economic and social development in the region and thereby prevent a build-up of migration pressures. It is clear, however, that the aid levels agreed upon— Ecu 4.7 billion for the period 1995-1999—were a result of political compromise rather than rigorous needs analysis. It is highly doubtful, in any case, that this aid will have any real impact on migration trends in the region (4).

Numerous interregional discussions and negotiations touching on migration over the last 10 years reveal the limits to effective cooperation on this issue between the EU and non-member countries in the southern Mediterranean. Despite overall agreement that closer cooperation should be fostered, it has not been at all clear, once representatives of the various countries involved gathered around a single table, how this cooperation should proceed. The North African governments' demands in the early 1990s for a charter on migrants' rights, for example, were not taken up, reflecting not only the sensitivity of this issue on the European side, but also the weak bargaining position and questionable strength of purpose of the Maghreb governments in this area. The lack of interest in Tunisia's 1993 proposals for foreign debt to be recycled into productive investment and thus into job creation to reduce migration pressures similarly reflected the limited leverage enjoyed by the Maghreb governments in their efforts to steer the agenda (4).

CONCLUSION

Despite governments' efforts to reduce and restrict levels of international migration in western Europe, the region remains an important and dynamic centre of international migration, involving a diversifying range of migration flows from all over the world and in every economic and social sector. Migration is increasingly privatized; whether documented or unauthorized, its scope and development are determined increasingly by private individuals, companies, and other actors whose decisions and activities are largely independent of government preferences. The continuation of international migration both reflects and contributes to the intensification of international and global communication networks that connect European societies with the rest of the world and suggests that it will remain an enduring and, in most respects, enriching aspect of social, political, and economic life in the region for a long time to come.

ENDNOTE

[1.] The German pattern differed from other European countries in that this number represented a 6 per cent decline over previous levels.

REFERENCES

1. Basfao, K. and H. Taarji (Eds.) (1994). *L'Annuaire de l'Emigration: Maroc*. Fondation Hassan II, Rabat.

2. Collinson, S. (1994). *Europe and International Migration*, 2nd rev. ed. Pinter Publishers for the Royal Institute of International Affairs, London.

3. Collinson, S. (1996). Visa requirements, carrier sanctions, "safe third countries" and "readmission": the development of an asylum "buffer zone" in Europe. *Transactions* (Journal of the Institute of British Geographers), New Series, 21(1).

4. Collinson, S. (1996). *Shore to Shore. The Politics of Migration in Euro-Maghreb Relations*. Royal Institute of International Affairs, London.

5. Eurostat (1999). *Demographic Statistics: Data 1960-99*. Office for Official Publications of the European Communities, Luxembourg.

6. Eurostat (1997). *Migration Statistics 1996*. Office for Official Publications of the European Communities, Luxembourg.

7. Eurostat (1998). *Migration Between the Mediterranean Basin and the EU in 1995, Statistics in Focus: Population and social conditions 1998 (3).* Office for Official Publications of the European Communities, Luxembourg.

8. *Migration News Sheet. Monthly Bulletin on Immigrants, Refugees and Ethnic Minorities,* various issues. Migration Policy Group, Brussels.

9. Morrison, J. (1998). *The Cost of Survival: The Trafficking of Refugees to the UK.* The Refugee Council, London.

10. OECD (1999). *Development Co-operation. Efforts and Policies of the Members of the Development Assistance Committee,* 1999 Edition. Paris.

11. OECD (1998). *Trends in International Migration. SOPEMI Annual Report,* 1998 Edition. Paris.

12. OECD (1999). *Trends in International Migration. SOPEMI Annual Report,* 1999 Edition. Paris.

13. Safir, N. (1999). Emigration dynamics in Maghreb. In R. Appleyard (Ed.), *Emigration Dynamics in Deveoping Countries,* vol. 4. Ashgate, for IOM/UNFPA, Aldershot, England.

14. Schoorl, J.J., B.J. de Bruijn, E.J. Kuiper and L. Heering (1997). Migration from African and eastern Mediterranean countries to western Europe. In *Mediterranean Conference on Population, Migration and Development. Proceedings* (Palma de Mallorca, 15-17 October 1996), Council of Europe, CE (835), December 1997, pp.123-211.

15. Tapinos, G. (1997). Development cooperation and international migration: the European Union and the Maghreb. In *Mediterranean Conference on Population, Migration and Development. Proceedings* (Palma de Mallorca, 15-17 October 1996), Council of Europe, CE (835), December 1997, pp.123-211.

16. Transatlantic Learning Community (2000). *Migration in the New Millenium.* Bertelsmann Foundation, Gütersloh, Germany.

SOUTH AMERICA

INTRODUCTION

In the past two decades, international migration in South America has been profoundly transformed as a result of changes in economic, social, and political conditions. Historically an immigration region, all of the countries of South America were affected. European immigration was especially important in the nineteenth and early twentieth centuries. Following the course of both economic development and political conditions, the nature of recent migration trends changed in quantitative, directional, and qualitative ways: the extracontinental immigration of earlier days gave way to predominantly intraregional movements and outflows to the United States.

Labour flows—closely related to comparative advantages in national labour markets—dominate the migration scenario in South America. For many decades, migration push and pull were governed by the balance between the search for better working conditions and the growing needs of more developed countries in

Lelio Marmora, IOM's Regional Representative for the Southern Cone and Director of the Master's Degree Programme on International Migration Policies jointly sponsored by the University of Buenos Aires and IOM in Buenos Aires, Argentina, contributed to this chapter.

the region for workers at all skill levels. Progress in communication and transportation, combined with the deterioration of middle-class living conditions, facilitated the establishment of ongoing out-migration to neighbouring—and even distant—countries. Migration helped alleviate economic strains and contributed to development of the country of origin while aiding individuals and families to find solutions to personal crises.

To explain the dynamic relationship among countries in the region, this analysis is divided into two large blocks of countries:

- The Southern Cone—Argentina, Bolivia, Chile, Paraguay, Uruguay, and, for the purposes of this analysis, Brazil, from which migrants travel to Uruguay and Paraguay;

- The Andean region—Colombia, Ecuador, Peru and Venezuela.

This chapter discusses movements within and between the two blocks as well as migration flows to the United States from both.

THE SOUTHERN CONE

The countries in the Southern Cone differ by levels of development: Argentina, Brazil, Chile, and Uruguay have higher relative development, industrialization, urbanization, and lower population growth rates; Bolivia and Paraguay in comparison are among the poorest countries in South America and have higher population growth rates.

Although one might expect migration flows from the latter two countries to the more developed countries, the migration story is more complex. All of these countries have vast depopulated areas and low population densities. Approximately 1.3 million migrants were residing outside their country of origin in the early 1990s, up from 1 million in 1980 (Tables 37 and 38). Within the Southern Cone, Argentina presents the strongest pull factors, attracting migrants from all of the other countries in the region.

TABLE 37.

MIGRATORY MOVEMENTS IN THE SOUTHERN CONE IN THE 1980s

| PLACE OF BIRTH | PLACE OF RESIDENCE | | | | | | |
	Argentina	Bolivia	Brazil	Chile	Paraguay	Uruguay	TOTAL
Argentina		14,669	26,633	19,733	43,670	19,669	**124,374**
Bolivia	115,616		12,980	6,298	500	211	**135,605**
Brazil	42,134	8,492		2,076	98,730	12,334	**163,766**
Chile	207,176	7,508	17,830		1,530	1,440	**235,514**
Paraguay	259,449	978	17,560	284		1,422	**279,693**
Uruguay	109,724	193	21,238	989	2,310		**134,454**
TOTAL	**734,099**	**31,840**	**96,380**	**29,380**	**146,770**	**35,076**	**1,073,406**

Sources: Data from national censuses of the 1980s.

TABLE 38.

MIGRATORY MOVEMENTS IN THE SOUTHERN CONE IN THE 1990s

| PLACE OF BIRTH | PLACE OF RESIDENCE | | | | | | |
	Argentina	Bolivia	Brazil	Chile	Paraguay	Uruguay	TOTAL
Argentina		14,669	54,600	34,415	49,166	19,669	**172,519**
Bolivia	146,460		49,140	7,729	600	211	**204,140**
Brazil	34,850	8,492		4,610	108,526	12,334	**168,812**
Chile	247,673	7,508	42,230		2,398	1,440	**301,249**
Paraguay	253,522	978	33,000	683		1,422	**289,605**
Uruguay	135,858	193	25,000	989	3,210		**165,250**
TOTAL	**818,363**	**31,840**	**203,970**	**48,426**	**163,900**	**35,076**	**1,301,575**

Source: Partial updating of census data in Table 1, prepared by J. Gurrieri for the
IOM/OAS/Argentine Government Inter-American Course on International Migration,
Mar del Plata, Argentina, on the basis of national censuses of Argentina, 1991;
Brazil, 1991; Chile, 1992; and Paraguay, 1991.

Argentina also led the way in extraregional migration, with the highest number of citizens residing in the USA (as measured in 1980 and 1990). In 1990, the percentage of Argentines in the total flow had declined somewhat and given way to a growing presence of Bolivian and Brazilian nationals; the percentage of Chileans, Paraguayans, and Uruguayans in the north-bound flow remained stable.

IMMIGRATION TRENDS

Argentina played a dominant migration role in the Southern Cone. As a relatively more developed nation with an educated and highly urban population concentrated in a single metropolis, historically it saw the need to expand and diversify its population and labour sources. Traditionally, Argentina was a receiving country. Large immigration flows, mostly from Europe, continued from the nineteenth to early twentieth centuries and again after the Second World War. In the 1970s, geography and proximity played a large role in labour migration and in political migration from Uruguay, Paraguay, and Brazil. In recent decades, however, bordering countries provided the primary source of migrants. Of a total of 35 million people in Argentina (according to the 1991 census) the foreign-born sector comprised 2 million, approximately 50 per cent of whom were Latin American nationals.

The most recent census reveals that more than 80 per cent of intraregional migrants from the Southern Cone settle in Argentina. The number of immigrants from bordering countries grew from 571,000 in 1970 to 753,000 in 1980 and 818,000 in 1991. Between 1980 and 1990, migration increased from Bolivia, Chile, and Uruguay, and slightly decreased from Brazil and Paraguay. In the 1990s, border immigrants who settled in Argentina were Paraguayans (31 per cent), Chileans (30 per cent), Bolivians (18 per cent), Uruguayans (17 per cent), and Brazilians (4 per cent). Conversely, Argentine nationals make up some 10 per cent of the migrants living in its neighbouring countries.

Currently, flows are basically legal movements resulting from a series of bilateral accords among countries in the region in the 1960s. A relatively small proportion of individuals is in unauthorized status, mostly temporary migrants in border areas. Very precarious estimates of their number vary between 3 and 5 per cent of all immigrants.

Migration from the Andean region to the Southern Cone, a relatively uncommon practice, appears to be rising (Table 39). In 1993, following significant structural changes in Peru, immigrants from that country flooded Argentina. In only three months, an estimated 12 thousand Peruvians, whose socio-economic characteristics were generally of a higher level than other Southern Cone migrants, arrived and established a new urban-urban migration pattern (34). The flow persists, although at a slower rate. No exact information on their number is available (35).

TABLE 39.

POPULATION BORN IN THE SOUTHERN CONE COUNTRIES BY COUNTRY OF RESIDENCE IN THE ANDEAN REGION

PLACE OF BIRTH	PLACE OF RESIDENCE				
	Colombia	Ecuador	Peru	Venezuela	TOTAL
Argentina	27,854	121	5,025	9,070	**42,070**
Bolivia	390	240	3,210	1,936	**5,776**
Brazil	3,221	662	2,926	5,359	**8,285**
Chile	1,496	4,769	5,976	20,820	**33,061**
Paraguay	137	90	194	494	**915**
Uruguay	316	406	399	5,454	**6,575**
TOTAL	33,414	6,288	17,730	43,133	100,565

Sources: **Chilean immigrants in Colombia, Ecuador. and Venezuela:** data analysed by The United Nations Economic Commission for Latin America (ECLAC) on the basis of national censuses (1990).
Southern Cone immigrants in Peru: ECLAC 1981, quoted by Altamirano, T. in *Migración: el fenómeno del siglo*. Catholic Pontiff University of Peru, Fondo Editorial, 1996, Lima.
Brazilian immigrants in Colombia, Ecuador, and Venezuela: Report from the Division of Consular Assistance, Ministry of Foreign Affairs of Brazil (1996).
Argentine immigrants in Colombia: data of 1993 quoted by S. Ríos Begambre, in: *Las migraciones en América del Sur. El caso Colombiano.*
Argentine and Bolivian immigrants in Ecuador: ECLAC, according to the 1990 census.

In the 1990s, immigration from Asia and eastern Europe added a new twist to Argentina's immigration story. Traditional immigration from the Republic of Korea (23) and Taiwan (Province of China) was replaced by relatively small inflows from Mainland China. The principal sources of the new eastern European immigration are Ukraine and Russia. After a 1994 administrative decree permitting the unlimited entry of eastern Europeans, some 4,121 Ukrainians, 1,095 Russians, and 328 from other countries in that region were granted temporary residence, renewable annually.

Because fluctuations in the international economy in 1997-1998 forced Argentina to make severe structural adjustments, salary and employment conditions were created that served to continue to attract migration into Argentina. The harshness of the economic adjustments appeared to affect older waves of migrants more than recent migrants, who had fewer local obligations and were less established. The Argentine economy, which was increasingly exhibiting a tendency to high concentration of incomes, left new migrants in the same precarious labour conditions as their compatriots at home. Thus, few migrants returned home, and new migrants continued to head directly for the most densely populated urban areas. Because of the slight salary differential between Argentina and their home countries, migrants—especially Peruvians—began for the first time to send money home, rather than return with the savings. Estimates of the value of these remittances to Peru range as high as US$ 2-3 million monthly or about US$ 100-150 per migrant. According to IMF, about US$ 32 million was remitted by migrants in Argentina in 1997.

A number of recent studies addressing the impact of migration upon Argentina conclude that, while the overseas movements generated remarkable changes in the population and the economic, social, and cultural structure of Argentina historically, later regional and border migration subjected newcomers to precarious —and in some cases, illegal—living and work conditions that hamper their complete economic and social integration into Argentine society.

Despite the difficulties migration may bring to bear upon the migrants, these movements seem to cause no negative impact upon Argentina's social structure. Immigrants are incorporated into Argentine labour markets where they play an additional and/or complementary role. Recent studies on their insertion into the labour market indicate that migrants do not affect unemployment rates (24), do not appear to influence the access of native-born workers to health services and education (12, 2), and do not affect public safety, as the rate at which foreigners stand trial on criminal charges is no greater than their share of the total population (21).

Notwithstanding these findings, Southern Cone government, public, and media concern about the potentially negative impact of migration created controversy and debate—both in favour of and against more restriction migration measures. The effects of economic austerity, amidst rising crime and 12.4 percent unemployment, led to a congressional proposal to take further restrictions against unauthorized immigration in Argentina. Polls indicate 77 per cent of Argentines favour such measures (29).

EMIGRATION TRENDS

Information on the causes, conditions, and consequences of migration for countries of origin remains elusive. In the 1970s, political conditions generated pressure for emigration from some countries in the region. Untold numbers of refugees fled to Argentina and Venezuela, thousands of others to Europe and the United States. The subsequent assumption of power by democratic governments associated with economic revitalization created conditions for return flows to Argentina, Uruguay, and Chile; however, the exact magnitude of those returns may never be known. The change from authoritarian to democratic rule was also accompanied by the liberalization of migration measures and, in turn, by an increase in unauthorized migration.

In the 1990s, some older cross-border movements—such as from Chile to Argentina—waned. The recovery of the economies in the traditional countries of origin, along with political change, contributed to reduced emigration. Today, because of ongoing economic integration processes in the Southern Cone countries and in the Andean region, however, the flows that do take place involve not only unskilled, but also skilled, labour. National labour markets previously governed by protectionist rules under military governments were opened to facilitate labour productivity and international competition.

CHILE. In 1990, 370 thousand Chileans resided abroad—in contrast to the roughly 182,000 in 1970. During this period, the number of emigrants grew from 2 to 3 per cent of Chile's total population, largely because of political emigration (22). Their top destinations were Argentina, Venezuela, and the United States.

The migration of Chileans to Argentina is the oldest and most significant outflow in terms of volume. The migrant flow was rural-to-rural, unskilled agricultural workers who crossed the border to work in seasonal employment in Argentina. Over time, the seasonal character of the migration changed and migrants gradually became more permanent, especially in the sparsely populated areas of Patagonia that recently were integrated into the economy (31). In recent decades, Chileans migrated internally along with Argentines and immigrants from Bolivia, Paraguay, and Uruguay, and eventually settled in the outskirts of the urban centre. The characteristics of Chilean migrants in Argentina are more diverse than others;

they work in all employment sectors—urban services, construction, mining, and rural harvesting and shearing.

In recent years, Chileans with high-level professional skills began migrating to Venezuela, while those with moderate-level skills moved to the United States. As the return of professionals and others who fled the country for political reasons in the 1970s is not well documented, its impact cannot be fully evaluated.

BOLIVIA. Approximately 75 per cent of Bolivian migrants currently head for Argentina, where they are among the least educated immigrants. Bolivia's extremely uneven development conditions set the stage for seasonal migration to gain reliable supplementary income. The Bolivian outflow has a long history, although migration was relatively small until the 1960s. Migrants traditionally settled along the Argentine side of the border, mostly in Salta and Jujuy; but now migration extends from the border provinces to Argentina's metropolitan areas where Bolivians occupy the lower rungs of industry and construction. Networking among migrants from the same villages facilitates migrants' employment, housing, and social life. Highly participative community associations—more characteristic of this immigrant group than of others in Argentina—help organize the migrants' lives and their contacts with home.

The remaining 25 per cent of Bolivian emigrants are divided among less-skilled workers who travel to Chile and highly skilled workers who settle in Venezuela and the United States (1, 28).

PARAGUAY. The largest community of South American immigrants in Argentina is composed of Paraguayan nationals. The Catholic Church in Paraguay estimates 800,000 Paraguayans have emigrated to Argentina, although Argentine official sources place the figure at closer to 250,000. This long-standing migration began as a seasonal agricultural flow and, like other migration flows in the region, took on a distinct urban character. Paraguayan immigrants engage in construction, handicrafts, and domestic service.

URUGUAY. Unlike other immigrant groups who take low-status jobs, Uruguayan nationals work mostly in urban, professional activities. Thus, their presence places some competitive pressures on Argentine labour. For Uruguay, however, the brain drain from its middle class is the most important feature of its emigration (3, 27).

BRAZIL. It is estimated that 1.5 million Brazilian nationals reside abroad. Their principal destinations are the United States, western Europe, Japan, and neighbouring countries, especially Paraguay. Recent estimates are that out of every 10 Brazilian emigrants, four reside in the United States, three in Paraguay, one in Europe, and one elsewhere. In 1991, nearly 800,000 foreigners (0.52 per cent of the total population) resided in Brazil, some 28 per cent from Argentina, Bolivia, Paraguay, Uruguay and Peru, and the rest from Europe, Asia, and other regions (26). While the number of Brazilians living in Argentina remains sizeable (168,000), they are among the only immigrant groups in Argentina whose numbers dropped somewhat between 1980 and 1990 (Table 38), perhaps owing to the more open political and economic environment at home.

REGIONAL MIGRATION POLICY

A long tradition of bilateral and multilateral accords has facilitated legal movements in the Southern Cone. Since the 1960s, these accords have permitted free transit among Argentina, Bolivia, Brazil, Chile, Paraguay, and Uruguay (25). Together with the repeated amnesties for unauthorized migrants enacted by Argentina (in 1958, 1965, 1974, 1984, and 1992-1994), they provided a flexible framework for the transit and stay of international migrants. Migration was restricted only during the authoritarian regimes of the 1970s.

Undeniably, the political situation in the 1970s generated conditions for outmigration from all the neighbouring countries toward Argentina. The later return of these exiles was facilitated by the reinstatement of democratic governments, combined with the critical economic situation in Argentina. As a result of successive liberal and restrictive migration policies, however, unauthorized immigration rose notably. Argentina responded several times with regularization or amnesty campaigns. Although such measures did not modify the basically restrictive rules in force, their exceptional character did help resolve the marginality of unauthorized migrants. Recently, however, the country has pursued a more coordinated response to unauthorized migration.

Two recent developments are responsible for altering the policy context: the founding of the Southern Cone Common Market, Mercosur; and a series of bilateral agreements. While Mercosur currently does not have a working group specifically for migration issues, migration emerged as a topic in the Working Group (SGT10) on Customs Matters, when it discussed migration facilitation and control mechanisms, and the Working Group (SGT 11) on Labour Matters, which made progress in addressing the needs of border labour markets and their migration dynamics (20).

Two bilateral agreements concluded by Argentina and Chile in 1972 and by Argentina and Bolivia in 1978 (25) provide for the protection of migrant workers and regulations for temporary movements. More recently, on the initiative of the respective presidents, Argentina signed bilateral agreements with Bolivia and Peru in 1998.

These recent agreements not only include regularization of unauthorized migrants, but provide more flexible terms for labour migrants who intend to settle in receiving countries. For these nations to have taken such steps away from unilateral action toward bilateral agreement is a positive sign of regional integration on migration. While Argentina's interest is management of the flows and better protection of the rights of migrants, the countries of origin, too, are motivated by their desire to regularize the status and thereby better protect the rights of their nationals.

THE ANDEAN REGION

The Andean region currently experiences temporary and permanent labour migration flows, as well as political and forced migration, mostly in the form of internal displacement (Table 40). Venezuela, a traditional immigration country, is the destination of most international migration flows within the region. Colombians represent by far the largest source of migrant flows, with Ecuadorians a distant second. Peru, for its part, has experienced an emigration boom in the past decade. Owing to domestic violence related to counterinsurgency, drug trafficking, and other matters, civilians in both Colombia and Peru—numbering in the hundreds of thousands—experienced internal displacements. Since the 1980s, out-migration from the region has become a permanent feature.

Although 1 million or so persons have migrated in each of the Andean and Southern Cone subregions, the exchange between the two blocks is not significant.

TABLE 40.

MIGRATORY MOVEMENTS IN THE ANDEAN REGION

PLACE OF BIRTH	PLACE OF RESIDENCE				
	Colombia	Ecuador	Peru	Venezuela	TOTAL
Colombia		8,755	2,374	598,893	**610,022**
Ecuador	113,263		1,801	23,370	**138,434**
Peru	53,044	1,157		27,748	**81,949**
Venezuela	94,469	3,117	1,489		**97,587**
TOTAL	**260,776**	**13,029**	**4,176**	**650,011**	**927,992**

Sources: ECLAC, IMILA Project: Colombia, 1993; Ecuador, 1990; Peru, 1993; Venezuela, 1990.

TABLE 41.

POPULATION BORN IN ANDEAN REGION COUNTRIES BY COUNTRY OF RESIDENCE IN THE SOUTHERN CONE

PLACE OF BIRTH	PLACE OF RESIDENCE						
	Argentina	Bolivia	Brazil	Chile	Paraguay	Uruguay	TOTAL
Colombia		529	862	1,666			**3,057**
Ecuador		243		2,667			**2,910**
Peru	6,583	5,805	1,829	7,649	622		**22,488**
Venezuela		300	647	2,397			**3,344**
TOTAL	**6,583**	**6,877**	**3,338**	**14,379**	**622**		**31,799**

Sources: **Peruvian immigrants in Paraguay:** Dirección General de Estadísticas, Encuentas y Censos *Annual Statistical Report,* 1994.
Peruvian immigrants in Argentina 1985-1990: *Annual Statistical Report of Peru,* 1991.
Andean region immigrants in Chile: data analysed by ECLAC on the basis of national censuses (1992).
Andean region immigrants in Brazil: Instituto Brasileiro de Geografia e Estadística, 1991 Demographic Census.
Andean region immigrants in Bolivia: ECLAC, 1992 census.

Migrants from the Southern Cone residing in the Andean region number just over 100,000 (Table 39), mostly holdovers from the previous political situation in the south, while Andean migrants to the Southern Cone number slightly over 30,000 (Table 41). Recent information indicates an increasing trend of Peruvians migrating to Argentina, as noted above.

TABLE 42.

**IMMIGRATION FROM SOUTHERN CONE AND ANDEAN REGION
COUNTRIES IN THE UNITED STATES**

	1980 CENSUS		1990 CENSUS	
	Migrants	%	Migrants	%
SOUTHERN CONE				
Argentina	68,887	39.2	92,563	32.0
Bolivia	14,468	8.2	31,303	10.8
Brazil	40,919	23.3	82,489	28.6
Chile	35,127	20.0	55,681	19.3
Paraguay	2,858	1.6	6,057	2.1
Uruguay	13,278	7.6	20,766	7.2
TOTAL	**175,537**	**100.0**	**288,859**	**100.0**
ANDEAN REGION				
Colombia	143,508	45.1	286,124	46.5
Ecuador	86,128	27.0	143,314	23.3
Peru	55,496	17.4	144,199	23.4
Venezuela	33,281	10.5	42,119	6.8
TOTAL	**318,413**	**100.0**	**615,756**	**100.0**

Source: J. Martínez Pizarro, IMILA Project.

Migration to the United States from the Andean countries is double that of the north-bound flow from Southern Cone countries (Table 42). Colombians in the United States are as numerous as Ecuadorians and Peruvians together.

The 1997-1998 international economic crisis that began in Asia reverberated in Venezuela. Unlike Argentina, where migrants found it in their interests to stay through the crisis, migrants in Venezuela left, sparing Venezuela any additional consequences of competition for scarce jobs and resources.

IMMIGRATION TRENDS

Immigration has been significant to Venezuela throughout the twentieth century. During the first part of the century, Venezuelan immigrants came primarily from Italy and other European countries. By 1961, however, the number of Colombian immigrants equalled that of Italian immigrants, each group encompassing about 20 per cent of a total of 526,000 registered foreigners. Prevailing unauthorized flows to Venezuela in the 1960s and 1970s included growing rates of Colombian nationals. There were additional inflows from Ecuador, Peru, and Bolivia in the 1970s (16).

The most important increase in migration accompanied the rise of oil prices in 1973 and the nationalization of oil production in 1975. Since the 1980s, the context and contour of Venezuela's immigration changed course several times as a result of ensuing economic developments. The concurrent establishment of authoritarian governments in the south brought emigrants from Argentina, Chile, and Uruguay.

The oil boom was short-lived. When oil prices fell and the Venezuelan economy went into crisis in the 1980s and the 1990s, the return of Colombian migrants became the prevailing trend. Colombia's economic recovery in the 1980s contributed to this return. As a result of political transition towards democracy at home, Argentines, Uruguayans, and Chileans also returned. The economic advances of the European Union created adequate conditions for the return of large numbers of European citizens (9).

Venezuela currently is experiencing a dual migration phenomenon: continued unauthorized inflows of unskilled Colombians to rural areas; and significant exodus of both regular and unauthorized urban skilled migrants from many countries. The most recent census (1990) recorded a total of 1,025,849 foreigners, or 5.7 per cent of the total population—51.7 per cent Colombians, followed by Peruvians and Ecuadorians (32). Approximately 1.5 million Colombians reside in Venezuela, only one-half of whom are registered with the Colombian Embassy; the rest are assumed to be unauthorized. About one-half of the 100,000 Ecuadorians living in Venezuela are unauthorized.

Southern Cone migrants remain in Venezuela in significant numbers despite returns. Of some 180,000 Chileans believed to have sought refuge there, roughly 40 to 50 per cent returned. Approximately 20,000 Argentines, mostly from Buenos Aires, continue to live in Venezuela, along with 6,000-7,000 Brazilians and fewer than 2,000 Paraguayans (32).

In recent years, Venezuela received increasing inflows of Peruvian and Ecuadorian citizens and new migration from the Caribbean basin, especially the Dominican Republic, Guyana, and Haiti (9). The latter migrants often enter by air on tourist visas, but become unauthorized as they exceed the time and work limits of their visas. Other Caribbean migrants are known to arrive unauthorized by sea via Curaçao and Trinidad. Significant unauthorized flows of Chinese migrants also use the sea route via Curaçao (10).

Migration in Venezuela continues to be dominated by Colombians who engage in unskilled agricultural labour in rural areas and service and construction work in urban centres (16). South Americans in Venezuela from countries other than Colombia are primarily professionals, managers, and other white-collar workers. Chileans, for example, are university professors and technical professionals; Paraguayans are mostly in medicine, architecture, engineering, dentistry, and business.

Immigration to Venezuela has far-reaching economic, social, and cultural implications. There is, however, little evidence of any negative impact of migration on public safety; crime rates among immigrants do not exceed that of the overall population (32). The burden of immigrants on state services aroused concern in the 1970s. More recently, however, new local and regional economic, political, and social developments triggered the return of technical, professional, and agricultural workers. Technical and professional posts vacated by departing immigrants were filled by qualified, skilled native labour.

Local labour alone cannot cover unmet needs in seasonal and agricultural production, given the decrease in fertility levels among the Venezuelan population. In the 1990s, competition between the similar agricultural sectors of the Venezuelan and Colombian economies generated a relative shortage of temporary labour in Venezuela while, at the same time, improving salaries and living conditions in some sectors of Colombia's rural economy (36). Analyses of the labour market impact of migration in Venezuela show that the foreign labour is indispensable for the development of agriculture. With increases in the participation of women in domestic service, the personal services sector in the country has grown (10).

In the early 1990s Venezuela, long without an immigration plan, attempted to implement a specific programme to promote the immigration of skilled labour.

Then-President Carlos Andrés Pérez, who appointed a Presidential Commission for Selective Immigration (COPRISE), sought immigration of skilled labour from eastern Europe. Although the plan did not meet with much success, Rafael Caldera's following administration took up the selective immigration banner and created the National Immigration Commission in 1996 to revise and update laws regarding migration and to design an immigration policy. A new immigration and alien control law under development has not yet been sent to the Congress. Discussion of the selective immigration issue appears sidetracked by public debate on Venezuela's current and very real problems with unauthorized migration.

EMIGRATION TRENDS

COLOMBIA. The deepening of the armed conflict in Colombia in the 1990s produced renewed outflows, despite the condition of the Venezuelan economy. Estimates of just those internally displaced by violence during the period 1985-1994 vary between 550,000 and 625,000 persons (5); a more recent, but controversial, estimate puts the figure at 920,000 (7, 8). The violence put pressure on flows out of the country as well.

The displacement is reminiscent of *La Violencia*, a period of prolonged and intense civil violence in Colombia from 1946 to 1966, which started the first significant emigration decades ago. *La Violencia* resulted in the displacement of an estimated 2 million persons from rural to urban areas.

In 1992, some 1.9 million Colombians resided abroad. While it is difficult to determine with any precision, it is reported that nearly 600,000 Colombians resided in Venezuela in 1990 (Table 40). Moderate levels of migration move people from Columbia to other border countries, such as Ecuador, where 50,000 emigrants arrived between 1974 and 1980 following the oil boom; currently, more than 8,000 Colombians reside legally in Ecuador (16, 33).

Nevertheless, significant Colombian outflows were directed to other destinations, both for reasons explained above and because new opportunities opened up in Europe, the United States, and Asia. Contacts with friends and family already in the United States, where a sizeable Colombian community exists in New York, helps maintain a steady flow to that country. Research shows that an important motivating factor in these decisions to migrate is the pursuit of advanced education and training (36, 30). As the conflict intensified, however, the numbers of Colombian asylum seekers in the USA also increased in the late 1990s.

PERU. Until recent decades, out-migration was rare among Peruvians. In 1970, only 45,000 Peruvians resided abroad, nearly one-half in the United States and most of them skilled, white-collar workers. In 1980, the Venezuelan Foreign Registry listed Peruvians among its most skilled immigrants (28). More recently, as a result of economic and political changes, Peru's emigration is higher than ever, estimated at between 300,000 and 500,000 persons (34). Peruvians seek residence in Europe, the United States, Japan, and Argentina. An additional serious problem has been internal displacement due to violence. Estimates commonly cite approximately 600,000 persons (140,000 families) displaced between 1981 and 1993.

ECUADOR. A traditional country of origin, Ecuador registers sizeable out-migration both within the region and to the United States. At the same time, the country is an important haven for Colombian and Peruvian nationals fleeing violence (13).

REGIONAL MIGRATION POLICY

Present-day migration policies in the region are characterized by a double trend: while governments increase restrictive measures, they also seek improved management of migration flows through bilateral and multilateral action.

In the 1990s era of free trade and globalization, the Council of the Cartagena Agreement (JUNAC) attempted to renew interest in migration issues and ultimately reached agreement on a project for the free transit and stay of professionals in member countries. The Andean Regulations on Labour Migration, the multilateral agreement governing migration that was part of the Andean Pact signed in 1969, provided for the administration of labour movements and regularization of migrants in the 1970s and 1980s. Unfortunately, in the late 1980s the enforcement and application of the Andean Regulations weakened—as did the Andean Pact.

CONCLUSION

In South America, the intraregional migration flows are long-term and predictably will continue long into the future. Argentina and Venezuela continue to be the main host countries, but each is experiencing a slower rate of absorption of migrants, especially Chileans and Colombians respectively. Most recently, Peru has emerged as a net emigration country. There is no expectation of major changes in the scale of flows, although from a qualitative standpoint the economic integration processes in the region (Mercosur and Andean Group) produced an increase in movements among higher-skilled workers. Inevitably, as integration processes gain strength, they will positively influence the free mobility of labour.

Owing as much to relative differences in economic opportunity as to broadening social networks among migrants, flows from South America to other regions have increased and are likely to continue to increase, especially towards the United States. A similar permanent but weaker outflow to Europe (particularly from Southern Cone countries) is also expected to continue.

Extraregional flows to South America are established streams. There is a growing trend of immigrants from the Republic of China, a somewhat smaller flow from the Republic of Korea, and potential for new movements from eastern Europe, especially Ukraine and Russia.

While there are no indications of prospective changes in the restrictive nature of migration in the region, the rise of to the top of countries' agendas of the need for policy changes bodes well for increasingly cooperative approaches.

REFERENCES

1. Ardaya Salinas, G. (1997). *Nuevo Modelo de Desarrollo y Migraciones en Bolivia.* International Organization for Migration, La Paz, Bolivia.

2. Ávila, M., N. Grana, S. Valef, M. Miranda, and S. Scaruli (1986). *Inserción de la Población Chilena en las Escuelas Provinciales de Comodoro Rivadavia.* Universidad Nacional de la Patagonia, Comodoro Rivadavia, Argentina.

3. Balán, J. (1985). *Las Migraciones Internacionales en el Cono Sur.* Hemispheric Migration Project, Georgetown University and IOM, Washington, DC.

4. Base-Investigaciones Sociales (1997). *Evolución del Proceso Migratorio en la Ultimas Décadas.* Asunción, Paraguay.

5. Conferencia Episcopal de Colombia (1995). *Derechos Humanos. Desplazados por la Violencia en Colombia.* Bogotá, Columbia.

6. Comisión Latinoamericana de Demografíca (1982). *Censos Nacionales: Análisis Comparativo.* Santiago, Chile.

7. Consultoría para Derechos Humanos y Desplazamiento (1997). *Elementos para un Sistema de Información sobre Desplazados y Derechos Humanos, Santafé de Bogotá.*

8. Consultoría Permanente sobre Desplazamiento Interno en las Américas (1997). *Informe Final. Misión in Situ de Asistencia Técnica sobre Desplazamiento Interno en Colombia.* Costa Rica.

9. Dávila, R. (1998). *Addressing the Employment of Migrants in an Irregular Situation.* Paper presented to the Technical Symposium on International Migration and Development, The Hague, Netherlands.

10. Florez, J. and C.Y. Chen (1992). *Impact of Migration in the Receiving Countries: Venezuela.* Commission for International Cooperation in National Research in Demography-IOM, Geneva.

11. Gurrieri, J. (1992). *Migraciones e Integración en el Cono Sur: Diagnóstico de la Situación.* Paper presented to the Seminario Internacional sobre "Las migraciones en el proceso de integración de las Américas", Bogotá, Colombia.

12. Gurrieri, J. and L. Mármora (1990). *La Población Extranjera en Mendoza en la Década del 80.* IOM (unpublished), Buenos Aires.

13. León Albán, J. (1997). Las Migraciones en el Ecuador (unpublished), Quito, Ecuador.

14. Maguid, A. (1995a). *La Migración Internacional en Argentina, Características Recientes.* Latin American and Caribbean Demographic Centre/Centro Latinoamericano de Demografía, Córdoba, Argentina.

15. Maguid, A. (1995b). L'immigration des pays limitrophes dans l'Argentine des années 90, mythes et réalités. *Revue Europénne des Migrations Internationales*, 11(2).

16. Mármora, L. (1985). *Las Migraciones Laborales en Venezuela.* Organization of American States, Washington, DC.

17. Mármora, L. (1988). La fundamentación de las políticas migratorias internacionales en América Latina. *Estudios migratorios Latinoamericanos*, 3(10).

18. Mármora, L. (1990). *Los Movimientos Migratorios Internacionales en los Países Andinos.* Paper presented to the Primer Seminario Andino sobre Migraciones, Caracas, Venezuela.

19. Mármora, L. (1997). *Las Políticas de Migraciones Internacionales.* Alianza-IOM. Buenos Aires, Argentina.

20. Mármora, L. and M. Cassarino (1997). Las migraciones y su tratamiento institucional en el Mercosur. *Relaciones Internacionales,* 7(12).

21. Mármora, L.H., and J. Gorini (1995). *Impacto de las Migraciones en la Estructura de Seguridad de la Argentina.* Secretaría de Población, Ministerio del Interior, Buenos Aires, Argentina.

22. Martínez Pizarro, J. (1997). *Panorama de la Migración Internacional en Chile.* Centro Latinoamericano de Demografía, Santiago, Chile.

23. Mera, C. (1997). *La Inmigración Coreana en Buenos Aires: Multiculturalismo en el Espacio Urbano.* Eudeba, Buenos Aires, Argentina.

24. Montoya, S. and M. Pertircara (1995). Los migrantes limítrofes: aumentan el desempleo? *Novedades económicas,* 17(170).

25. Organización Internacional para las Migraciones (IOM) (1990). *La Migración en los Procesos Regionales y Subregionales de América Latina.* Paper presented to the Seminario Internacional Latinoamericano, La Paz, Bolivia.

26. Patarra, N. (1997), *Movimentos Migratórios Internacionais no Brasil Contemporaneo: Algumas Características e Tendencias.* Departamento de Sociología, Nucleo de Estudios de Populaçio/Universidade Estadual de Campinas, Rio de Janeiro, Brasil.

27. Pellegrino, A. (1997). *Memorandum sobre la Situación Migratoria en Uruguay en las Ultimas Décadas* (unpublished), Montevideo, Uruguay.

28. Rapado R. (1985). *Las Migraciones Laborales en el Perú.* Organization of American States, Washington, DC.

29. Reuters (1999). Argentina, Chile to call immigration conference, Buenos Aires, 16 February.

30. Ríos Begambre, S. (1997). *Las Migraciones en América del Sur: el Caso Colombiano* (unpublished), Bogotá, Colombia.

31. Rodrígues Allendes (1986). *Las Migraciones Laborales en Chile.* Organization of American States, Washington, DC.

32. Suárez Sarmiento, C.G. (1996). Diagnóstico sobre las Migraciones Caribeñas hacia Venezuela (unpublished), Caracas, Venezuela.

33. Torales, P. (1979). *Las Migraciones Laborales en la Frontera de Colombia con Panamá.* UNDP-ILO Project, Bogotá, Colombia.

34. Torales, P. (1993). *La Migración de Peruanos a la Argentina.* IOM, Buenos Aires, Argentina.

35. Torales, P. (1997). *Las Migraciones del Perú* (unpublished), Lima, Perú.

36. Urrea Giraldo, F. (1992). *Principales Tendencias de los Procesos Migratorios en Colombia y la Internacionalización de la Economía.* Paper presented to the Seminario Internacional sobre las migraciones en el proceso de integración de las Américas, Bogotá, Colombia.

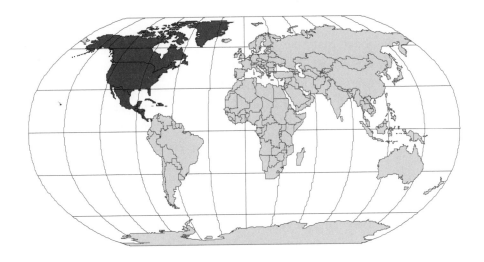

NORTH AMERICA, CENTRAL AMERICA, AND THE CARIBBEAN

INTRODUCTION

The North American migration system includes the world's major emigration and immigration destinations, defined in volume (migration between Mexico and the USA) or in per capita terms (the Dominican Republic or El Salvador and Canada). Between 1 and 2 million Mexicans enter the USA for more than three months each year, and about 300,000 settle there. There were 36,000 immigrants admitted to the USA from the Dominican Republic in 1996—about 0.5 per cent of that country's residents emigrated legally to the USA in that year.[1] The USA receives almost 1 million legal immigrants a year, plus 300,000 unauthorized foreigners who settle, making it the largest recipient of foreigners welcomed into another country as permanent residents and intending future citizens. Canada receives about 200,000 immigrants a year, giving it one of the world's highest per capita intakes of planned immigrants.

Philip Martin, Professor in the Department of Agriculture and Resource Economics, University of California at Davis, CA, USA, contributed to this chapter.

IMMIGRATION TRENDS

Canada and the United States are the principal countries of immigration in this region. Next, Mexico is host to labour migrants (most unauthorized) from Central America and elsewhere. In addition, within Central America, migrants—particularly from Nicaragua—move to Costa Rica. Also, in the Caribbean, Haitian migrants move into the Bahamas, the Dominican Republic, and other islands.

CANADA

Canada has relatively high levels of immigration, generous social welfare programmes, and a significant refugee intake. Canada had its highest ever level of immigration in 1993 when 256,000 immigrants were admitted (Table 43). Canada anticipates about 200,000 to 225,000 immigrants a year; thus it annually adds the equivalent of 0.75 per cent to its population via immigration (4). About 17 percent or 5 million Canadian residents were foreign-born in 1997.

Canada has three major avenues of entry for legal immigrants: family unification, which accounted for 28 per cent of immigrants in 1999; economic migraton or independent skilled workers/business investors, 57 per cent; and refugees, 12 per cent (Table 44) (4).

TABLE 43.
IMMIGRATION TO CANADA, 1975-1998

Immigration

Year	Immigration	Year	Immigration	Year	Immigration
1975	187,881	1983	89,517	1991	230,781
1976	149,429	1984	88,239	1992	252,842
1977	114,914	1985	84,302	1993	255,819
1978	86,313	1986	99,219	1994	223,875
1979	112,093	1987	152,098	1995	212,491
1980	143,117	1988	161,929	1996	225,833
1981	129,618	1989	192,001	1997	215,840
1982	121,147	1990	214,230	1998	174,072

Source: Department of Citizenship and Immigration, Calendar years.

TABLE 44.

IMMIGRATION TO CANADA BY CLASS, 1996-1999

	1996	1997	1998	1999[1]
Economic	120,286	125,486	94,984	102,500
Family	68,342	59,963	50,885	51,200
Other	8,855	6,174	5,417	4,400
Refugees	28,360	24,217	19,824	21,500
Total	225,843	215,840	174,072	180,000

Note: [1]Projected.

Source: Department of Citizenship and Immigration

Of the 174,000 immigrants admitted in 1998, 11 per cent were from Mainland China, 9 per cent from India, and about 5 per cent each from Hong Kong, Taiwan (Province of China), and the Philippines. Social networks have developed to closely link sending and receiving locales, especially Hong Kong and the Canadian cities of Toronto and Vancouver. The 1998 admissions from Hong Kong (8,000) were down sharply from 22,000 in 1997. China has become the biggest single source of immigrants to Canada.

More than one-half of Canada's recent immigrants were born in Asia, including 25 per cent born in Hong Kong and Mainland China, and 19 per cent were born in Europe.[2] Immigrants are concentrated in three cities: Toronto, Vancouver, and Montreal. In 1996, about 71 per cent of recent immigrants, compared to 25 percent of Canadian residents, lived in these cities.[3]

Canada accepted about 20,000 refugees in 1998, including 10,200 who were already in Canada, 7,000 sponsored by the Canadian Government, and 2,200 who were privately sponsored. Their principal countries of origin were Bosnia and Herzegovina, Sri Lanka, the Islamic Republic of Iran, Afghanistan, Croatia, and Somalia. In addition, foreigners arrive in Canada and apply for asylum; about 25,000 cases are referred for adjudication each year. The Immigration and Refugee Board reviews applications for asylum and grants refugee status to about 40 per cent.

Canadian immigration has fluctuated over time. Before restrictive legislation was enacted, inflows were dominated by economic conditions in Canada and countries of origin. Beginning in the 1880s, qualitative restrictions on immigrants were imposed. For example, Chinese immigration was barred in 1885 and the 1906 Canadian Immigration Act called for controls on the US border.

In March 1931, in the midst of the Depression, most immigration to Canada was halted, reducing immigration from 1.2 million in the 1920s to 140,000 in the 1930s. However, in the aftermath of the Second World War, Canada permitted European immigrants to enter under a "bulk labour" scheme and admitted 40,000 Hungarians in 1956-1957 after the Soviets crushed the Hungarian uprising. Canada's "white only" immigration policy ended in 1962, and the point system for selecting immigrants was launched in 1967. The Immigration Act of 1976, the basis of current immigration policies, went into effect in 1978.

The 1976 Act established a point system to select non-family or independent immigrants. This system assesses foreigners wishing to immigrate for economic reasons against nine major criteria on which an applicant can score a maximum of 107 points. For example, language skills (knowing English and/or French) can earn an applicant a maximum 15 points, education up to 16 points, educational training factor (ETF) 18, occupational factor 10, experience 8, arranged employment 10, personal suitability 10, age 10, and demographic factor 10. Applicants must score at least 70 points to immigrate.

Canada also has a programme that permits investors and entrepreneurs to immigrate, but assesses them on a different scale with a maximum of 45 points. Beginning on 1 April 1999, business investor immigrants must have operated a business before immigrating, have a net worth of at least C$ 1 million and invest at least C$ 500,000 for at least five years in a business or in funds managed by Canadians that preserve businesses and jobs; these new rules double previous net worth and investment requirements. Entrepreneurs must convince immigration authorities that they can establish or purchase a business that will create at least one job for a Canadian. Self-employed immigrants can receive up to 30 points if they can demonstrate that they can create a job for themselves in a manner that contributes to the Canadian economy.

Immigration is regulated by the Department of Citizenship and Immigration. The Canadian constitution makes immigration a shared responsibility between the federal Government and the provinces. Quebec, Manitoba, New Brunswick, and British

Columbia have signed federal-provincial agreements that transfer to the provinces some immigration responsibilities.

Quebec is the only province that selects its own independent immigrants and temporary workers. Immigrants can enter Quebec under one of three programmes: the secured job offer programme that provides immigrant visas to qualified persons with job offers from Quebec employers; the occupations in demand programme that permits the entry of foreigners with skills that are in short supply in Quebec; and the occupational employability and mobility programme that is aimed at attracting professionals. Quebec received 27,300 immigrants in 1997; about 36 per cent spoke French, 20 per cent spoke English, and 44 per cent spoke neither French nor English. About three-fourths of Quebec's immigrants settled in Montreal.

In the 1990s, there were concerns that too many immigrants were admitted to Canada, that too many were becoming dependent on welfare assistance, and that too many asylum seekers were abusing the system. In 1997, Citizenship and Immigration Minister Lucienne Robillard appointed a three-member independent panel to suggest changes in Canada's immigration system. The review was justified as a means to "examine the suitability of the immigration and refugee legislation to continue to provide the flexibility and direction needed to respond to emerging issues and migration trends in the twenty-first century".

In January 1998, the Legislative Review Advisory Group chaired by Robert Trempe, a former deputy minister of immigration in Quebec, released its report *Not Just Numbers: A Canadian Framework for Future Immigration* (3). The report made 172 recommendations for changes in Canadian immigration and refugee policies, including the recommendation that prospective independent immigrants to Canada be required to speak English or French; some of those coming to join family members who were settled in Canada would have to pay a language study fee if they lacked English or French.[4]

In January 1999, Immigration Minister Lucienne Robillard introduced 60 pages of proposed changes to Canada's 1978 Immigration Act that would make it easier to detect and expel foreigners attempting to enter Canada with false documents. She noted that *Not Just Numbers* "did not show any justification for a radical change in direction, or a break from success of Canada's immigration policy".

However, Robillard's proposals were not implemented before she was replaced in August 1999 by former Ontario Health Minister Elinor Caplan. Between July and September 1999, migrant smuggling—the interception of four ships each attempting to smuggle over 100 Chinese migrants into Canada—triggered national debate. As a result, Caplan recommended toughening Canadian laws against alien smuggling, including stiffer penalties for smugglers and mandatory detention for suspected unauthorized migrants.

Canada admits about 11,000 farm workers each year—mostly from Jamaica and Mexico—to work on fruit, vegetable and tobacco farms. Under the Mexican Seasonal Agricultural Workers Programme, Canadian farmers have their need for Mexican workers certified and pay for the workers' transportation to Canada, their housing, and wages that are the higher of the prevailing or minimum wage. Mexican workers have 4 per cent of their pay deducted to cover the cost of administering the programme. The Mexican Government is enthusiastic about this seasonal worker programme and has urged the USA to implement a similar programme.

Canada traditionally has not had problems with illegal immigrants entering the country without inspection, in the way that Mexicans enter the USA. However, it has had problems with ineligible foreigners who arrive and seek asylum. Canada does not detain most asylum seekers while their applications are pending. This practice permitted a smuggling ring based in Hong Kong to fly Chinese to Vancouver where they applied for asylum, then transport them to Toronto, and then smuggle them into the USA through the St. Regis Mohawk Indian reservation on the New York-Ontario border. This alien smuggling operation was broken up by Canadian and US authorities in December 1998.

The flexibility of the Canadian immigration system was illustrated in 1997 when Canada imposed visa requirements on the Czech Republic in anticipation of large-scale migration of Czech gypsies. In August 1997, a film aired on Czech TV Nova implied that refugee status and welfare benefits in Canada were almost guaranteed to Czech gypsies. Some 1,000 Czechs flew to Canada the following month, and about half applied for asylum; economy-class airline seats to Canada were sold out for months. Even before the first decisions of the Immigration and Refugee Board, which granted refugee status to several Czech gypsies, Canada slowed the influx by imposing visa requirements on Czechs in October 1997. Canada received 1,216 asylum claims from Czech nationals in 1997.

In addition to unauthorized migrants and asylum seekers, a third migration issue involves war criminals. Canada is believed, in some cases, to have granted refugee and immigrant status to war criminals and terrorists. In July 1998, Canada announced plans to crack down on war criminals, proposing to spend C$ 50 million over three years to add resources to determine whether 320 Canadians were guilty of war crimes in their home countries. If found to have committed war crimes, they can be stripped of their Canadian citizenship and deported.

Canada officially is a multicultural country and encourages and—until recently—subsidized immigrant associations that preserve the culture of immigrants' countries of origin. As the major countries of origin shift from Europe to Asia, the percentage of non-whites in Canada is increasing. As recently as the 1930s, it was estimated that virtually all Canadians were white, and 80 per cent were of either British or French ancestry. In 1997, an estimated 13 per cent of Canadian residents were non-white.

Canada has one of the world's fastest routes to naturalization. Immigrants who are at least 18 years of age, have been legal permanent residents of Canada for at least three of the previous four years, can communicate in English or French, and have knowledge of Canada, including the rights and responsibilities of citizenship, are permitted to naturalize. Canada has recognized dual citizenship since 1977, and in 1996, 3 per cent of Canadians held dual citizenship.

THE UNITED STATES

The United States is a nation of immigrants. Under the motto *E pluribus unum*—from many one—US presidents remind citizens that they share the experience of themselves or their forebears leaving another country to begin anew in the USA.[5] Immigration thus permits immigrants to better themselves and strengthens the USA, leading the US Commission on Immigration Reform (CIR) to assert a widely held core value: "a properly regulated system of legal immigration is in the national interest of the United States" (16).

Immigration has costs as well as benefits, and these costs were the focus of policy attention in the USA in the mid-1990s. Criminal aliens, the costs of welfare and other assistance for legal and unauthorized immigrants, and illegal immigration were the subjects of major legislative changes in 1996. Polls suggest that a majority of Americans want both legal and illegal immigration reduced. However, immigration has faded from the headlines, in part because of the booming economy; the unemployment rate has been the lowest in three decades, with the economy generating an average of 10,000 net new jobs each workday.

Between 1991 and 1996, more than 6 million immigrants were admitted to the USA, an average of more than 1 million per year. However, more than 1 million immigrants were admitted in only one year (1991), the year that the USA recognized the presence of more than 1 million previously unauthorized immigrants who had been granted amnesty. Some had been in the USA for a decade or more. Normal immigration flows averaged 860,000 a year in the 1990s, up from 600,000 in the 1980s, 450,000 in the 1970s, and 330,000 in the 1960s.

During the second half of the 1990s, processing delays reduced levels of legal immigration. The United States admitted 660,477 legal immigrants in fiscal year 1998, which ended 30 September 1998 (Table 45). Among these immigrants were 284,270 immediate relatives, 191,480 family preference immigrants, 77,517 employment preference immigrants, 54,709 refugee and asylee adjustments, and 45,499 immigrants who entered under an immigration diversity programme. Of the total of 660,447 immigrants, 357,037 were abroad and received immigrant visas from the US Department of State; the remaining 303,440 immigrants were already in the USA and merely adjusted their status (11).

TABLE 45.
UNITED STATES IMMIGRATION DATA, FISCAL YEAR 1998

	Number of persons
Immigrants	660,477
Immediate relatives of US citizens	284,270
Other family-sponsored immigrants	191,480
Economic/employment-based	77,517
Refugees and asylees	54,709
Diversity immigrants	45,499
Other Immigrants	7,002

Source: Immigration and Naturalization Service.

The top source countries for US immigration in 1998 were Mexico (19.9 per cent), Mainland China (5.6 per cent), India (5.5 per cent), the Philippines (5.2 per cent), and the Dominican Republic (3.1 per cent). This list reflects the significant shift toward Latin American and Asian immigration that has taken place since 1960, when most immigrants came from Europe. Mexico is the largest single source of immigrants, comprising nearly 20 per cent of legal immigrants to the USA and more than 50 per cent of the unauthorized migrants. Most new immigrants reside in just six states: California, New York, Florida, Texas, New Jersey, and Illinois.

The current wave of immigration to the USA began with immigration reforms in 1965 that eliminated country-by-country quotas based on the number of persons from each country already in the United States. Under the preference system enacted in 1965, three major doors were opened to immigrants: family unification that permits entry of spouses, children, parents and siblings of US citizens and spouses and unmarried children of legal residents; employment-based admissions of immigrants who could contribute to the US economy or fill jobs for US employers; and refugees, with a particular focus on those resettled from overseas. In 1990, a fourth door was opened for up to 50,000 diversity immigrants a year— persons from countries that had sent fewer than 50,000 immigrants to the US over the previous five years—through a lottery for a US immigrant visa.

About 70 per cent of the immigrants admitted in 1998 entered via the family unification door (Table 45). The second largest group included immigrants and their families admitted for economic or employment reasons (12 per cent). The third-largest category was refugees and asylees (8 per cent), and the fourth group the 45,000 diversity immigrants who arrived in 1998.[6]

Non-immigrant is the term used in the United States to describe those who come to visit, work, or study. The number of these persons has more than doubled in the past 15 years, primarily because of the growing number of tourists. In 1996 (the last year for which statistics have been published), 19 million of the 25 million non-immigrants who arrived were tourists, followed by almost 4 million foreign business visitors. Foreigners also arrive to work temporarily in the United States: 227,000 temporary foreign workers arrived in 1996, ranging from Canadian hockey players to Mexicans who harvested tobacco in North Carolina, and from Indian computer programmers to British artists and entertainers.

Unauthorized foreigners—also referred to as illegal aliens, deportable aliens, and undocumented workers—are persons in the USA in violation of US immigration laws. No one knows exactly how many unauthorized foreigners are in the United States: the Immigration and Naturalization Service (INS) apprehended more than 1.6 million unauthorized aliens in 1996,[7] most caught just inside the US border with Mexico.

The INS estimated that there were 5 million foreigners living without authorization in the US in October 1996, up from 3.9 million in October 1992, suggesting that their number is increasing by 275,000 per year. Thus, about 2 per cent of US residents were unauthorized migrants. According to INS estimates, there were about 2.7 million unauthorized Mexicans, 335,000 Salvadorans, 165,000 Guatemalans, and 120,000 Canadians.

In the past, it was said that US immigration policy changed once a generation. In the last two decades, there were major changes in 1980, 1986, 1990, and 1996—and more are likely. The USA adopted the United Nations definition of a refugee in the Refugee Act of 1980; legalized 2.7 million unauthorized migrants and introduced sanctions on employers who knowingly hired unauthorized workers in the Immigration Reform and Control Act (IRCA) of 1986; and more than doubled the number of legal immigrants admitted for economic or employment reasons in the Immigration Act of 1990. All three of these major immigration laws affected immigration flows and integration patterns.

A major legacy of the IRCA, for example, was to increase legal and illegal immigration from Mexico. About 60 per cent of those legalized were Mexican, and in many cases only the husband in a rural Mexican family won legal immigrant status. When these legal immigrants decided to unite their families in the USA, the backlog of Mexican wives and children waiting to enter the USA as legal immigrants increased to almost 1 million in the mid-1990s. Many families did not wait for immigrant visas. There was an upsurge in unauthorized Mexico-US migration in the early 1990s, often of family members awaiting legal status, which in turn led to the creation of "mixed families", or families in which the legal status of members ranged from legal, to US citizen baby, to unauthorized. There was also an increased demand for schools and social services at a time when California was experiencing its worst recession in 50 years. This combination of factors set the stage in 1994 for Proposition 187, an ultimately unsuccessful attempt in

California to curtail public benefits for unauthorized immigrants, and in 1996 for another round of major immigration reforms.

The year 1996 was a watershed year for US immigration policy. Three major laws were approved, aimed at speeding the deportation of criminal immigrants, reducing the access of immigrants to welfare, and stepping up efforts to reduce illegal immigration: (1) the Anti-Terrorism and Effective Death Penalty Act; (2) the Personal Responsibility and Work Opportunity Reconciliation Act; and (3) the Illegal Immigration Reform and Immigrant Responsibility Act. All contained provisions aimed at immigrants, but only the immigration act was considered by congressional immigration subcommittees; the others were developed by justice and tax committees.

The second 1996 law, which reformed welfare, marked a radical change in the way both US citizens and immigrants are treated but especially restricted the access of immigrants arriving after 22 August 1996 to federal welfare benefits. Until this law was enacted, immigrants had most of the same rights and responsibilities as US citizens: they had to pay taxes and register for military service, but also had access to most social assistance programmes on the same basis as US citizens. The new law drew a sharp line between US citizens and legal immigrants; some of the restrictions on legal immigrants were later relaxed in 1997-1998.

The third 1996 law, aimed at reducing unauthorized immigration, authorized more Border Patrol agents, fences, and lights along the US-Mexican border. A more controversial feature was authorization for a pilot programme to test new methods for verifying authorization to work in the United States. The results of the pilot programmes are not yet available.

Stepped-up border controls seem to have changed migration patterns, but not deterred attempts at unauthorized entry, especially from young men. Partly as a result of policy shifts and the increased difficulty of crossing the border, more and more migrants are resorting to *polleros*—smugglers—to guide them across the border. To avoid authorities, these crossings are attempted in increasingly remote and difficult terrain, even though this poses greater threats to migrant safety. Ridding the border of crime, and thereby improving public safety, is one of the Government's top priorities in border enforcement.

Targeting migrant smugglers is part of this plan and an area in which the USA and other national authorities cooperate. There is evidence of increasing professionalization of smuggling operations, many of which show little regard for human life. Fearing apprehension by border authorities, smugglers have left migrants without water or protection from the hot sun. As smuggling fees increase and migrants find it difficult to pay all costs at once, smugglers "sell" migrants to businesses which cover the fees in exchange for indentured labour. In one of its most troubling forms, trafficking can amount to virtual slavery, particularly for women and children forced into sexually exploitative occupations.

US law enforcement strategies have been a mixture of disruption and deterrence. They include increasing legal penalties for alien smuggling, improving intelligence, breaking up smuggling rings, increasing arrests and prosecutions of smugglers, disrupting traditional routes and safe houses, and improving cooperation with state, local, and foreign law enforcement officials. Additional attention has been focused on the employers of smuggled aliens, including increased enforcement of labour laws and regulating marriage and modelling and escort services to ensure they are not involved in trafficking for forced prostitution. The INS also works with domestic and overseas airlines and other carriers of aliens to enlist their help in combating smuggling, offering training for carrier personnel in identifying fraudulent documents more accurately.

The USA further offers witness protection and other programmes for those who testify against smugglers. Often, successful prosecution of traffickers requires the cooperation of those who have been smuggled into the country, but they may fear recriminations if they must return home. The USA has a temporary visa category (S visa) that permits witnesses in organized crime and national security cases to remain in the USA during the trial. In some cases, permanent residence can also be obtained for cooperative witnesses. The USA is now exploring ways to strengthen these provisions to grant legal status to migrants who testify against smuggling operations.

IMMIGRANT INTEGRATION. Most immigrants come to the USA for higher wages and more opportunities, and their work has significant effect on the US economy and labour market. In 1997, the National Research Council (NRC) (13) released a comprehensive report on the economic effects of immigration that concluded "immigration produces net economic gains for domestic residents", adding

US$ 1 billion to US$ 10 billion per year to the country's GDP. The economic gain from immigration in an US$ 8 trillion economy is small, but positive.

Immigration slightly expands the size of the US economy. Its most debated effects are distributional: immigration benefits some residents and imposes costs on others. The beneficiaries include owners of capital and land, as well as skilled and professional US workers; the losers include unskilled US workers, including settled immigrants whose wages and opportunities may be limited by newcomers.

One of the most debated issues is whether immigrants with low education and few skills will enjoy upward mobility in the USA. Immigrants usually begin their American journey with lower earnings than US-born persons who have similar levels of education. However, immigrants may be more ambitious and entrepreneurial, enabling their earnings to quickly catch up and soon surpass those of similar natives—the so-called trampoline effect.

Even though the education levels of immigrants are rising, the education levels of the US-born are rising faster, creating a wedge between immigrant and US-born earnings. In 1970, the average immigrant earned 1 per cent more than the average US-born worker; by 1980, the average immigrant earned 10 per cent less than an average US-born worker; and by 1990, the wage gap had expanded to 17 per cent. The native-immigrant earnings gap is especially wide for Mexican and Central American immigrants; their average earnings were 25 to 40 per cent lower than natives' earnings in 1970 and 50 per cent lower in 1990.

Low earnings have raised concern about the fiscal impacts of immigrants: how do the taxes they pay compare with the costs of tax-supporter services they receive? The NRC estimated that the 89 million households headed by a US-born person each paid an extra US$ 170-230 in taxes in 1996 to cover the deficit of the 9 million immigrant-headed households—that is, immigrants collectively consumed more in publicly provided services than they paid in taxes (13). Moreover, the taxes paid by immigrants went largely to the federal Government, while the costs of the services that immigrants consumed were largely paid by state and local governments.

The NRC concluded that the long-term economic value of an immigrant depends on age at arrival and years of education: "if the policy goal were to maximize the positive contribution of immigration to public sector budgets, that could be achieved by policies favoring highly educated immigrants and not admitting immigrants over age 50" (13). However, on several occasions Congress has considered—and rejected—proposals for a point system like the Canadian programme that would give priority to economic/employment immigrants over family unification.

The CIR, a congressionally-mandated body, recommended in its final report in 1997 that the federal Government establish programmes to help immigrants integrate into US society. The CIR also noted that integration is the responsibility of immigrants and the communities in which they settle and emphasized that US business must do more to help immigrants develop language and other skills needed for advancement within the economy. "Those business groups in particular who lobby for high levels of immigration must make a far greater effort not only to support immigration, but also to support immigrants, through English classes, naturalization, and civic education (16)". In his first major speech on immigration in June 1998, President Clinton echoed the CIR. The President urged immigrants to do their part in joining the community: "Honor our laws. Embrace our culture. Learn our language. Know our history. And when the time comes, you should become citizens".

Although the USA has long encouraged immigrants to become naturalized US citizens, fewer than half of immigrants to the United States naturalize. For example, the immigrants admitted in 1977 were eligible to naturalize in 1982, but by 1995 only about 46 per cent had. Of those admitted in 1982, and thus eligible to naturalize after 1987, only 42 per cent had by 1995. Mexicans and Canadians traditionally have had low rates of naturalization.

This pattern may be changing, however. In most years until 1995, the INS received 200,000-300,000 naturalization applications. It received 543,000 applications in 1995, the first time that the number of foreigners wishing to naturalize topped 400,000 since 1944. In 1996 there were 1.3 million naturalization applications, and in 1997 about 1.6 million.

The upsurge in naturalization applications and new citizens was due in part to the 1995 "Citizenship USA" campaign that sought to assure applicants that most would be naturalized within six months. The surge in applications was caused by a combination of a number of other factors, including the requirement that immigrants replace their "green cards", approval of a proposition widely seen as anti-immigrant in intent by California voters,[8] and passage of the 1996 immigration laws that restricted immigrant access to welfare. Republicans accused Democrats of using Citizenship USA to add Democratic voters to the rolls before the November 1996 election. When investigators found that background checks on applicants were not always completed, naturalization procedures were changed, and the lag between application and naturalization lengthened to two or more years in 1998, although the waiting period declined subsequently to about one year on average.

EMIGRATION TRENDS

Mexico and parts of Central America and the Caribbean are net emigration areas, with most emigrants heading for the United States. Migration from Mexico has different origins from migration from Central America—Mexicans were recruited to work on US farms in the 1940s and 1950s, while many Central Americans migrated to the USA in the 1980s to avoid civil wars. In both cases, continued demand-pull in the USA, supply-push in the migrants' countries of origin, and the strengthening of social networks helped migration pressures and flows to snowball over time.

MEXICO

Mexico, the largest and richest of the major emigration countries south of the USA, had a population of 95 million in 1997 that was growing by 1.7 per cent or 1.6 million a year. In 1998, there were about 7.5 million Mexican-born persons in the USA, including 2 million naturalized US citizens, 3 million legal immigrants, and 2.5 million unauthorized migrants. In all, about 8 per cent of those born in Mexico had migrated to the United States.

Mexican-born US residents and workers traditionally have come from rural areas where the US and Mexican Governments authorized the recruitment of Mexican farm workers. Mexico was primarily a rural society until recently: about

25 per cent of Mexico's 97 million residents in 1999 lived on farms and in rural areas. Many Mexican men with homes and families in rural Mexico continue to be sojourners, coming to the USA for six to nine months each year, but the majority of Mexican-born US residents today are settlers who live in US cities; about half are women. Most Mexican-born persons in the United States have less than eight years of schooling and low US earnings and incomes.

For most of the twentieth century, the major relationship between Mexico and the USA was a migration relationship, and there were many disputes involving the treatment of Mexicans in the United States. Migration continues to be a function of several factors: demand-pull factors throughout the US economy, symbolized by the fact that about two-thirds of US hired farm workers in 1998 were born in Mexico and only about 20 per cent of the 4 to 5 million Mexican-born workers in the US labour force were employed in agriculture; supply-push factors in Mexico, as indicated by high levels of un- and under-employment, changes in agricultural and land policies that loosened ties to the land, and declining real wages that expanded the US-Mexican wage gap; and the strengthening of social networks that link transnational communities—the millions of former residents of Mexican villages and cities now established in the US who can provide the information and funds needed for others to enter the USA either legally or without authorization.

In 1991, Mexican President Salinas said that Mexico wanted to change its migration relationship with the USA into a trade relationship and formally requested that the USA negotiate a free trade agreement: "We want to export goods, not people". Mexico was the primary proponent of the North American Free Trade Agreement (NAFTA), which was approved after a close vote in the US Congress in October 1993 and went into effect in January 1994. Mexico, the USA, and Canada are parties to the Agreement.[9] It was hoped that NAFTA would lock national economic policy changes into an international agreement and thus encourage foreign investment, export-led growth, and job creation—most models projected about 100,000 net new jobs in Mexico each year because of NAFTA.

Most migration experts predicted that the closer economic integration symbolized by NAFTA would produce a migration hump, a temporary growth in Mexico-USA migration as Mexico restructures, especially its farm economy that employs about 25 per cent of Mexicans. US farmers can produce staple foods such as corn much more cheaply than Mexican farmers, so that up to 1 million of Mexico's 28 million residents are expected to leave their farms each year over the next decade. Most of them will move to mid-sized Mexican cities and border areas where *maquiladora* assembly plants are expanding, but some will migrate to the USA where they have family or friends.

NAFTA got off to a rocky start: Zapatista rebels launched an armed campaign in Chiapas on 1 January 1994; the leading presidential candidate was assassinated in March 1994; and the Mexican peso was sharply devalued in December 1994. Instead of job and wage growth, Mexico in 1995 suffered its worst recession in years, and many Mexicans responded by migrating to the USA despite stepped-up border controls. The USA apprehended 1.1 million foreigners—more than 95 per cent Mexican—in 1994, 1.4 million in 1995, 1.6 million in 1996, 1.5 million in 1997, and 1.7 million in 1998.

In 1995, Mexico lost jobs despite NAFTA, but employment in Mexico has since rebounded, reaching a new highest-ever level at the end of 1998. However, wages fell sharply in 1995, and they have not yet recovered to pre-NAFTA levels. In addition, the transformation of the Mexican economy continues, and farmers and farm workers squeezed by the elimination of government subsidies and cheaper imports are exiting agriculture.[10] Many of the rural residents leaving agriculture do not have the education needed to get good non-farm jobs in Mexico, which encourages some to migrate to the United States. Mexican Trade Minister Herminio Blanco in January 1999 reiterated that NAFTA was a very positive factor in Mexico's economic development and that it was achieving the goal of substituting trade for migration. However, he acknowledged that the benefits of export-led growth have not been widely shared: 300 firms, mostly multinationals, account for 70 per cent of Mexican exports.

The fastest growing sector of the Mexican economy in 1998—the *maquiladora* industry—was launched originally in the mid-1960s to deter Mexico-USA emigration. Foreign direct investment averaged US$ 11 billion a year between 1994 and 1997. Much of it went into *maquiladoras*, factory assembly operations that are permitted to import components duty free, assemble products with Mexican workers in Mexico, and then re-export the finished product, paying duty only on the value added by Mexican assembly operations.

There were about 4,045 *maquiladoras* with 1 million employees in June 1998, a doubling since 1995, up sharply from the 1,924 plants and 472,000 workers in 1990 (Table 46). M*aquiladoras* provide almost 10 per cent of the formal sector jobs in Mexico and about 30 per cent of the manufacturing jobs. Most *maquiladoras* are located along the US-Mexican border where unemployment is low; assembly plants recruit workers from the interior of Mexico. About 60 per cent of the employees in *maquiladoras* are young women, and most studies of the linkages between maquiladoras and migration conclude that the *maquiladora* workers do not use the assembly plants as a stepping-stone to the USA. However, the young men who often accompany women to border cities may migrate to the United States.

Projections of emigration for the mid- to long-term are more positive than today's figures would foretell. Changes set in motion in the 1970s and 1980s have set the stage for less Mexico-USA migration in the twenty-first century. Most important were demographic changes. Mexico had one of the world's most remarkable demographic transitions, with fertility falling from an average 6.1 births per woman in 1974 to 2.5 in 1996. This will sharply reduce the number of Mexicans turning 15 every year, from 1 million per year in the mid-1990s to 500,000 per year by 2010. Simultaneously, each 1 percent job growth adds 130,000 formal sector jobs

TABLE 46.
MAQUILADORAS **AND EMPLOYMENT, 1965-1998**

	Number of *maquiladoras*	Employment
1965	12	3,000
1970	120	20,327
1975	454	67,213
1980	578	119,546
1985	789	211,968
1990	1,924	472,000
1995	2,206	674,692
1998[1]	4,045	1,033,527

Note: [1]1998 data are for June 1998.

Source: US-Mexican Chamber of Commerce.

and 300,000 total jobs. If current levels of job growth continue at about 1 million formal sectors jobs added each year, Mexico should be able to absorb all new labour entrants, as well as a portion of the un- and under-employed, into formal jobs within the foreseeable future.

Mexico's policy has long focused on protecting its citizens in the USA. Mexico has 45 consulates in the USA, the most that any country has in another. US authorities have increased their cooperation with Mexican consuls, often notifying them, for example, when Mexicans are apprehended in the United States. Mexico took a further step toward strengthening its ties to citizens in the USA in 1996 when the Mexican constitution was amended to permit dual nationality; Mexicans becoming US citizens no longer lose their Mexican passports, and naturalized US citizens of Mexican origin can reclaim Mexican nationality. A second change permitted Mexicans to vote away from their registered residences, which opened the door for Mexicans living in the USA to vote in Mexican elections. The Federal Electoral Institute (IFE) in November 1998 issued a 14-volume study on the feasibility of absentee voting. The report focused on what the IFE estimated to be 7.1 million Mexican-born immigrants and 2.7 million adult children of Mexican-born parents in the USA who could be eligible to vote in the Mexican presidential election.

Remittances from Mexicans in the USA continue to be very important to the migrants' families and areas of origin as well as the Mexican economy. Mexico's central bank estimated that remittances were US$ 5.5 billion in 1998; about 25 per cent of the remittances arrived in Mexico during the last two weeks of December when an estimated 1.2 million Mexicans returned to Mexico for the holidays. Remittances have multiplier effects when they are spent in Mexico. Migrants often make contributions that improve the quality of life in their areas of origin, leading to new or improved schools, clinics, and roads. In some cases, remittances have been used to start sewing, agricultural, and other industries that create jobs for residents who do not emigrate.

NAFTA symbolized a new era of US-Mexican cooperation on difficult issues, including migration. Other notable steps that have increased US-Mexican cooperation on migration issues include the formal Binational Working Group on Migration, part of the Binational Commission between Mexico and the United States. Cooperative activities resulting from this ongoing dialogue include the

Binational Study of Migration, as well as the often quiet Mexico-USA cooperation to reduce the entry through Mexico to the USA of non-Mexicans, to prevent border violence, and to avoid deaths and injuries to migrants attempting unauthorized entry through remote areas of the border. These policy objectives were specifically agreed upon in the 1996 Joint Declaration on Migration signed by the presidents of both countries.

CENTRAL AMERICA

There were relatively few immigrants from the seven countries of Central America in the USA before the 1980s. Of the 1.1 million Central American immigrants who arrived in the USA over the past 175 years, 90 per cent arrived after 1980, compared to 60 per cent of the Mexican immigrants. In 1998, the 36,000 legal immigrants from the seven Central American countries were 5 per cent of the 660,000 US immigrants.

When El Salvador, Guatemala, Honduras, and Nicaragua were wracked by civil wars in the 1980s, many nationals of these countries fled to neighbouring countries as well as to the United States. US foreign policy concerns influenced decisions on whether to grant asylum to Central Americans in the USA. The granting of asylum to Nicaraguans and not to Salvadorans, reflecting US foreign policy goals of the time, prompted a suit against the INS that was settled in 1991. The so-called American Baptist Church or ABC settlement permitted Salvadorans, Guatemalans, and Nicaraguans who applied for temporary protected status (TPS) or asylum in the USA before 1990, but had their claims rejected, to have their applications reconsidered.

However, by the time that Central American asylum applications were reconsidered in 1997, many Central Americans had been in the USA a decade or more and had US-born children. In 1997, the USA approved the Nicaraguan Adjustment and Central American Relief Act permitting 200,000 Salvadorans and 50,000 Guatemalans to have their applications to remain in the USA considered under pre-1996 rules, which increases the chance that they will be allowed to remain. (Until 1996, foreigners in the USA for seven or more years, with good moral character, and whose removal would cause extreme hardship to themselves or their US families, could apply to remain in the USA as immigrants). The 150,000 Nicaraguans who arrived in the United States before 1 December 1995 were permitted to achieve immigrant status almost automatically.

In October-November 1998, Hurricane Mitch caused massive destruction in Honduras and Nicaragua. In response, the USA granted 150,000 unauthorized Nicaraguans and Hondurans in the USA temporary protected status to obtain work authorizations and remain in the country for at least 18 months in the hope that their remittances would speed reconstruction. The USA also temporarily stopped deportations of other Central Americans.

Both Central American presidents and news reports predicted that many of those displaced or made unemployed by the hurricane in Central America would attempt to migrate to Mexico and the United States. Honduran immigration director Reina Ochoa said in January 1999 that 300 Hondurans a day were leaving for the United States; the US consulate in the Honduran capital of Tegucigalpa reported that visa requests were up 40 per cent over year-earlier levels. Mexico, which had 150 agents on its 650-mile border with Guatemala and Belize, reported apprehending 5,800 migrants, mostly Honduran, on its southern border in December 1998, up from 2,900 in December 1997. Guatemala signalled its cooperation to prevent a mass migration of Central Americans northward by tightening border controls on 15 November 1998, despite an agreement among the four Central American nations to allow free movement. Salvadoran President Armando Calderón Sol called Guatemala's action "a step back in Central American integration".

El Salvador, the most densely populated country in Central America, is a special case in US immigration and asylum policy. During El Salvador's civil war, which ended in 1992, about 1 million of the 6 million Salvadorans migrated to the United States. Salvadorans in the USA remit about US$ 1 billion a year, making remittances more than three times more important than the country's leading export, coffee.

El Salvador takes a keen interest in US immigration policy. In February 1999, the President of El Salvador estimated that there were 1.2 million Salvadorans in the USA, including 450,000 who were unauthorized. President Calderón asked President Clinton during a March 1999 visit to provide TPS for Salvadorans in the

USA and to give legal immigrant status to the 200,000 Salvadorans whose applications for asylum were pending. He also requested assistance to help El Salvador deal with the return of Salvadorans convicted of committing crimes in the United States. For example, some of the 8,000 mostly young men deported from the USA to El Salvador between 1993 and 1998 re-established branches of Los Angeles gangs in El Salvador that have become a problem for local police.

There is considerable migration within Central America, generally from poorer to richer countries. Most Central American nations permit nationals of neighbouring countries to enter without visas for 72 hours, and some of these short-term visitors go to work. For example, there are believed to be 300,000-500,000 Nicaraguans working in Costa Rica, half of them illegally employed in agriculture, construction, or services at wages that are four to six times higher than in Nicaragua. Nicaraguans form more than 10 per cent of the 3.4 million Costa Rican residents, and they have relatively free access to Costa Rican education and health care systems.[12] Because of Hurricane Mitch, Costa Rica announced that it would not deport illegal Central Americans for six months. Mexico issues about 125,000 work permits to mostly Central American migrants each year, and other Central American migrants are employed illegally in Mexico to pick coffee beans or do unskilled construction work. Mexico also granted permanent resident status to Guatemalans living in refugee camps who chose not to repatriate.

CARIBBEAN

The 15 independent Caribbean nations, plus several dependencies, have some of the highest emigration rates in the world.[13] The largest four sources of migrants to the USA—Cuba, the Dominican Republic, Haiti, and Jamaica—include about 75 per cent of the 36 million Caribbean residents. Caribbean residents also migrate to former colonial powers in Europe, to Central and South America, and to Canada. In 1998, the USA received 75,000 Caribbean immigrants: 20,000 Dominicans, 17,000 Cubans, 15,000 Jamaicans, and 13,000 Haitians. The region is also used as a stepping-stone to the USA by traffickers smuggling migrants from China and other countries.

Cuba has been the major emigration country: there are more than 1 million Cuban-born persons in the USA, while almost 10 per cent of those born in Cuba are in the United States. Cubans migrated to the USA in three major waves—after

Castro came to power in 1959, during the Mariel boat lift in 1980, and in 1994. Since 1994, a US-Cuban migration agreement guarantees 20,000 immigrant visas for Cubans each year. Most Cuban immigrants settle in southern Florida where they are extraordinarily successful in business and politics, helping to turn Miami into a business and finance gateway to the Americas.

Some 350,000 Haitians have emigrated to the USA, including one-third who arrived in the 1990s. Per capital GNP in Haiti is US$ 400, the lowest in the western hemisphere. Haiti also has undergone political repression and turmoil. In the late 1970s, Haitians began to make the 720-mile trip from Haiti to Florida in boats, and 25,000 Haitians arrived during the Mariel boatlift in 1980. Beginning in 1981, Haiti allowed the US Coast Guard to stop boats in Haitian and international waters to determine whether they were carrying Haitians bound for the United States. If they were, the Haitians were often returned to Haiti. In 1991, following the military overthrow of Haiti's elected president, Haitians began fleeing the country in large numbers. The USA instituted a policy of direct returns, not permitting Haitians to apply for asylum.

Haitian migration became a crisis in summer 1994 when security in Haiti deteriorated significantly. Haitians picked up at sea were sent to the US base at Guantanamo Bay in Cuba, where they were provided temporary protection. After President Aristide was restored to power in 1994, most returned home. The US Congressional Black Caucus condemned the generous treatment of Cubans and the tough policies toward Haitians. In 1998, Congress approved the Haitian Refugee Immigration Fairness Act permitting 50,000 Haitians in the USA since 1995 to become immigrants. A poll of 1,400 Haitians conducted in that year by the US Embassy in Haiti found that nearly three-fourths of those surveyed would emigrate if they could.

Haitians also migrate to the neighbouring Dominican Republic. There are an estimated 500,000 Haitians in the Dominican Republic; about 6 per cent of Dominican residents may be Haitians. Most of the Haitians work on sugar and rice plantations, sometimes under such poor conditions that there have been investigations by the ILO. Migration is a point of tension between the Spanish-speaking Dominican Republic and Creole/French-speaking Haiti. About 40,000 Haitians also live in the Bahamas, including 10,000 in Freeport, making Haitians a significant share of the 280,000 residents of the Bahamas.

Both Haitians and Cubans continue to migrate to southern Florida in small boats: in 1998, the US Coast Guard intercepted 1,025 Cubans and 1,206 Haitians at sea, compared to 406 Cubans and 587 Haitians in 1997. Haitians stopped at sea are returned to Haiti, while Cubans are taken to Florida or to the US naval base on the south-eastern tip of Cuba at Guantanamo before being returned home. Cubans who reach Florida without being detected at sea are permitted to remain in the USA. After one year they may become permanent residents under a 1966 law, which explains why many Cubans turn themselves into the INS as soon as they land in Florida.

Another major Caribbean source of US immigrants is the Dominican Republic. Some 765,000 Dominicans have immigrated legally, most since 1985, and most settling in New York City. Dominican migration began in the 1960s after US involvement, including a 1965 invasion. The Dominican Republic has about 8 million residents, and US consulates in the Dominican Republic receive an average of 500 requests for immigrant and tourist visas daily, making the Dominican Republic third among US consulates in visa requests after the far more populous Philippines and Mexico. According to a 1997 poll, half of the residents of the Dominican Republic have relatives in the USA and two-thirds would move there if they could.

Dominican migration exemplifies transnational migration, the practice of maintaining ties to two countries. The current president of the Dominican Republic, Leonel Fernández Reyna, went to elementary and high school in New York City, and has said he may return to the USA after he leaves the Dominican Presidency. The Dominican Republic made dual citizenship legal in 1994, and Dominican politicians regularly campaign for votes in New York City.

Some 536,000 Jamaicans emigrated to the USA in one of the oldest migrations in the region—only 20 per cent of the Jamaicans arrived in the 1990s. Jamaicans were recruited to work in US agriculture beginning in 1943, and until the early 1990s about 10,000-12,000 arrived annually to cut sugar cane in Florida and pick apples on the East Coast. Since then, sugar cane harvesting in Florida has been mechanized, and Mexico replaced Jamaica as the major source of non-immigrant farm workers. Especially in the 1940s and 1950s, large numbers of Jamaicans also migrated to the United Kingdom.

Remittances from migrants in the USA are a major source of foreign exchange in the Caribbean; "labour" is a major export of many of the island nations. Remittances to Cuba were estimated to be US$ 800 million in 1998; in 1995, IMF reported that remittances to the Dominican Republic were US$ 796 million and to Jamaica US$ 503 million. In 1997, the 15-nation Caribbean Community (Caricom) signed the Bridgetown (Barbados) accord to lay the basis for trade and economic cooperation between the United States and the Caribbean. Caricom, established in 1973, would like to turn the Caribbean into a single market to facilitate trade and investment.

Many of the families receiving remittances report that money from abroad is 30-50 per cent of their total income; dollar remittances have been credited with accelerating the drive to "dollarize" Latin American economies, that is, to use the US dollar as legal tender in an effort to stabilize currencies.

Puerto Rico represents a special case of Caribbean migration. Puerto Ricans have been US citizens since 1917, and in 1998 there were about 2.7 million residents of Puerto Rican origin on the mainland and 3.8 million in Puerto Rico. This internal migration responds to changing economic conditions in Puerto Rico and the mainland, especially in New York and Chicago, where most mainland Puerto Ricans live. Higher wages and lower unemployment on the mainland encouraged emigration until the mid-1970s, when minimum wages in Puerto Rico were raised and job creation was induced by special tax breaks. As the US welfare system expanded, the combination of a narrowing wage gap as well as the availability of food stamps and other assistance reduced net migration to nearly zero.[14]

REGIONAL TRENDS

Although unilateral policy-making continues to dominate, migration issues within North America increasingly are handled through bilateral and regional mechanisms. NAFTA provided an important stimulus to regional cooperation, although the trade negotiations avoided direct discussion of the most controversial issue: unauthorized movements from Mexico to the United States. Nevertheless, NAFTA created a new environment of cooperation between the two countries that has permitted freer exchange of views on migration. Moreover, both countries recognize that increased trade offered the best hope for reducing emigration pressures.

NAFTA has some immigration-related provisions. Chapter 16 of NAFTA permits 64 types of professionals—for example, accountants, engineers, and lawyers—to work in the other participating countries. The professional seeking to work in another member country goes to the port of entry, shows an offer of employment, a professional credential and passport, and is admitted under a one-year visa that can be extended indefinitely. NAFTA professionals may bring their families with them. The spouses of US professionals may work in Canada under certain conditions, but the spouses of Canadian and Mexican professionals may not work in the United States.

In 1996, some 34,438 Canadian professionals and 243 Mexicans, including their spouses and dependent children, moved into the USA under this NAFTA provision; in 1997, 10,800 professional US citizens moved to Canada. There is no limit on how many professionals can cross the border between the USA and Canada, but the number of Mexican professionals who can enter the USA under NAFTA provisions is limited to 5,500 thousand per year until 2003.

A second form of regional cooperation, the Regional Conference on Migration—the Puebla Process—is an ongoing migration consultation that involves 11 countries, mostly in North and Central America. The Dominican Republic is the group's only Caribbean member. Member governments seek cooperation on a long-term strategy for understanding and managing migration problems and opportunities. Since the first meeting in Puebla, Mexico, in 1996, the consultations have developed a plan of action that focuses on development of migration policy, study of the linkages between migration and development, enforcement against traffickers, return of extraregional migrants, promotion of migrants' human rights, and cooperation on other technical matters. In addition to the members, representatives of several South American governments and international organizations attend sessions as observers. Consultations also are held with representatives of nongovernmental organizations. The International Organization for Migration serves as secretariat to the process.

The annual vice-ministerial meetings, along with interim technical sessions and seminars, focus governmental efforts on better understanding of the processes of migration and on cooperative responses. Mexico, Canada, El Salvador, and the United States have hosted these meetings.

CONCLUSION

The North American migration system is likely to continue to include some of the world's major source, transit, and destination countries for migrants in the twenty-first century. Canada and the United States are debating changes to their immigration systems, administration, and enforcement; but both countries continue to see themselves as countries of immigration—countries that welcome newcomers—believing that immigrants who better themselves by migrating also enrich their new country.

Mexico, Central American countries such as El Salvador, and Caribbean islands such as Haiti, the Dominican Republic, and Jamaica are likely to continue to be major sources of immigrants, with 5 to 15 percent of persons born in these countries living abroad as migrants. Migration within the North American system is likely to become more complex, for example, as Nicaraguans migrate to Costa Rica and the USA, Guatemalans to Mexico and the USA, and Haitians to Canada, the Dominican Republic, and the USA. NAFTA and other trade liberalizing regimes may begin to substitute trade for migration. Transit migration is likely to affect many of the countries in the North American migration system as Asians and others headed for one North American country transit through another (as Chinese migrants transit through Canada and Mexico to the USA).

The migration challenges facing North America are likely to strengthen such forums for discussions of migration issues as the Regional Conference on Migration—Puebla Group. This and other forums are likely to play an ever stronger role in ensuring that North American countries guarantee the human rights of all migrants and work cooperatively to reduce smuggling and exploitation.

ENDNOTES

[1.] US immigration data are recorded by US fiscal, not calendar, year.

[2.] In 1996, about 16,000 Canadians emigrated to the USA, and 5,000 US citizens emigrated to Canada. An estimated one-third of the Canadians who migrate to the USA return to Canada within ten years.

[3.] Ontario had 2.7 million or 54 per cent of Canada's immigrants in 1997, British Columbia 22 per cent, and Quebec 15 per cent; about 42 per cent of metro-Toronto's residents are immigrants.

4. Available on the Internet at **http://cicnet.ci.gc.ca/legrev/e_pubs.html**

5. The exceptions are Native Americans, slaves, and those who became US citizens by purchase or conquest, such as French nationals who became US citizens with the Louisiana Purchase, Mexicans who became US citizens with the settlement ending the Mexican War, and Puerto Ricans who became US citizens as a result of the US victory over Spain in 1898.

6. Nationals of countries that sent fewer than 50,000 immigrants to the USA over the past five years are eligible to enter an annual lottery for one of up to 50,000 diversity visas. Some 6 to 7 million applications were made during the month-long application period that opened in October 1998. Nationals of the United Kingdom, Canada, China (including Taiwan [Province of China]), Colombia, the Dominican Republic, El Salvador, Haiti, India, Jamaica, Mexico, Poland, the Philippines, the Republic of Korea, and Viet Nam could not apply in 1998.

7. Apprehensions record the event of capturing an unauthorized alien and are not a count of individuals; one alien apprehended five times is recorded as five apprehensions.

8. In 1999, Proposition 187 was nullified by the court after several years of litigation on its constitutionality. The court actions precluded its ever having been implemented.

9. Canada and the USA have had a free trade agreement since 1989.

10. For most of the twentieth century, Mexico has had a unique land tenure system, the *ejido*. The 1917 Mexican Constitution included Article 27, which permitted large private land holdings to be redistributed to create communal *ejido* farms for peasants. The 27,000 *ejidos* in Mexico in the early 1990s included half of Mexico's arable land and had 15 million residents, one-sixth of the population. *Ejido* farmers and their heirs retained the right to the land only as long as they actively worked and lived on it. Article 27 was repealed on 27 February 1992; since then, *ejido* farmers may sell or rent their land, and foreigners and corporations can buy or rent farm land in Mexico.

11. There were 10,216,940 permanently insured workers in Institute Mexicano del Seguro Social, the Mexican social security system, in October 1998, up 380,000 or 4 per cent from the year before.

12. Costa Rican Immigration Director Eduardo Vilchez Hurtado asserted in 1998 that Nicaraguan immigration "is interfering with our system of social services and job availability. We [Costa Rica] need to regain control over our borders. We need to be able to determine who enters our country and who doesn't. . . . Costa Rica needs the migratory groups that come to fill vacancies in the manual labour work force. But these should be considered migratory workers who must return to their country once the harvest is finished. It must be a cyclical migration". Quoted in Juanita Darling, "Nicaraguans seeking work are finding it harder to sneak into Costa Rica as patience wears thin", *Los Angeles Times*, 28 July 1998, p. A1.

13. During the 1960s and 1970s, many former Caribbean colonies became independent countries. Since 1983, most islands have voted against independence, including Puerto Rico in 1998.

14. In 1996, about 40 per cent of Puerto Rico families received some form of federal welfare assistance.

REFERENCES

CANADA

1. Dirks, G.E. (1995). *Controversy and Complexity: Canadian Immigration Policy During the 1980s*. McGill Queens University Press, Montreal, Canada.

2. Reitz, J.G. (1998). *Warmth of the Welcome: The Social Causes of Economic Success for Immigrants in Different Nations and Cities*. Westview Press, Boulder, CO.

3. Trempe, R., S. Davis and R. Kunin (1997). *Not Just Numbers: A Canadian Framework for Future Immigration*. Ottawa, Citizenship and Immigration, 31 December. **http://cicnet.ci.gc.ca/english/about/policy/lrag/emain.html**

4. **http://cicnet.ci.gc.ca/** Citizenship and Immigration Canada.

5. **http://www.citzine.ca/** Citzine, the web magazine for Canadians.

6. **http://www.irb.gc.ca/** Immigration and Refugee Board of Canada.

7. **http://www.statcan.ca/** Statistics Canada.

UNITED STATES

8. Binational Study of Mexico-U.S. Migration (1997). *Migration between Mexico and the United States*. US Commission on Immigration Reform, Washington, DC.

9. Cornelius, W.A., P.L. Martin and J.F. Hollifield (Eds.) (1994). *Controlling Immigration: A Global Perspective*. Stanford University Press, Stanford, CA.

10. Duignan, P. and L. Gann (Eds.) (1998). *The Debate in the United States over Immigration*. Hoover Institution, Stanford, CA.

11. Immigration and Naturalization Service, US Department of Justice (1999). *Legal Immigration, Fiscal Year 1998, Annual Report of the Office of Policy and Planning*, Statistics Branch, No. 2, May.

12. Martin, P.L. and E. Midgley (1999). Immigration to the United States. *Population Bulletin*, 54(2). Population Reference Bureau, Washington, DC.

13. National Research Council (1997). *The New Americans: Economic, Demographic, and Fiscal Effects of Immigration*. National Academy Press, Washington, DC .

14. Portes, A. and R.G. Rumbaut (1996). *Immigrant America: A Portrait*. University of California Press, Berkeley, CA.

15. Suro, R. (1998). *Strangers Among Us: How Latino Immigration is Transforming America.* Knopf, New York, NY.

16. US Commission on Immigration Reform (1997). *Becoming an American: Immigration and Immigrant Policy*, Washington, DC. **http://migration.ucdavis.edu/MN-Resources/ resources.html**

MEXICO AND CENTRAL AMERICA

17. Bean, F.D., et al. (Eds.) (1998). *At the Crossroads: Mexico and U.S. Immigration Policy.* Rowan & Littlefield, Lanham, MD.

18. Binational Study of Mexico-U.S. Migration (1997). *Migration between Mexico and the United States*. US Commission on Immigration Reform, Washington, DC.

19. Castillo García, M.A. and S.I. Palma Calderón (1999). Central American International Emigration: Trends and Impacts. In R. Appleyard (Ed.), *Emigration Dynamics in Developing Countries, Vol. III: Mexico, Central America and the Caribbean*, Ashgate for IOM/UNFPA, Aldershot, England and Brookfield, VT.

20. Consulate General of Mexico in New York. On-line at **http://www.quicklink.com/mexico/ ingles/ing.htm**

21. Escobar Latapí, A., F.D. Bean, and S. Weintraub (1999). The Dynamics of Mexican Emigration. In R. Appleyard (Ed.), *Emigration Dynamics in Developing Countries, Vol. III: Mexico, Central America and the Caribbean*. Ashgate for IOM/UNFPA, Aldershot, England and Brookfield, VT .

22. Escobar Latapí, A., F.D. Bean, and S. Weintraub (1998). Migración y Desarrollo en Centro y Norteamérica: Elementos para una Discusión. Paper presented at the Conferencia Migración y Desarrollo en Centro y Norteamérica organized by the IOM and the Economic Commission for Latin America and the Caribbean, Mexico City, 21-22 May.

CARIBBEAN

23 Chamberlain, M. (Ed.) (1998). *Caribbean Migration: Globalized Identities*. Routledge, New York, NY.

24. Diaz-Briquets, S. and S. Weintraub (Eds.) (1991). *Determinants of Emigration from Mexico, Central America, and the Caribbean*. Westview Press, Boulder, CO.

25. Gmelch, G. (1992). *Double Passage: The Lives of Caribbean Migrants Abroad and Back Home*. University of Michigan Press, Ann Arbor, MI.

26. Grasmuck, S. and P.R. Pessar (1991). *Between Two Islands*. University of California Press, Berkeley, CA.

27. Pessar, P.R. (Ed.) (1996). *Caribbean Circuits: New Directions in the Study of Caribbean Migration*. Center for Migration Studies, New York, NY.

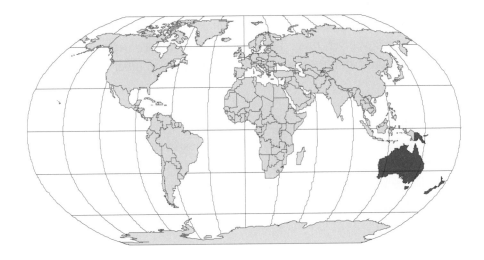

OCEANIA

INTRODUCTION

A "sea of islands", Oceania comprises two highly developed countries (Australia and New Zealand), the island nation of Papua New Guinea, and the small States of Melanesia, Micronesia and Polynesia. The region is characterized today by several types of permanent and temporary population flows in and out of the region.

Both Australia and New Zealand have a history of permanent immigration from the United Kingdom and Ireland, as well as temporary labour migration from nearby Asian and Pacific countries. Since the 1970s, economic alignment and globalization have played a role in shifting immigration patterns in which immigration from Asia began to exceed that from Europe. Well developed immigration systems in these two host countries resemble those in North America and, like them, currently aim at reducing immigration and making it more selective. Reduction in permanent immigration notwithstanding, both countries have generous humanitarian policies that welcome refugees from around the world.

Graziano Battistella, Director of the Scalabrini Migration Center and Editor of the *Asian and Pacific Migration Journal* based in Quezon City, Philippines, contributed to this chapter.

While Australia and New Zealand experience some out-migration, the island nations of Oceania frequently have significant portions of their population working overseas at any given time. The smaller island States are characterized by circular migration within the region and out-migration to other countries on the Pacific rim.

Profound changes in migration patterns throughout Oceania marked the last quarter century. These patterns reflect the changes in economic regionalization and globalization of markets for goods and labour. For the most part, however, these nations escaped the worst impacts of the economic crisis from which Asia is slowly emerging.

IMMIGRATION TRENDS

Australia and New Zealand are the principal destinations for migrants in this region.

AUSTRALIA

Abundant land, a growing economy, and an open door greeted immigrants to Australia for more than a century. From the early years as a colony of the British Empire, Australia grew with the infusion of predominantly British and Irish immigrant labour. European immigrants continued to settle in Australia in the twentieth century. By the 1970s and 1980s, however, European immigration began to wane and, in the interests of international competitiveness, the country took steps to attract well qualified immigrants from other regions. Economic changes, including vast deregulation of industry, made this developed economy even more attractive to immigrants. The combination of the pull of the economy, the aggressive search for new markets, and opportunities for Asian business investment led to the shift in origin of immigration. Quality education, political stability, and abundant jobs continue to attract immigrants from Asia and South Africa, the sixth leading country of origin of Australia's immigrants.

Australia continues its long tradition as an immigration country. Like other developed countries in Europe and North America, however, Australia has begun to set in place a more selective immigration policy to ensure immigrants will be well received and will contribute to the overall economy and society. This more restrictive policy stems from concerns about the magnitude and diversity of recent immigration. Currently, nearly 25 per cent of the population in 1996 is foreign-born, according to the Australian Bureau of Statistics. In addition to permanent immigration, a growing number of temporary residents are admitted for their skills each year—50 per cent of whom come from Europe. Since The Second World War, some 5.7 million people have immigrated to Australia and 580,000 refugees have been granted resettlement.

For the fiscal year 1999-2000, the official migration programme anticipates the admission of up to 82,000 persons: 70,000 immigrants (32,000 family members, 35,000 skilled migrants, and 3,000 in the special eligibility category) and 12,000 refugees or persons in a refugee-like situation—particularly from the countries of the former Yugoslavia, the Middle East and Africa. Actual arrivals normally fall short of the established ceiling (Table 47). Considering non-programme arrivals who come mostly from New Zealand, however, the overall intake each year comes close to the expected programme totals. More immigrants to Australia come from New Zealand than any other country. In recent years, overall immigrant arrivals were highest in 1988-1989 (145,300); total immigration reached nearly 100,000 in 1995-1996, before dropping off again.

In addition to immigrants, Australia gives temporary residence to people with special employment skills (37,000 in 1997-1998) (10), including corporate and independent business executives, specialists, university professors, and medical practitioners who may stay for six months to four years. Also admitted in a temporary category are individuals who can contribute to the fields of sport, culture, or international relations. There are no limits on the maximum number of temporary entrants, with the exception of a seasonal student employment programme. In 1998-1999, a total of 97,000 temporary residents were first admitted to Australia. While 45 per cent of all temporary residents were from the United Kingdom and Ireland, 27 per cent originated in Asia, and 12 per cent in North America. In addition, just over 66,000 new visas were granted to students in 1998-1999, mostly (73 per cent) from East and South-East Asian countries (Table 48).

TABLE 47.
AUSTRALIA'S IMMIGRATION PROGRAMME AND ACTUAL ARRIVALS, 1992-1993 TO 1997-1998

	1992-93	1993-94	1994-85	1995-96	1996-97	1997-98	1998-99
Programme							
Family	45,300	43,200	44,500	56,700	44,580	31,310	30,500
Skill	21,300	18,300	30,400	24,100	27,550	34,670	35,000
Special eligibility	1,400	1,300	1,600	1,700	1,730	1,110	3,500
Humanitarian	11,800	12,700	13,200	15,052	11,903	12,020	12,000
Total	**79,800**	**75,500**	**89,700**	**97,552**	**85,763**	**79,110**	**80,000**
Actual arrivals							
Family	32,102	33,580	37,078	46,458	36,490	21,142	21,501
Skill	22,137	12,794	20,210	20,008	19,697	25,985	27,931
Special eligibility	304	349	434	511	393	217	175
Humanitarian	10,939	11,350	13,632	13,824	9,886	8,779	8,790
Total	**65,482**	**58,073**	**71,354**	**80,801**	**66,466**	**56,123**	**58,397**
Non-programme							
Migration[1]	10,848	11,695	16,074	18,338	19,286	21,204	25,746
Total arrivals	**76,330**	**69,768**	**87,428**	**99,139**	**85,752**	**77,327**	**84,143**

Note: [1]Mostly New Zealanders.

Source: Department of Immigration and Multicultural Affairs. *Immigration Update, June Quarter 1999.*

TABLE 48.
TEMPORARY ENTRIES TO AUSTRALIA, 1998-1999

	Students		Temporary residents	
	First entry	Total arrivals	First entry	Total arrivals
Oceania	1,750	5,279	1,573	3,081
Europe and former USSR	7,904	11,786	56,146	97,139
Middle East and North Africa	487	949	941	1,907
South-East Asia	22,898	65,765	4,192	10,399
North-East Asia	19,156	51,555	15,673	36,822
Southern Asia	6,716	11,773	2,627	4,851
Northern America	4,661	7,439	11,752	31,163
Central and South America	1,787	2,494	1,330	2,061
Africa	1,377	2,182	3,054	5,174
Other	2	26	6	21
Total	**66,739**	**159,246**	**93,011**	**194,123**

Note: Total arrivals comprises First entry, Re-entry and Not stated. The total may differ from the sum of its components in the table due to rounding.

Source: Department of Immigration and Multicultural Affairs. *Immigration Update, June Quarter 1999.*

Thanks to its immigration policy and geographical configuration, Australia succeeded in limiting irregular immigration. At the end of 1997, there were approximately 51,000 overstayers in Australia, most of whom arrived as visitors (76 per cent). However, although Australia is relatively far to reach by boat for unauthorized entrants and the Government requires a visa from citizens of all countries (except New Zealand), a surge of unauthorized arrivals occurred in the second part of 1999. A total of 242 boats were intercepted in 1998-1999, carrying 926 people. In 1989 only three boats were intercepted and, as of October 1998, only 3,127 boat people had arrived since 1989 (mostly Chinese and Sino-Vietnamese). Of these arrivals, 672 were granted entry, 2,400 departed, and 55 are still in the country (10). Reacting quickly to the fear of uncontrolled immigration, the Border Protection Legislation Amendment Bill was adopted with bipartisan support. Its purpose is to discourage asylum claims as a way of entering Australia. The bill contains a provision that denies entry to asylum seekers if before reaching Australia they travelled through another nation in which they could have received asylum, i.e., a signatory to the relevant Geneva Convention.

Asia is the region of origin of most of today's immigrants to Australia because of declining flows from Europe. Europe is the second leading region of origin, followed by Oceania (mostly New Zealanders). Currently, 32 per cent of all immigrants come from Asia and 23 per cent are from Europe (Table 49). Although New Zealand (22 per cent) and the United Kingdom (10 per cent) remain by far the single most important countries of origin, China is third on the list of countries of origin (7 per cent) and five more of the remaining top 10 countries of origin are Asian countries (Table 50).

The states of New South Wales (41.8 per cent) and Victoria (20.5 per cent) in the south-east are destinations for two-thirds of immigrant arrivals. New South Wales has the highest number of immigrants in all categories. Western Australia (40 per cent) and Queensland (39 per cent) have the highest proportion of skilled migrants, while Tasmania (27 per cent) had the highest proportion of entrants under the humanitarian stream.

Of the overall foreign-born population, the United Kingdom is still by far the number one place of birth, followed by New Zealand, Italy, Viet Nam, and Greece. China, the Philippines, and India are also among the top 10 places of birth (9). Among the second generation, Asian countries do not figure prominently in the

TABLE 49.

AUSTRALIA: SETTLER ARRIVALS BY REGION, 1987-1988 AND 1997-1998

	1987-1988		1997-1998		1998-1999	
	Number	Per cent	Number	Per cent	Number	Per cent
Oceania	25,700	17.9	17,792	23.0	22,501	26.7
Europe and former USSR	43,600	30.4	19,501	25.2	19,608	23.3
Middle East & North Africa	10,000	7.0	5,790	7.5	5,195	6.2
South-East Asia	29,500	20.6	9,700	12.5	10,934	13.0
North-East Asia	12,700	8.8	10,214	13.2	10,869	12.9
Southern Asia	6,700	4.7	5,333	6.9	5,316	6.3
Northern America	3,100	2.1	2,049	2.6	1,624	1.9
S. & C. America and Caribbean	4,600	3.2	667	0.9	773	0.9
Africa (excl. North Africa)	7,600	5.3	6,256	8.1	7,246	8.6
Total (including "not stated")	**143,190**	**100.0**	**77,327**	**100.0**	**84,143**	**100.0**

Sources: Department of Immigration and Multicultural Affairs. *Fact Sheet 2,*
http://www.immi.gov.au/facts/index.htm
Department of Immigration and Multicultural Affairs. *Immigration Update, June Quarter 1999.*

TABLE 50.

AUSTRALIA: SETTLER ARRIVALS BY TOP 10 COUNTRIES OR TERRITORIES OF BIRTH, 1997-1998 AND 1998-1999

	1997-1998		1998-1999	
Place of birth	Number	Per cent	Number	Per cent
New Zealand	14,723	19.0	18,677	22.2
United Kingdom	9,193	11.9	8,785	10.4
China	4,338	5.6	6,133	7.3
South Africa	4,281	5.5	5,024	6.0
Philippines	2,769	3.6	3,318	3.9
Yugoslavia	-	-	2,912	3.5
India	2,786	3.6	2,557	3.0
Indonesia	1,917	2.5	2,491	3.0
Vietnam	2,311	3.0	2,137	2.5
Hong Kong (SAR)	3,194	4.1	1,918	2.3

Source: Department of Immigration and Multicultural Affairs. *Immigration Update, June Quarter 1999.*

population because of their recent arrival. Projections of the future ethnic composition in Australia indicate that in the year 2025 Europeans will comprise 77.6 per cent of the population, Asians 15.5 per cent.

Australia has a well defined immigration policy, similar in many ways to policies in North America. The migration programme is based on principles established in the 1970s with the repeal of the "White Australian" policy that had effectively limited immigration to Europeans. Today, ceilings are set annually for the admission of immigrants on the basis of skill, family ties, and humanitarian reasons. Policy preferences have shifted toward skills-based admissions over admissions based on family reunification. For prospective immigrants who do not have close family ties or an established job connection, admission is determined on the basis of a general point system that rates an individual by skill, age, and English language ability. The 1972 Trans-Tasman Travel Agreement between Australia and New Zealand allows the exchange of population without numerical restriction.

Current policy may best be described as the promotion of multiculturalism. Earlier positions—from which this policy evolved—promoted the assimilation of immigrants (1901-1966) into the existing culture and society of Australia and integration of immigrants (1966-1972) if not wholly into the existing cultural ways, into the economy. Multiculturalism is based on the right of all Australians to their cultural heritage, to equality of treatment and opportunity, and to the need to pursue economic efficiency by utilizing the skills of Australians regardless of background. What is expected in return is immigrants' overriding and unifying commitment to Australia, acceptance of the basic principles and structures of the Australian society, and the acceptance of the right of others to express their views and values (10). A new National Multicultural Advisory Council (NMAC) was established to advise the Government on multicultural issues. While polls generally confirm an overwhelming support for multiculturalism, they also reflect concerns that multiculturalism sows divisiveness in the society.

Each year, the establishment of the immigration ceiling becomes an occasion for public discussion of the relative merits of expanding or conserving current immigration levels. In 1998, the debate stirred by the controversial position of former member of Parliament Pauline Hanson against Asian immigrants was the latest occasion for heated discussion and resulted in a bipartisan reaffirmation of nondiscriminatory principles in immigration policy (19). Although Hanson was not re-elected in 1998—indicating that voters have distanced themselves from the divisive positions she expressed—her defeat cannot be considered the end of the debate.

At the same time that the basic principles of immigration policy were being reaffirmed, some policy measures were taken to discourage the entry of immigrants into Australia by limiting their benefits in the first period of settlement. Beginning in 1993, for example, immigrants were ineligible for unemployment and sickness benefits during the first six months after arrival. In 1996, the period of ineligibility was extended to two years. In addition, the cost of visas and English language courses was sharply increased (6). Such policies replicate similar restrictions imposed in North America and respond to the same objective of reducing the role of the welfare state and reducing pressure from immigrants likely to become a public charge. However, the unwanted consequence of these policies is likely to be greater difficulty for immigrants in their attempts to function meaningfully and to begin to contribute to the host society. In the end, the cost for the State to provide for non-integrated immigrants may be higher than what is saved through the denial of benefits.

The ultimate objective of immigration policy is to encourage immigrant settlers to commit themselves to citizenship. Permanent residents are eligible for citizenship after living in the country for two out of the previous five years, including 12 months out of the previous two years.

Discussion of the foreign-born population generally differentiates those who come from English-speaking backgrounds from those with non-English speaking backgrounds. According to the 1996 census, 23 per cent of the population was born overseas, while 9 per cent came from English-speaking backgrounds and 14 per cent from non-English-speaking countries. The foreign-born population has a higher median age (42 years) than the Australia-born (29 years). It lives predominantly in urban areas; only 8 per cent reside in rural areas as compared to 17 per cent for the non-immigrant population. Immigrants, particularly from non-English-speaking backgrounds, tend to own their own house and to be married at a higher rate than the Australia-born population.

Marriage within the ethnic group is more common among those with a non-English-speaking background, as is a lower rate of divorce. Young immigrants from non-English-speaking countries attend school in Australia more than the Australia-born. In 1992, 60 percent of 15- to 24-year-olds from non-English backgrounds were enrolled in an educational institution, compared with 50 per cent of the Australia-born and those from English-speaking countries. How ever, immigrants from English-speaking countries had a higher percentage of persons with post-secondary education.

The economic performance of those who came from non-English backgrounds is lower than the Australia-born, while English-background immigrants fare better than the Australia-born. Immigrants from a non-English-speaking background have a lower participation in the labour force (53 per cent compared to 65 per cent for the Australia-born), higher unemployment (7.9 per cent, compared to 6.3 per cent in July 1999) (11), and a higher participation in unskilled occupations (30.6 per cent, compared to 21.0 per cent). Broad summaries obviously do not give justice to the various differences concerning the individual ethnic groups, however. Indicators are generally more favourable for immigrant groups that have a long history of presence in Australia, such as Italians, Greeks, and Maltese, while recently arrived migrants appear to be in a more difficult situation.

New Zealanders top the list of immigrant nationalities. The 1996 census in Australia registered 291,000 New Zealanders who actively participate in the labour market (76.6 per cent participation compared to 66.3 per cent for Australia-born), but who also show a higher unemployment rate (9.3 compared to 9.0 per cent) (10).

A specific review based on the 1991 census profile of Chinese immigrants—the third leading country of origin today—revealed that more than one-half of the immigrants from China to Australia arrived between 1986 and 1991. A high percentage of Chinese men (82 per cent) and women (61 per cent) are in the labour force, working as traders, labourers, machine operators, professionals, and managers. About one-half of Chinese immigrants owned their own home in Australia, more than one-half spoke English well or very well, and about 56 per cent had acquired Australian citizenship (17).

Discussion of immigration often is rooted in perceived fears. Nationals fear an "invasion" by immigrants, loss of jobs to immigrants, downward pressure on salaries, and a lower quality of life. Conservationists fear an excessive burden imposed by immigrants on welfare, diminished national identity and cohesion, and damage to the environment. In this regard, the debate in Australia is not very different from that in North America or Europe. However, Australia benefited from extensive research on migration issues, particularly in recent years. On some issues regarding the impact of immigrants, research has been less than definitive. The absence of clearly positive impacts of immigration on all issues allows for differing positions to emerge even within the two broad camps of conservationists and expansionists (16). Nevertheless, there is some consensus on various issues— with the caveat that general conclusions do not necessarily apply equally to all immigrants.

According to a review of research on the economic impact of immigration (21), the overall impact of immigration has been positive, if not significantly so. Specifically, no evidence shows that immigration increased unemployment. The review points out that migrants present higher skill levels than the domestic work force and that they contribute substantially to the construction industry, which has a significant impact on the rest of the economy. Further, contributions by migrants to Government revenues (in taxes) is greater than migrants' burden on the Government. Although the positive impact of immigration to the economy does not appear particularly strong in the research, the negative impact is even weaker (16). An inquiry into the different immigration flows concludes that migrants in the skilled category have higher salaries, higher levels of expenditure and, therefore, a more positive impact on the economy than migrants in the family reunification category. These findings prompted the Government to provide more opportunities for skilled immigration than for family reunification in recent years (10).

On the social impacts of immigration (15), no evidence indicates that immigrants undermine the social cohesion in Australia. Instead, even non-English-speaking immigrants are found to succeed in achieving upward social mobility, particularly over the long term. Various areas of concern remain, particularly in regard to youth unemployment, high rates of occupational injury among non-English-speakers, and difficulties in accrediting qualifications earned in other countries. Refugees constitute a group with higher difficulties for integration and advancement in Australian society, particularly because of lower skills and qualifications.

With regard to the labour market impact (22), the relative lower achievements of immigrants is best explained by poor English language skills and their recent arrival. The unemployment rate among immigrants is inversely proportional to English-language skills (Table 51). Consequently, beginning July 1999, immigrants in occupations that require English must demonstrate a vocational knowledge of the language before obtaining a visa (10). The fact that immigrants received relatively lower wages as compared to others with similar years of education was explained by the considerable differences in educational systems between countries of origin and Australia. However, when migrants are equipped with post-secondary qualifications, they are said to experience, on average, the same unemployment rate as all persons born in Australia. Those without post-secondary qualifications experience a much higher unemployment rate (10). The higher rate of occupational injury among migrants derives from the type of industry in which migrants find a job—traditionally jobs shunned by the domestic work force. In the last 30 years, fewer immigrants found employment in the manufacturing sector; only 19 per cent in manufacturing in 1998, down from 40 per cent in 1966 (10).

TABLE 51.
AUSTRALIA: UNEMPLOYMENT RATE BY ENGLISH-SPEAKING ABILITY, 1998 (PERCENTAGES)

English-speaking ability	Months after arrival		
	6 months	18 months	42 months
English is first language	17	10	4
Speak English very well	32	16	9
Speak English well	45	20	12
Do not speak English well	60	35	30
Do not speak English at all	76	55	42

Source: Department of Immigration and Multicultural Affairs. *Fact Sheet 65,* **http://www.immi.gov.au/facts/index.htm**

A 1998 survey of immigration issues (6) confirmed findings that immigrants have a positive impact on the country. Additionally, the survey reflects no support for patterns of ethnic segregation in Australia, but finds trends of disadvantage and exclusion for some groups of migrants. Entrants under the humanitarian programme are more welfare-dependent and take longer to improve their position than other immigrants. As for social cohesion, evidence suggests that Australia is successful in integrating people of different cultural backgrounds without forcing them into a homogeneous identity. "There is no evidence that such 'multiple identities' lead to social divisions or weaken Australian culture" (6).

NEW ZEALAND

On the surface there are many similarities between New Zealand and Australia in migration terms. Though they are similarly closely related in historical ties to the United Kingdom and in the predominance of immigration from the United Kingdom and Ireland, New Zealand took a concerted approach in the 1970s to create links with the emerging Asian economies. Immigration from Asia rose with these ties. At the time Europe was preoccupied with building its own economic community and immigration from Europe declined. Outflows from New Zealand to Australia began to increase to the point that—despite the new immigration—net migration levels in New Zealand remained low and were negative in 1998-1999.

Like Australia, New Zealand is an immigrant country built on an indigenous population of Polynesian origin. Immigration from the United Kingdom and Ireland began even before the Treaty of Waitangi between the British Crown and the Maori tribes on the island that established New Zealand as a colony of the United Kingdom in 1840. Traditionally, New Zealand was a supplier of agricultural products to the United Kingdom in exchange for industrial products. Immigration continued to reflect these economic ties into the twentieth century.

In the 1970s, changes in the international economy, particularly the adherence of the United Kingdom to the European Economic Community, brought about changes in immigration policy. Unrestricted entry for citizens of the United Kingdom and Ireland was discontinued. New Zealand shifted its economic interest toward Asia and the Pacific and allowed immigration from the Pacific Islands. However, immigrants were admitted to alleviate labour shortages in particular sectors and citizens of traditional countries of origin (mostly Europe and the United States) were granted priority.

The history of migration between New Zealand and Australia is a long one and is commonly examined as trans-Tasman migration, indicating a flow in both directions. In history, it was not always Australia that gained in net immigration. The 1972 Trans-Tasman Travel Agreement set in motion a three-to-one outflow from New Zealand to Australia that acquired the characteristics of "brain drain" (12). Recently, this imbalance became more pronounced. Frequently, however, New Zealanders return after acquiring qualifications and skills outside the country. The net flow does not refer to migration of New Zealand- or Australia-born migrants alone, however, and includes migrants and/or their children from other areas of the world that first settled in one or the other country and then moved. Australia is the major destination of outbound New Zealanders.

In 1997-1998, some 30,000 foreign citizens were approved for residence in New Zealand, a decline from the recent high of 56,000 persons in 1995-1996 (Table 52). Applications for permanent residence have similarly declined during this period across all but the family reunification category (Table 53).[1]

TABLE 52.
NEW ZEALAND: PEOPLE APPROVED FOR RESIDENCE BY REGION AND NATIONALITY, 1992-1998

	1992	1993	1994	1995	1996	1997	1998
Africa	552	3,157	4,752	3,177	3,866	4,729	4,530
Europe	4,953	7,007	9,750	10,736	9,238	7,298	6,737
Middle East	331	595	826	2,988	1,591	993	675
Asia	14,816	14,878	22,738	33,362	21,983	11,314	11,308
America	997	1,021	1,566	1,243	1,436	1,076	1,215
Pacific Islands	3,859	2,702	3,006	4,097	4,428	4,145	4,378
Not defined	152	142	190	282	158	246	522
Total	**25,660**	**29,502**	**42,828**	**55,885**	**42,700**	**29,801**	**29,365**

Sources: New Zealand Resident Information Management System (RIMS) to 30 June 1997, thereafter New Zealand Management Information System (MIS).

An ethnic shift is evident in recent immigration to New Zealand. In 1998 (calendar year) 38.5 per cent of immigrants originated in Asia, while 22.9 per cent came from Europe (Table 54). The United Kingdom (14 per cent) remained the top country of origin in the 1990s, followed closely by China (11 per cent) and South Africa (7 per cent). Samoa (5 per cent), Fiji (3 per cent), and Tonga (2 per cent) were the only Pacific Island States to reach the top 15 countries of origin between 1992 and 1997 (Table 55). Net immigration gains in the 1990s were largely from Asian countries, while immigration from the Pacific posted negative gains and immigration from Europe continued to decline (2).

New Zealand also attracts foreign students (20,000 in the 1997-1998 business year). In general, no numerical limits are placed on student entries that increasingly are of Asian origin. Only students from China are subject to a quota.

TABLE 53.
APPLICATIONS TO NEW ZEALAND AND PEOPLE INCLUDED
BY CATEGORY, 1992-1998

APPLICATIONS[1]

Year	Business	Family	General skills	Humanitarian	Other	Total
1992	967	4,628	4,105	835	2,239	**12,774**
1993	389	4,496	6,521	675	1,342	**13,423**
1994	659	5,394	9,840	765	1,872	**18,530**
1995	611	7,065	13,540	1,170	1,670	**24,056**
1996	471	8,471	9,247	708	1,581	**20,478**
1997	56	8,800	5,305	927	1,055	**16,143**
1998	57	8,560	4,851	953	695	**15,116**

PEOPLE[1]

Year	Business	Family	General skills	Humanitarian	Other	Total
1992	3,917	5,977	10,271	1,467	4,031	**25,663**
1993	1,417	5,526	18,920	1,460	2,180	**29,503**
1994	2,449	6,679	28,819	1,703	2,818	**42,468**
1995	2,117	9,075	39,877	2,378	2,445	**55,892**
1996	1,622	10,846	26,472	1,423	2,346	**42,709**
1997	163	11,433	14,262	2,109	1,838	**29,805**
1998	184	11,722	13,515	2,546	1,367	**29,334**

Notes: [1]Applications = Number of principal applicants;
People = Number of people included in applications.

Sources: New Zealand Resident Information Management System (RIMS) to 30 June
1997, thereafter New Zealand Management Information System (MIS).

TABLE 54.
PEOPLE APPROVED FOR RESIDENCE IN NEW ZEALAND
BY REGION AND NATIONALITY, 1992-1998

	1992	1993	1994	1995	1996	1997	1998
Africa	552	3,157	4,752	3,177	3,866	4,729	4,530
Europe	4,953	7,007	9,750	10,736	9,238	7,298	6,737
Middle East	331	595	826	2,988	1,591	993	675
Asia	14,816	14,878	22,738	33,362	21,983	11,314	11,308
America	997	1,021	1,566	1,243	1,436	1,076	1,215
Pacific Islands	3,859	2,702	3,006	4,097	4,428	4,145	4,378
Not defined	152	142	190	282	158	246	522
Total	**25,660**	**29,502**	**42,828**	**55,885**	**42,700**	**29,801**	**29,365**

Sources: New Zealand Resident Information Management System (RIMS) to 30 June 1997,
thereafter New Zealand Management Information System (MIS).

TABLE 55.

NEW ZEALAND: TOP 15 COUNTRIES OR TERRITORIES BY PERSONS
APPROVED FOR RESIDENCE, 1992-1993 TO 1997-1998

	1992-93	1993-94	1994-95	1995-96	1996-97	1997-98	Total	Per cent
United Kingdom	3,907	4,753	7,297	5,352	5,500	4,840	31,649	14
China	2,316	2,058	5,742	5,445	4,950	4,220	24,731	11
South Africa	958	4,244	2,661	2,312	3,607	3,366	17,148	7
India	1,084	1,568	2,838	3,633	2,311	2,433	13,867	6
Samoa	1,482	983	1,525	2,282	2,387	1,835	10,494	5
Fiji	905	704	920	1,067	1,422	1,746	6,764	3
Tonga	1,367	587	871	798	949	932	5,504	2
Philippines	597	473	835	1,448	872	776	5,001	2
Sri Lanka	515	822	1,274	1,410	601	747	5,369	2
USA	629	699	811	808	752	740	4,439	2
Rep. of Korea	2,991	3,289	4,554	2,665	579	592	14,670	6
Taiwan (Prov. of Ch.)	2,827	3,601	7,573	12,325	664	537	27,527	12
Iraq	66	333	1,261	2,100	759	493	5,012	2
Hong Kong	3,699	2,687	2,708	2,599	1,122	438	13,253	6
Malaysia	1,698	1,004	668	533	253	337	4,493	2
Other	4,606	5,716	9,223	9,660	6,955	6,646	42,806	18
Total	**29,647**	**33,521**	**50,761**	**54,437**	**33,683**	**30,678**	**232,727**	**100**

Sources: New Zealand Resident Information Management System (RIMS) to 30 June 1997,
thereafter New Zealand Management Information System (MIS).

The ceiling on admission of students from the People's Republic of China was set at 4,000 students for 1998-1999.

Increasing economic relations with Asian countries brought an end to the preferential treatment of immigrants from Europe and the United States in 1986 and the adoption of a new Immigration Act in 1987. A further change occurred with the introduction in 1991 of a point system to rate immigrants, which facilitated immigration from East Asia (Table 54). Immigration from Mainland China, Hong Kong, Taiwan (Province of China), and the Republic of Korea increased immediately, doubling net immigration from these sources from 17,281 in 1987-1991 to 35,000 in 1991-1995. During the same periods, immigration from the Pacific Islands dropped by nearly one-half from 22,000 to 13,000. The point system obviously was intended to give preference to skilled immigrants who could contribute to the economic restructuring brought about by globalization (2). Nevertheless, an arrangement with Samoa that permits an annual total of 1,100 immigrants is still operative.

Currently, New Zealand admits immigrants under various categories that include general skills (50 per cent), family reunification (45 per cent), humanitarian (1 per cent), business investors (1 per cent), and Samoans (3 per cent). The increase in immigration applications in the general skills category in 1995 (some 14,000 as against nearly 10,000 in 1994) generated fear that immigration was going beyond the implicit—but never specified—annual target of 25,000 immigrants. Thereafter, the point system was revised, so that automatic permits are not granted even if the requirements have been fulfilled.

Proficiency in English—of both the applicant and the whole family—has become a critical requirement. Failure to pass the test forces the immigrant to deposit a bond (NZ$ 20,000) that is refunded if the test is passed within one year of immigration. The measure is intended to diminish Government expenses for English training and has a direct impact on Taiwan (Province of China), Mainland China, and the Republic of Korea, three major sources of immigration (Table 55). Migration authorities establish the "pass mark", or the number of points necessary for admission, on a weekly basis for general skill migrants and business investors. Thus, authorities allow for constant monitoring and management of immigration inflows within an undefined, but politically acceptable, margin.

New Zealand holds a number of temporary work agreements with Asian countries and island nations in the Pacific. In addition, the Government issues temporary work visas in a broad range of special employee categories including, among many others, international fishing vessel crews, entertainers, sports figures, and slaughterhouse workers.

The increased Asian component of immigration—mostly Chinese—was met with apprehension in public opinion, primarily because of the geographic concentration of Asians in Auckland (80 percent) and the formation of distinct Asian communities. Because their arrival and search for homes overwhelmed existing demand, at one point the price of real estate increased out of range for some in the local market. Parents who commute between their business in Asia, particularly in Hong Kong, and their family in New Zealand add to the concerns about recent immigrants (14). The language needs of the high number of Asian students in schools are cited as an additional burden.

Investment by East Asian businesses (NZ$ 285.5 million) in 1995 was more than 10 times greater than European foreign investment (NZ$ 16.4 million). This pattern confirmed New Zealand's strategy of development with Asian partnerships, but also left New Zealanders with the perception that wealthy Asians lack long-term commitment to New Zealand (2). Immigrants are now required to spend at least six months of each of two consecutive years in New Zealand, becoming residents for tax purposes.

Asian and South African immigration also had an impact on the dislocation of the indigenous population in the labour market. In the late 1980s, in economic restructuring, one in five Maori workers lost their jobs to skilled workers from abroad. Debate followed on biculturalism (which gives preferential treatment to the indigenous population) versus multiculturalism (which provides the same opportunities for all migrants). Undoubtedly, such debate will continue in the attempt to "accommodate both the bicultural initiatives and the new orientation to Asia for migrants, markets and capital" (2).

EMIGRATION TRENDS

Migration from the Pacific Islands—particularly labour migration—has received extensive research attention. The dispersion from the islands, comprising 22 States traditionally aggregated into three major indigenous groups, makes it very difficult to arrive at solid generalizations concerning population movements. In addition to the traditional inter-island and internal mobility, increasing permanent and labour migration has been observed since the 1970s. The permanent relocation to the metropolitan States of the Pacific Rim received most attention.

People of Pacific Island ethnicity living abroad were estimated at approximately 400,000 in the mid-1990s, mostly in New Zealand (170,000), the United States (145,000), Australia (84,000), and Canada (16,700). These migrants correspond to 75 per cent of the Polynesian population. Perhaps 30 to 40 per cent of Tongans and Samoans are living abroad (1). The out-migration may not be very impressive in comparison to the total Pacific Island population (about 6 million), but it is very significant for the small States of Polynesia and Micronesia. The three regions present distinct migration patterns: mostly international migration from Polynesia;

internal migration in Melanesia; and a combination of both in Micronesia, which also is characterized by an inflow of migrant workers (8).

Analysis of Pacific Island migration points to population and environmental issues as the principal determinants of the flows. Concerns about such catastrophic events as rising sea levels that would submerge the islands do not measurably increase migration pressure. However, population pressure on the remaining agricultural land is a factor, particularly because of the complex issue of the land rights of migrants who have left for a long time and might not return (1).

Several different analyses of the causes and impacts of Pacific Island migration dominate the research. One perspective, modelled on dependency theories, attributes much of the cause of migration to the colonial legacy and the penetration of foreign capital and western models into the traditional island social and economic system (7). In contrast, a second perspective attributes migration to rational decision-making among kinship groups who are responding to labour surplus conditions brought about by the infusion of foreign capital (3). More recently, it was argued that demographic factors, the fertility transition and mobility embedded in cultural traditions are equal—if not more important—migration pressures (13). The Pacific diaspora has long been embedded in the local culture. Skills are developed elsewhere as mobility increases and strong ties are maintained with the place of origin. The myth of return is particularly strong among Pacific islanders abroad; however, permanent return is rare (1).

The importance of remittances—both monetary and in kind—to the sustainability of these economies is conclusive. Research indicates that remittances do not decline over time and that remittances are sent back to the Islands for capital accumulation, not just consumption. Such findings led to recommendations that policy facilitate the accumulation of migrant savings in the islands of origin (5).

The future development of migration from the Pacific Islands is very much dependent on the development of those economies within an international context of increasing globalization. In this regard, economic and communication flows tend to favour linkages with the metropolitan countries, rather than among the Pacific Islands. This, together with the establishment of migrant networks that ensure that most Pacific Island countries have some entry into Pacific Rim nations, suggests that opportunities for migration will continue to be strongly considered.

CONCLUSION

The new millennium is opening with the renewed relevance of migration for the countries of Oceania, particularly Australia. Progressively restrictive migration policies have their counterpoint in increased demand for immigration. As such demand is not met, attempts to enter in unauthorized ways increase, renewing old debates that were never set to rest: should Australia considerably increase its population, up to 50 million by the middle of the next century—as some groups advocate—or should it limit its population growth—as others, particularly environmentalists, demand? The threat of Australia being invaded by unauthorized immigrants is exaggerated. The number of asylum claimants in 1998-1999 (8,257) is far below the number of such claimants in the United Kingdom (51,795) or Germany (98,644). However, Australia is close to a region in which ethnic strife is on the rise. Since the crisis in East Timor, in which Australia took a leading peacekeeping role, there is further unrest, such as in Aceh, not to mention unsolved problems in the Middle East. Australia appeals to many different people trying to escape such intolerable situations.

In the attempt to manage migration before unwanted population movements that do not respond to their tradition or interest overwhelm them, the countries of the South Pacific increasingly participated in intergovernmental initiatives concerning migration with Asian countries. These official discussions, although carried out between regions with widely different migration systems, promise to advance both the understanding of contemporary changes in migration movements and the capabilities of governments to ensure orderly migration within an increasingly globalized context.

ENDNOTES

1. Unless otherwise stated, New Zealand immigration data were obtained from the New Zealand Resident Information Management System (RIMS) up to 30 June 1997, and thereafter the New Zealand Management Information System (MIS) at **http:// www.immigration.govt.nz**

REFERENCES

1. Bedford, R. (1997). *International Migration, Identity and Development in Oceania: Towards a theoretical synthesis*. Paper presented at the International Food Policy Research Institue Conference on International Migration at Century's End: Trends and Issues. Barcelona, 7-10 May.

2. Bedford, R. and P. Spoonley (1997). Aotearoa/New Zealand. In P. Brownlee & C. Mitchell (compilers), *Migration Issues in the Asia Pacific*. Asia-Pacific Migration Research Network, Wollongong, NSW.

3. Bertram, I.G. and R.F. Watters (1985). The MIRAB economy in South Pacific microstates. *Pacific Viewpoint*, 26(3):489-519.

4. Brown, R.P.C. and J. Connell (1995). Migration and remittances in the South Pacific: towards new perspectives. *Asian and Pacific Migration Journal*, 4(1).

5. Brown, R.P.C., J. Foster, and J. Connell (1995). Remittances, savings, and policy formation in the Pacific Island States. *Asian and Pacific Migration Journal,* 4(1).

6. Castles, S., W. Foster, R. Iredale and G. Withers (1998). *Immigration and Australia. Myths and Realities*. Allen & Unwin, St. Leonards, NSW.

7. Connell, J. (1991). Island microstates: the mirage of development. *The Contemporary Pacific*, 3(2):251-287.

8. Connell, J. and R.P.C. Brown (1995). Migration and remittances in the South Pacific: towards new perspectives. *Asian and Pacific Migration Journal*, 2(1).

9. Department of Immigration and Multicultural Affairs (1997). *Immigration Update, June Quarter 1997.*

10. Department of Immigration and Multicultural Affairs (1998). *Fact Sheet* (various numbers), Accessed on 5 November 1998.

11. Department of Immigration and Multicultural Affairs (1999). *Immigration Update, June Quarter 1999.*

12. Elliott, J.L. (1993). New Zealand: The coming of age of multiracial islands. In D. Kubat (Ed.), *The Politics of Migration Policies*. Center for Migration Studies, Staten Island, NY.

13. Hayes, G. (1992). The use of scientific models in the study of Polynesian migration. *Asian and Pacific Migration Journal*, 1(2).

14. Ho, E., R. Bedford, and J. Goodwin (1997). "Astronaut" families: a contemporary migration phenomenon. In *East Asian New Zealanders: Research on New Migrants*. Asia-Pacific Migration Research Network, Albany, NZ.

15. Holton, R. (1994). Social aspects of immigration. In M. Wooden, R. Holton, G. Hugo and J. Sloan (Eds.), *Australian Immigration: A Survey of the Issues*. Bureau of Immigration and Population Research, South Carlton, Vic.

16. Hugo, G. (1994). Introduction. In M. Wooden, R. Holton, G. Hugo and J. Sloan (Eds.), *Australian Immigration: A Survey of the Issues*. Bureau of Immigration and Population Research, South Carlton, Vic.

17. Khoo, S-E., et al. (1994). Asian immigrant settlement and adjustment in Australia. *Asian and Pacific Migration Journal,* 3(2/3).

18. Lindquist, B.A. (1993). Migration networks: a case study in the Philippines. *Asian and Pacific Migration Journal*, 3(1).

19. Mackie, J. (1997). The politics of Asian immigration. In J.E. Coughlan and D.J. McNamara (Eds.), *Asians in Australia: Patterns of Migration and Settlement*. Macmillan, Melbourne, SA.

20. Organisation for Economic Co-operation and Development (1998). *Trends in International Migration.*

21. Wooden, M. (1994a). The economic impact of immigration. In M. Wooden, R. Holton, G. Hugo and J. Sloan (Eds.), *Australian Immigration: A Survey of the Issues*. Bureau of Immigration and Population Research, South Carlton, Vic.

22. Wooden, M. (1994b). The labour-market experience of immigrants. In M. Wooden, R. Holton, G. Hugo and J. Sloan (Eds.), *Australian Immigration: A Survey of the Issues*. Bureau of Immigration and Population Research, South Carlton, Vic.